SEVERANCE

THE EARLY PRACTICE OF CHÖ

SEVERANCE

THE EARLY PRACTICE OF CHÖ

THE HEART ESSENCE OF PROFOUND MEANING

BY JAMYANG GÖNPO

Translated, edited, *and* annotated *by* Sarah Harding

Foreword *by* Lodrö Tulku Rinpoche

Wisdom

Publisher's Acknowledgment

The publisher gratefully acknowledges the generous help of the Tsadra Foundation in sponsoring the production of this book.

Wisdom Publications
132 Perry Street
New York, NY 10014 USA
wisdom.org

Library of Congress Cataloging-in-Publication Data
Names: Gönpo, Jamyang, author. | Harding, Sarah, 1951– translator. | Rinpoche, Lodrö
    Tulku, writer of foreword.
Title: Severance: the early practice of Chö: the heart essence of profound meaning /
    by Jamyang Gönpo; translated, edited, and annotated by Sarah Harding;
    foreword by Lodrö Tulku Rinpoche.
Description: New York, NY, USA : Wisdom, [2025] | Includes bibliographical references
    and index. | Text in English. Translated from Tibetan.
Identifiers: LCCN 2024052550 (print) | LCCN 2024052551 (ebook) |
    ISBN 9798890700001 (hardcover) | ISBN 9798890700100 (ebook)
Subjects: LCSH: Spiritual life—Tantric Buddhism. | Tantric Buddhism—Tibet
    Region—Doctrines.
Classification: LCC BQ8936 .G66 2025 (print) | LCC BQ8936 (ebook) |
    DDC 294.3/925—dc23/eng/20250116
LC record available at https://lccn.loc.gov/2024052550
LC ebook record available at https://lccn.loc.gov/2024052551

ISBN 979-8-89070-000-1   ebook ISBN 979-8-89070-010-0

29 28 27 26 25   5 4 3 2 1

Cover art by Livia Liverani. Cover image courtesy of Eric Colombel. Cover design by Philip Pascuzzo. Interior design by Tim Holtz. An earlier translation of the verses in chapter 1 appeared in *The Treasury of Precious Instructions: Essential Teachings of the Eight Practice Lineages of Tibet, Volume 14: Chöd*, by Jamgön Kongtrul Lodrö Taye, translated by Sarah Harding, © 2016 by Tsadra Foundation. Reprinted by arrangement with Shambhala Publications, Inc., Boulder, CO. www.shambhala.com.

Contents

Foreword

The great eleventh-century Tibetan Buddhist teacher and yoginī Machik Labdrön transmitted the wisdom teachings of the supreme Prajñāpāramitā by means of unconventional instructions suitable for bodhisattvas. The practice of detachment from grasping for a self and the subsequent liberation from the sufferings of dependent arising can be traced back to a central teaching of Buddha Śākyamuni, who also prophesied the coming of Machik Labdrön and her teachings.

Master Jamyang Gönpo's thirteenth-century commentary (*The Big General Guide to Severance*) is a timeless and authoritative work for all those interested in Machik Labdrön's Chö practice and traditions, which have evolved over the centuries.

A more profound subject and a more insightful Chö master and scholar than Jamyang Gönpo is hard to find. Even among the Chö masters who appeared later, few could articulate and express the essence of Machik Labdrön's method for the realization of emptiness as skillfully as this great Chö master. He is indeed an undisputed authority. It is therefore of great benefit that we encounter this text in our lifetime; even more so if we can read through it, analyze it, and meditate on it.

This magnificent translation (of *The Heart Essence of Profound Meaning*) from the Tibetan by Lama Sarah Harding, who is endowed with great linguistic expertise and understanding of the essence of the text, is a true delight. Thanks to her great commitment, a wider audience can now enjoy these precious explanations.

My great appreciation also goes to the Tsadra Foundation for supporting and enabling this important project.

Any merits generated by this undertaking will undoubtedly produce immeasurable results for all involved, and open the door to liberation for all beings.

The Sixth Tulku Lodrö Rinpoche, Lobsang Jampa Khedup Namgyäl
September 2024
The Chöd and Meditation Center, Ganden Chökhor, Switzerland

Lodrö Tulku Rinpoche's Account of His Chö Lineage

Oral Transmission (union of two lineages)

The first lineage begins in the early twelfth century with the *Profound Teachings of Chö* (*Zab don thugs kyi snying po*):

Machik Labdrön
Gyalwa Döndrup
Jamyang Gönpo (or Thönyön Latön)[*]
Sönam Rinchen
Lodrö Rabné

The second lineage also begins in the early twelfth century, thirteen or fourteen years later, with the *Whispered Oral Transmission of the Ḍākinīs* (*Mkha' 'gro snyan brgyud*):

---

[*] Thönyön Latön is sometimes named instead of his contemporary, Jamyang Gönpo. In his commentary, *Opener of the Wisdom Eye*, Master Balmang Könchok Gyaltsen (1764–1853) writes that these two masters are interchangeable.

Wisdom Ḍākinī

Chönyi Rangdröl

Lodrö Rabné

They are combined into a single lineage through Lodrö Rabné with the title *The Peaceful, Profound Tradition of the Ḍākinīs (Zhi ba lam zab)*:

Lodrö Rabné, Machik Köncham, Jangchup Rinchen, Jetsun Palsang, Sönam Wangchuk, Thakpo Sangpo and Rikzin Lodrö Gyatso (two tantric brothers), Dorjé Gyaltsen, Sangyé Sangpo, Sangyé Lodrö, Sönam Lhundrup, Damchö Tsomo, Karma Dargyé, Jampa Lhawang Rikzin, Geré Ngawang Phunzok, Kalsang Tsoknyi, Kalsang Chöwang, Chöden Kalsang, Losang Rabten, Gelek Palsang, Losang Yeshé, Gendun Gyaltsen, Gelek Rabgyé, Jikmé Gyaltsen, Jampa Namdröl (Ninth Khalkha Jetsun Dampa Rinpoché), Jampa Namgyal (Sixth Lodrö Tulku Rinpoche).

Compiled by the Sixth Tulku Lodrö Rinpoche, Switzerland, 2024

Preface

The Tibetan Buddhist practice called Chö (*gcod*), translated as "severance" or "cutting," has held a fascination for scholars and practitioners far and wide since its development in Tibet in the eleventh century. I joined that fan base after learning and engaging in the practice during a three-year retreat from 1976 to 1980 under the direction of the late Kalu Rinpoché. Over the years since then, I have researched and translated innumerable texts on the subject, both very ancient and somewhat more modern. As I worked with such a wide range of material, I began to notice a surprising trend in the very earliest texts, teachings that were attributed to the progenitor of this tradition herself, Machik Labdrön (1055–1149). That is, they were noticeably lacking in details, with some not even mentioning the widespread practice of visualizing the dismemberment of one's body and preparing it as an offering to various spirits—the normally unseen gods and demons—that has become the hallmark of Severance. I have written of this before, with what I consider a good case for that observation (see the appendix). I was therefore excited to discover the very early commentary translated here, *A Big General Guide to Severance*, and its implementation in the *Seven-Day Severance Retreat*, written by a certain Jamyang Gönpo (b. 1208). He was a disciple of Machik Labdrön's son Gyalwa Döndrup, among others, so the practice that he received would thus have been very close to what Machik herself taught. This text predates any other known commentary on Machik Labdrön's teachings. Like the other early source texts of Severance, it minimizes the body sacrifice. Although disowning and relinquishing the body is certainly mentioned, it is given far less emphasis than one would expect;

Severance here focuses instead on the practitioner's reactive emotions. It appears as yet another way to understand the very Buddhist idea of nonself and the suffering experienced through clinging to that self—a fear-based obsession. In other words, this early text displays Severance as it has always been described: a teaching of the Perfection of Wisdom (Prajñāparamitā) and a profound application of its intent.

Acknowledgments

I offer everlasting gratitude to my teachers, Venerable Kalu Rinpoché, Deshung Rinpoché, and the great masters of their generation. They are missed. I also offer sincere thanks to Eric Colombel and the whole team at Tsadra Foundation for their support of my work and for letting me choose a subject of much interest to me. Translating a single subject by a single author is a great respite from anthologies—although I love those too, don't get me wrong! Through their kindness, I was able to travel to Zurich to meet and confer with Lodrö Tulku Rinpoche, a strong proponent and knowledge holder in this rare lineage of Severance, as well as many other Severance traditions. I am so grateful for my brief time with him, which was facilitated by his very helpful Swiss entourage, especially Natascha Gassmann. This in-person exchange was most treasured, and it was also serendipitous to obtain the recent publication of his teachings on this same material, *The Profound Heart Essence: Prajnaparamita and the Practice of Chod.* I also appreciate retroactively his early support for another foray into this tradition as it developed in the Gelukpa school, by the scholar Carol Savvas in her 1990 dissertation. I am likewise thankful for the help I received from other Tibetan informants on my never-ending questions: Acharya Lama Tenpa Gyaltsen, Ringu Tulku Rinpoché, Kunga Lama, and his friend the Tibetan doctor Tenzin Leksang. Many thanks to Gregory Forgues, the research director at Tsadra Foundation, who was so very helpful with demonology, astrology, and weird rituals. And as always, I am grateful to all my colleagues on whom I rely in this eccentric cabal of Buddhist translators. I am grateful to Daniel Aitken at Wisdom Publications, where my very first book was published, for agreeing to continue the author-publisher relationship, and in particular to the editor Brianna Quick and her fresh perspective. And as ever, thanks to my indexer and Sanskrit mentor, L.S. Summer. On another note, I would like to thank the participants of several retreats and online intensives—my test audience—who stuck with me as I navigated these often heady translations and teachings. The best feeling in the world is when people actually appreciate and put into practice what I spend my life trying to articulate.

Lama Jamyang Gönpo

Courtesy Norton Simon Art Foundation. Asia: China, Tibet; Lama Jamyang
Gonpo (?), c. 1500; Bronze, 4-1/2 in. (11.4 cm).

Translator's Introduction

Severance

So much on Severance has been written in European languages, not to mention the vast literature in Tibetan, that the following brief summary should be enough to introduce the subject and provide a context for the texts translated here.

Chö (*gcod*), translated here as "severance," is a Tibetan term referring to a cycle of Tibetan Buddhist practice and to the lineage initiated by the Tibetan woman Machik Labdrön some time during the eleventh to twelfth centuries. It is primarily associated with the Perfection of Wisdom (Skt. Prajñāpāramitā), a set of sutras attributed to Buddha Śākyamuni that represent the second phase of Buddhist teachings that developed in India, which has been called the "middle turning" of the wheel of Dharma. The Tibetan term for Severance is normally spelled *gcod*, but is often used interchangeably with its homonym *spyod* (Skt. *caryā*), meaning "conduct" or "activity." *Caryā* is used often in the Perfection of Wisdom literature to describe the activity of a bodhisattva, the enactment of their realization of emptiness and compassion. The substitute by Tibetan authors of the spelling *gcod* seems to reflect its vernacular usage to indicate something that is decided or resolved once and for all. For instance, the phrases *thag gcod pa* (literally, "to cut the rope"), or *rtsa ba nas bcad pa* (literally, "to cut from the roots"), are both idiomatic expressions that have nothing to do with actual cutting. This identification of the term "severance" with the Perfection of Wisdom terminology of "practice" and "conduct" exactly reveals its intent—to act out (*spyod*) in a decisive way (*gcod*) one's own integration of that perfect wisdom. (See the glossary of terms for more on this.)

In Tibet itself, Severance was one of the many new sects that flourished in the second dissemination of Buddhism from India (950–1350 CE). It has been classified as a branch of Shijé (*zhi byed*), or "Pacification," one of the eight practice lineages, or "chariots," delineated in a particular Tibetan scheme to organize the vast amount of material that entered Tibet from India.[1] However, no actual text on Severance has been discovered in the early texts of Pacification. Despite this quandary, its classification has afforded a kind of validation in being connected with the sources of Buddhism through the great Indian master Dampa Sangyé.

There is no doubt, however, that Machik Labdrön herself is the sole progenitor for the teachings and the lineage. This remarkable woman was born in a village called Tsomer in lower Tamshö in Ei Gangwa, in the Labchi region of central Tibet.[2] She became known as Labkyi Drönma, "the Light of Lab," or sometimes Labkyi Drölma, "the Liberator of Lab." The respectful title Machik, "One Mother," was bestowed later, and is shared with several other important women of the time. It must be conceded, however, that Machik Labdrön's exceptionally compassionate practice of dealing with negative forces by feeding them seems particularly motherly. She showed remarkable abilities from an early age, and later gained mastery of speed reading. This led to a job as a chaplain in a patron's house, where she met her future partner, providing her biographers with a fascinating narrative revealing the problematic status of female masters in Tibet. The recitation of the Perfection of Wisdom texts also led to her epiphany about the sections on *māra*, which can be translated as "devil," "demon," or [spiritual] "death." She also had visionary relationships with the bodhisattva Tārā and the Great Mother (*yum chen mo*), the personification of the Perfection of Wisdom. These, and her important connection with the Indian master Dampa Sangyé, were the inspiration for what became one of the most widespread practices in Tibet.

The early Severance teachings represent aspects derived from both sutra and tantra sources. Their focus is on the understanding of emptiness that severs fixation on the reification of the self and the resultant conduct based on compassion for others. The impediments that prevent such realization, the *māras*, were a point of departure. As time went on, specific techniques and methods of practice (Skt. *sādhana*) accrued to this philosophy. While the main practice has remained the cultivation of insight and the enactment of separating consciousness from the body, the post-meditation practice known as *lü jin* (*lus byin*, "giving the body") developed elaborate visualizations and ritual accoutrements that came to dominate popular practice. The sources for this aspect are obscure and may well come from the surrounding culture of the Tibetan plateau, harking back to Bön and other pre-Buddhist practices. Some elements associated with shamanic practices are enacted in the Severance rituals, despite their Buddhist soteriological assertions. And many of the spirits that are mentioned occupied Tibetan territories long before the advent of Buddhism.

With its beautiful melodies and lurid visualizations, Severance quickly became popular in Tibet for exorcism, healing, and other practical usages. Its followers did not establish monasteries, as the lifestyle of the roaming mendicant was emphasized, but Severance was incorporated into most Buddhist schools in Tibet. Their liturgies are drawn from the works of Labdrön's descendants, or from the visionary experiences of yogis and yoginīs, or found as treasure texts, or *terma* (*gter ma*). In recent years, Severance has gained popularity worldwide, with many iterations in current practice.

Invisible Forces

Severance is the practice of facing one's fears. There is much that concerns spirits in the literature because they were a principal source of fear in Tibetan culture. And yet they defy categorization or comparison with the spirits of other cultures. Though many of their names were assigned by Tibetan translators of Sanskrit based on names of the spirits of India at the time of the Buddha, the spirits of Tibet were part of the landscape long before Indian Buddhism found its way over the Himalayas. Whether they are the same spirits that were commonly thought to occupy the subcontinent is doubtful and, in any case, impossible to know. Not only that, but it seems each subculture and valley in Tibet, even each village, may have had different ideas about their invisible neighbors. (For the names of specific spirits, see glossary 2.)

The one centrally important idea taken from Indian Buddhism that appears throughout Severance literature regarding these unseen forces is *māra*, "devil" or "evil." In Sanskrit, *māra* is a nominalized form of the verbal root *mṛ-*, "to die," and can be associated with actual death or spiritual death. It was personified in the Perfection of Wisdom scriptures and elsewhere as the familiar figure of the Buddha's antagonist or tempter, a role similar to the "devil" in other religious traditions. The Tibetan translation of *māra* as *bdud* (pronounced "dü" with a silent final "d") is complicated, since there were already hordes of *bdud* in Tibet before the advent of Buddhism. Nevertheless, in the context here, it is used to indicate hindrances to the attainment of enlightenment. This is what gives Severance its full name: Dükyi Chö Yul (*bdud kyi gcod yul*), "the devil/evil that is the object to sever." It is not only the personification of evil as so many demons to be severed, but also of any reification of objective reality (*yul*: "object") as intrinsically existing—the most salient point of all Perfection of Wisdom teachings, or even of all Buddhist teachings.

There were four *māra*s in the teachings of the Buddha: that of the five aggregates, afflictive emotions, actual death, and complacency ("divine child").[3] These four obviously interrupt or prevent spiritual development. Machik Labdrön would eventually focus on four other devils: the tangible devil, the intangible devil, the devil of exaltation, and the devil of inflation.[4] These are thoroughly described in the course of this commentary. All of them come down to the last one—the devil of inflating a nonexistent self into reified existence. Machik says:

That which is called "devil" is not some actual great big black thing that scares and petrifies whomever sees it. A devil is anything that obstructs the achievement of freedom. Therefore, even loving and affectionate friends become devils [with regard to] freedom. Most of all, there is no greater devil than this fixation to a self.[5]

The other important term in Severance literature is "gods and demons," or perhaps just "god-demons" (*lha 'dre*). (Or even the familiar duality, "angels and demons.") These are manifestations of unseen forces conceived of as benevolent or malicious, the helpers and harmers of negotiated existence. There is not much discussion of gods separately from demons in Severance practice. Rather, the terms are signals of our overall perception of the phenomenal world as basically dualistic, either good or bad. But this binary is shifty at best, which should be the first clue to its emptiness.

Severance has remained essentially an instruction on coping with stressful situations that provoke fear and, beyond that, a way to actively seek out such circumstances in order to test one's realization of perfect wisdom. This is clearly evident and relentlessly repeated in these works by Jamyang Gönpo.

Jamyang Gönpo

Jamyang Gönpo was primarily an important lineage holder in the early development of the Lower Drukpa Kagyü. All the available biographical sketches about him are found in the context of that school.[6] Those sources put his birth in the region of Upper Nyang (Myang/Nyang stod) in southern Tibet, not far from the Bhutanese border, in the Earth Male Dragon year, 1208. He was entrusted to the care of a Lopön Tsangtön, who caught a glimpse of the protector ("gönpo") Six-Armed Mahākāla during a related ritual, and so gave his ward the name Sönam Gönpo. Some of his amazing abilities are described from his early years, such as his ability to spontaneously enter meditation states, and his easy memorization and comprehension during his studies with Lopön Chetön Sangyé, Chetön Gönpo, and Yuthok Jogyal, among others. His mother died when he was ten years old, after which he traveled to Yeru, in Tsang,[7] and took ordination with Lama Martön at Serding Monastery. He received the ordination name Sherab Jungné. There he received many instructions and spent his time in seclusion meditating at Oyuk.[8] He became a fully ordained monk with Lama Martön, Dunglungpa, and Chungpo, and he received many important instructions from Trophu Lotsāwa. Then he spent fourteen years meditating on "a single seat" and did not eat meat for seventeen years. After hearing of the fame of Lopön Uripa (Lorepa), he traveled to Uru to study with him. Lorepa became Jamyang Gönpo's principal guru, and he stayed with him until Lorepa passed away.[9]

Lorepa Wangchuk Tsöndru is considered the founder of what is known as the Lower Drukpa (*smad 'brug*) transmission. This was an offshoot of the Drukpa Kagyü school that began with Tsangpa Gyaré, the first Drukchen Rinpoché, who was also from Upper Nyang.[10] Lorepa studied with Tsangpa Gyaré at Drukgön ("Dragon Monastery") and received many cycles of teaching, including what is called *The Five Capabilities*. After his teacher passed away, Lorepa took on the life of a wandering yogi, staying in meditation retreats in many places, including what is now Bhutan, where he founded the monastery of Tharpaling in Bumthang. His longest sojourn was for seven years in a monastery he founded in 1234 called Uri (Bdu ri). That is how he gained the alias Uripa (Dbu ri pa or Dbus ras pa). Lorepa's collected works are available in Tibetan in five volumes. The instructions known as *The Five Capabilities* became the signature teaching of the Lower Drukpa branch.[11] Of his many thousands of disciples, there were three who were known as the "three learned ones." Among them was Jamyang Gönpo, whose only extant writing on the Drukpa doctrine is his contribution to Lorepa's instructions on *The Five Capabilities*.[12]

Jamyang Gönpo continued his studies with Lorepa and many other masters, receiving a thorough education in Buddhist literature and ritual. It was during one empowerment that he received his secret name, Dönyo Dorjé, a Tibetan translation of the buddha Amoghavajra. At one point he was nominated to supervise some rites to avert an attack by Mongol troops. He was very effective; the people said, "Such a wise monk. He must be Mañjuśrī himself." Thus, he earned the name Jamyang Gönpo, which is Mañjughoṣanātha in Sanskrit. All his names and their Sanskrit equivalents become important later in discerning the "signatures" of his compositions. At the request of the people of Upper and Lower Nyang, Lorepa appointed him their teacher. He founded the monastery of Kurulung on the border of Upper and Lower Nyang. Jamyang Gönpo was forty-three years old when his master Lorepa passed away at the age of sixty-four. Jamyang Gönpo continued his work for the benefit of beings up until he disappeared on a visit to Wutai Shan in China, the holy site of Mañjuśrī. Most records just declare his death date as unknown. However, Kunkhyen Pema Karpo's few lines about him in *The Sun that Opens the Lotus of the Doctrine* explain it differently:

Jamyang Gönpo's activities took place in Lower Nyang Kuri (Uri?). The *Profound Heart Essence of Object Severance* and *Disclosing the Vajra Words of the Path of Methods* were done by him. His secret name was Dönyö Dorjé. Later [in life] at Five-Peak Mountain in China, he [passed] without leaving his body.[13]

Names and Dates

There has been some confusing information on the identity of Jamyang Gönpo. As seen above, the biographical sketches place him solidly within the Lower Drukpa tradition, with only a few mentions of a Severance connection. But in the widely consulted archives of the Buddhist Digital Resource Center there are two people with that name: one called "Lorepa's disciple," who was born in 1208, an earth dragon year, and another called "Nyangtö Jamyang Gönpo," who was born in 1196, a fire dragon year. But it seems more than a coincidence that Lorepa's Jamyang Gönpo is also from Upper Nyang, only spelled as *myang* rather than *nyang*. The confusion on BDRC may have originated in an appendix of chronology in the *Big Tibetan-Chinese Dictionary*, where not only are these two Jamyang Gönpos differentiated, but we are further confounded by the statement that both Nyangtö Jamyang Gönpo *and* Dönyö Dorjé were born in 1196.[14] As we have seen, Jamyang Gönpo's secret name of Dönyö Dorjé is attested in multiple sources, so that would be another unlikely coincidence. Khamnyön Dharma Sengé (a.k.a. Jikdral Chökyi Sengé), in his later *Religious History of Pacification and Severance*, addresses this directly:

> Also, the main mantra tradition known as Profound Meaning from Dönyö Dorjé is the one that is well known among all Nyingma, Ganden, and so forth. Its lineage line from Chögyal Terdak Lingpa to my two gurus appears clearly in the lineage supplication. Paṇchen Dönyö Dorjé, Sangyé Tenpa, and Jamyang Gönpo are all the names enumerated. However, some say they are individual emanations and list two lamas in the supplications.[15]

Jamyang Gönpo in the Severance Lineage

Most of the available information about Jamyang Gönpo comes from his Drukpa Kagyü connection, and yet in terms of literary output he is mainly known now for his contributions to the Severance tradition. He is listed by Jamgön Kongtrul and others directly after Machik Labdrön's son, the wisdom-lineage holder Gyalwa Döndrup.[16] And yet others describe him not as a direct heir but as a visionary who received a direct transmission from Machik in meditative experiences.[17] Perhaps his status is clarified by Könchok Gyaltsen (1764–1853):

Machik's five main disciples were Gyalwa Döndrup, Khambu Yalé, Tönyön [Samdrup], Khugom Chöseng, and Dölpa [Kyemé] Sangtal. Jamyang Gönpo is said to be associated with any [or all] of those five as guru-disciple. Although he was not an actual disciple of Machik, since he was a disciple in visionary experience, his tradition is considered equal to that of Gyalwa Döndrup and the others, and has been authenticated. He created the source text of *Heart Essence of Profound Meaning*, and therefore it is known as the lineage of Severance that comes from Jamyang Gönpo, or the Severance of Profound Meaning.[18]

This would explain why Jamyang Gönpo's source text is included with Machik Labdrön's works in the collections of Severance source texts. Jamyang Gönpo himself also cites the words of Gyalwa Döndrup in the *Big General Commentary*; the quotation gives the impression of direct personal advice and doesn't seem to be in the records of Gyalwa Döndrup's compositions, which are mainly poems.[19] Despite some paucity of information on their connection, there is no reason to think Jamyang Gönpo did not receive these teaching in some kind of personal interaction with Gyalwa Döndrup, if not also in visions of Machik. On the other hand, his work is so very similar in style and terminology to writings of his Kagyü guru Lorepa, which are missing only the actual word *gcod*, that it seems he may have creatively synthesized these two traditions of Drukpa Kagyü and Severance himself, rather than merely passing them on.

Jamyang Gönpo's Literary Output in the Severance Tradition

Jamyang Gönpo had a distinctive way of signing his compositions as "the Śākya monk, holder of the vajra" (*shākya dge slong rdo rje 'dzin pa*) and either Mañjughoṣanātha (translating Jamyang Gönpo) or Prajñāsvabhāva (translating Sherab Jungné, his novitiate name).[20] The texts definitively self-identified in this way that were available to me are as follows:

- *Heart Essence of Profound Meaning: The Quintessence of All Source Texts and Esoteric Instructions on Severance, the Perfection of Wisdom,* "signed" Prājñāsvabhāva
- *The Big General Guide to the Profound Meaning,* Mañjughoṣanātha
- *The Seven-Day Severance Retreat Experiential Guide,* Prājñāsvabhāva
- *Lives of the Lineage Gurus of the Heart Essence of Profound Meaning,* Prājñāsvabhāva
- *A Structural Analysis of the Profound Heart Essence,* Mañjughoṣanātha
- *The Ten Door Openers: Personal Advice on Severance,* Mañjughoṣa

In addition to these, two more texts were named by Khamnyön Dharma Sengé as also composed by Dönyö Dorjé (his secret name) in the *Religious History of Pacification and Severance*.[21] However, the first clearly names a different author in its colophon: "*Sam 'od,*" short for Samten Öser, and I suspect the second one is the same. Which brings us to a second conundrum.

Samten Öser and the Gyalthang Tradition of the *Heart Essence of Profound Meaning*

Twelve lineage generations after Machik Labdrön, a visionary named Samten Öser (fl. fifteenth century) from Gyalthang had powerful direct encounters with her in his meditation. Adopting the title *Heart Essence of Profound Meaning of Severing Evil,* nearly identical to that of Jamyang Gönpo's work,[22] he authored a number of texts on the subject. Later this was called the "new pronouncement" (*bka' gsar ma*), which included eight subjects or branch appendices (*le'u yan lag brgyad,* not to be confused with Machik's three sets of eight appendices). At first glance, this similarity of titles and subject matter is rather confusing. However, Samten Öser had a very distinct style of narrative, which makes it easy to distinguish his creations from those of Jamyang Gönpo. Although he doesn't "sign" his name in the colophons, he makes no bones about claiming special status. In the first chapter, "Pearl Rosary of Legendary Tales," after describing his encounter with Machik, he states:

> Since then, I thought, "I am inseparable from Machik. I am Machik. Without me, there is no other Machik." This is a very big secret pronouncement. . . . There is no one in the transmission between me and Machik. The teaching that I have is what Machik had. All people who practice the Severance of Evil, request the teachings from me. I am not just proud. [!] You folks who hear the Severance of Evil from this man, your merit is greater than the cloudy mountain that stands before you.²³

The Gyalthang tradition seems to have gained the ascendency, at least in some schools. Sometime later, the abbot of Jonang, Kunga Drölchok (1507–1566), received the lineage of these teachings and included them in his great anthology known as *The Hundred Guidebooks of Jonang*. The third of Samten Öser's chapters, called "Wish-Fulfilling Gem: An Instruction on the Inner Meaning," became the basis for the sixth guidebook. Kunga Drölchok remarks:

> Among the many versions [of Severance], I had supreme confidence in the new pronouncement composed by Lama Gyalthangpa Samten Öser in the *Eight Branch Appendices*. From start to finish, this work is excellently adorned with new revelations that were actually given to him by Mother Lapdrön, the secret ḍākinī of timeless awareness, and that were unknown in the earlier recensions on Severance.²⁴

There is no mention of Jamyang Gönpo. Kunga Drölchok's recognized incarnation, the illustrious Tāranātha (1575–1634), received this same lineage and composed *Object Severance Empowerment Known as Opening the Sky Door*. This, in turn, was received by Jamgön Kongtrul Lodrö Thayé (1813–1900), marking the continuation of the Gyalthang tradition in the Kagyü schools[25]—and, it would seem, the eclipsing or confounding of the original.

The Texts Translated Here

The source text, *Heart Essence of Profound Meaning*, is a long poem in forty quatrains and opens our present volume. Jamgön Kongtrul included it with other source texts in the Severance section of his *Treasury of Precious Instructions*, and added the following note: "This is the primary source of most of the later instructions. There are many commentaries and guidebooks and such."[26] Two of those commentaries are presented in this volume.

The text translated here as *The Big General Guide to Severance* is a direct explanation of this source text, taking each verse or couplet and commenting on its meaning. Autocommentaries on verse compositions are very common in Tibetan and Indian literature. The idea was to memorize the verses after studying the commentaries, such that the deeper meanings will be brought to mind with fewer words to remember. Jamyang Gönpo uses the opportunity of a commentary to compose a wide-ranging description of the Severance practice that can be used for all occasions. Early Severance texts such as this are not restricted to one school of Tibetan Buddhism, though as time went on sect-specific liturgies developed. The single overall directive of *The Big General Guide* is to seek out and directly confront difficult circumstances. This acts as both a means to recognize emptiness— the lack of intrinsic existence of all phenomena—and a testing ground of one's former realizations and studies of that emptiness from the Perfection of Wisdom and other sources. The commentary also presents a brief survey of basic Buddhist philosophy and the various tenet systems and respective vows, all in order to demonstrate the superiority of the Severance approach. But there is much more here than abstract theory and its enactment in the field. Such an ancient text includes a great deal of cultural information on situations that might terrify or disgust a native Tibetan. These are given as examples, but the modern practitioner may certainly substitute their own phobias with little alteration of the intent. Especially, the detailed descriptions of how to immerse oneself in the very things that horrify—such as snorting the contents of smallpox abscesses or sleeping in the bedding of lepers—should serve to convince anyone that Severance is not primarily a healing method, as it has often been construed. Apart from these forays into ancient lore, the text is notable for its lack of instruction on ritualized Severance involving body sacrifice, which later works emphasize. Its primary message is to practice letting go of clinging to the self and reification of existence. It seems in this way to be closest to the actual teachings of Machik Labdrön. The past Severance masters of course realized this, but the simple message could become lost in the complex overlays of ritual and visualization. A good example of that is from Tenzin Namdak, who concludes an extensive description of such practices with these words:

> . . . the conceptual patterns that fixate on the duality of recipients of generosity—the guests of samsara and nirvana—and the giver of that generosity are your own awareness: lucid clarity, dharmakāya, mahāmudrā, beyond the realm of the intellect, and devoid of thought or utterance. The necessity of the purity in that state of suchness is crucial. This is the reason that the vital points of Mother [Machik's] Severance cycle—*The Great Bundle of Precepts, Another Bundle*, the *Appendices*, and the root and commentaries of the *Heart Essence of Profound Meaning*, the secret Severance of the great Drukpa renunciate [Jamyang Gönpo], and so forth—must be conclusively ascertained through the three means of understanding, experience, and realization.[27]

The third translation in this volume, *The Seven-Day Severance Retreat Experiential Guide*, is a very concise and precise instruction on putting the main intentions of the teachings into practice in the setting of a one-week retreat. After a brief introduction on who should do this and when and how, the practice of giving away the body as food is described briefly for the first day's practice. The remaining days are each divided into three short instructions for setting out to practice, and three short instructions for arrival at a practice place. The instructions contain no rituals, visualizations, deities, instruments, or liturgies.

These two texts form part of a trilogy by Jamyang Gönpo, which he introduced at the conclusion of his history of the transmission in *The Lives of the Lineage Gurus of the Heart Essence of Profound Meaning*. Although the third part is not included in this book, his introduction is presented here for context and anticipation:

> These days, all the instructions of Severance may be subsumed into one, the experiences of all Severance adepts rolled together, and the advice of all gurus wrapped up in a single place and sealed. These instructions include the whole extent of the Severance cycle taught by the Lord Mother, with nothing left out. It is presented as three subjects: the presentation as a general guide (*spyi khrid*), the extension as an experiential guide (*nyams khrid*), and the instructions as personal advice (*zhal gdams*).
>
> Since the *General Guide* is support material, it cultivates an understanding of all Severance. The *Experiential Guide* is for establishing the practice. Once it is laid aside as a guidance, it will become part of one's experience. The *Personal Advice* is for dispelling hindrances and enhancing practice. It contains ten door-opening instructions: (1) the empowerment opens the door to the Dharma, (2) the sādhana opens the door to blessings, (3) the introduction opens the door to the sky, (4) dispelling hindrance

opens the door to auspicious connections, (5) enhancement opens the door to qualities, (6) lucid dreaming opens the door to daytime and nighttime practice, (7) transference opens the door to liberation, (8) intermediate state practice opens the door to lucid clarity, (9) altruism opens the door to awakened activity, and (10) philosophy opens the door to excellence. Those are the instructions. Since they are personal advice, they are given after the [initial mind-nature] introduction of Severance and its successful practice. Supplements are explained as part of the *General Guide*.²⁸

Perhaps this third text in the trilogy will be translated by the time practioners are ready to lay aside the guidance after making it part of their experience.

My Sources

The title of the two texts by Jamyang Gönpo translated here are *Zab don gyi spyi khrid chen mo* and *Bdud gcod nyams khrid zab mo* (or *Gcod kyi lag len nyams khrid du bskyang ba gnyan khrod zhag bdun ma*). The verses of the source text on which they are based, *Bdud kyi gcod yul gyi gzhung* (or *Shes rab kyi pha rol tu phyin pa gcod kyi gzhung dang man ngag mtha' dag gi yang bcud zab don thugs kyi snying po*), have been extracted from the commentary and are presented first. I have based the translations primarily on the digital edition printed in thirteen volumes, which I am calling the Dingri Volumes. These were based on a collection in the library of Kyabje Zhadeu Trulshik Rinpoche, who even wrote a small booklet in commemoration of their publication, which was sponsored by the Tsadra Foundation in 2013. I used this collection mainly for its breadth of inclusion and clarity of printing. However, all versions of ancient texts, especially those digital versions that are highly edited by well-meaning typists, tend to stray from whatever the elusive original may have been. In this case, for example, the greater parts of a structural outline for the *Big General Commentary* were superimposed on the text. While this may have been derived from the author's own outline in *A Structural Analysis*, it proved to be confusing and only partially helpful. Therefore, I have retained some of those as section headings where they are clarifying, and only included the actual outline forms that were also present in the three other versions that I consulted. Those versions are as follows.

Practices of the Severance Collection and So Forth is said to be "reproduced directly from a rare manuscript collection from Limi, Nepal." It is a copy of a handwritten text and referred to throughout as the "Limi version." This version seems to be the oldest and most reliable, or at least the most interesting. This is the only one that contains all the texts mentioned in the introduction that are attributed to Jamyang Gönpo.

Then there is a series called *The Collected Works of Kunkhyen Longchen Rabjam*. The final volume 26 contains some of the familiar source texts of Severance. In the foreword it is said that the tulku Jampal Khyenrab newly discovered these ancient texts from a household in Bhutan in 2003. The editor continues to say that though they are attributed to Longchenpa Drimé Öser (1308–1364), modern scholars should carefully investigate whether that is the case. I think I can say that they are definitely *not* authored by that great Nyingma master, despite each text being appended with his name. Some of them also mention Pema Lingpa (1450–1521), considered a rebirth of Longchenpa. Another source has informed me that the texts in this last volume, unlike the others in the series, were actually collected by a son of Pema Lingpa called Sedawa (probably Thuksé Dawa Gyaltsen) and found at Tsetok Gonpa.[29] It appears to be quite scrambled, as there is a large section missing from Machik's source text *The Great Bundle*. Also, the history text is copied verbatim from Jamyang Gönpo's *Lives of the Lineage Gurus* up to a point, and then adds a variant lineage and history, creating much confusion. I've called it "Longchenpa version" for lack of a better abbreviation, and hope that this doesn't add to the confusion.

Finally, I checked with another hand-copied collection called the *Cycle of Severance of Evil: the Heart Essence of Profound Meaning*, described as "A collection of Gcod texts reflecting the teachings of Padma-gliṅ-pa. Reproduced from a manuscript collection from Padma-bkod."[30] It includes texts by Jamyang Gönpo without naming him. In this version, the colophon of the *Big General Guide* and several of the other texts state that it is the "Severance of the stainless tradition and the practice of Pema Lingpa." "Stainless" (*dri med*) in this case probably indicates Longchen Drimé Öser. I am not certain of the text's connection with the above collection. However, there were enough variations between the two to warrant examination of both. Strangely, the *Seven Day Retreat* text in this collection is marked with the signs of a treasure text (*gter tseg*). This collection is called "Peling version" in the endnotes, since it is said to be related somehow to the great treasure revealer of Bhutan, Rikzin Pema Lingpa.

I also had a photocopy of a handwritten text given to me by Lodrö Tulku Rinpoche in Zurich of the *Seven-Day Retreat*. It concludes with clarifying remarks on the authorship. Furthermore, I received Lodrö Rinpoche's book *The Profound Heart Essence: Prajnaparamita and the Practice of Chod*, which is an edited English translation from the German. It was a delight to discover Jamyang Gönpo's tradition in such good hands.

All of these witnesses have any number of variations, usually in the spelling of words, but often enough whole phrases, so many so that I found it impossible to note each one. However, I generally checked the important ones with my Tibetan informants to identify their preferred version. And in a funny way those variations helped my understanding of the intent. But this volume is very far indeed from being a critical edition, and I am guilty of the scholarly sin of picking and choosing without a transparent paper trail. It is, after all, a book for practitioners.

Technical Note

The root verses quoted in the *Big General Guide* appear in italics. When portions of those verses are duplicated by the author in his comments, they are bolded. As explained above, the headings of sections are taken selectively from the author's structural outline. Words added by the translator to streamline or clarify the author's intent appear in square brackets. Information added by the translator that might be helpful to the reader, such as word alternatives or Tibetan and Sanskrit equivalents, appear in parentheses. The phonetics of Tibetan names and words follow the recommendations in the Wisdom Publications' Style Guide, except in the cases of contemporary Tibetan authors, where their own preferences are retained. Transliterations of Tibetan words follow the extended Wylie system. Sanskrit diacritics are used throughout, except for naturalized Sanskrit terms such as sutra, mandala, and Mahayana. When the Tibetan retains the Sanskrit of a particular term, so does the translation.

1

Root Verses
Heart Essence of Profound Meaning

The Quintessence of All Source Texts and Esoteric Instructions on Severance, the Perfection of Wisdom[31]

Homage to the guru and Mother of the Victors.

1.

Dharmakāya free of elaboration, unutterable, unthinkable, unimaginable
   realm of space;
saṃbhogakāya fully possessing major and minor marks;
nirmāṇakāya as anything to tame anyone for their benefit:
I bow down to your consummated aspirations, emptiness, and compassion.

2.

Mahayana Dharma overcomes the four devils,
neither inhibits nor indulges samsara and nirvana, the perfections' meaning,
and makes adverse conditions the path; the Lady Mother's approach:
I write the meaning of Severance instructions that befriend adversity.

3.

[The master should be] realized in the words and meanings, well adorned
     with loving-kindness, endowed with eight skills;
their personal benefit completed, emptiness and compassion accomplished,
     and skilled in correcting faults.
[The disciple should] have faith, diligence, devotion, armor, and fortitude;
desire protection from fear; aspire to higher status; and hope to gain
     omniscience.

4.

[To one who] becomes a vessel for hearing the profound through receiving
     supreme empowerment,
introduce the seeking mind itself through the path of accumulation and
     purification.
Fortunate ones should adhere to this path of the victorious ones
in order to sever the lack of realization, false realization, partial realization,
     and doubts.

5.

The devils are the afflictions, divine child, aggregates, and death lord.
The special four are tangible, intangible, exaltation, and inflation.
In charnel grounds, desolate valleys, temples, lone trees, deserted houses,
     and so forth:
sleep in places where your mind is anxious and afraid.

6.

At night, the terrifying gods and demons gather and concepts arise.
This is the time to sever doubts, dispel obstructions, and enhance progress.
Those who desire omniscience go for refuge and supplicate.
Having supreme awakening mind is the path for all migrators to gain
     freedom.

7.

The resident [practitioner] is lent to the devil, and the ground [master] and
    guest mix as one.

The escort is entrusted to the enemy, and you are fearless, free in a secure
    stronghold.

The patient is entrusted to demons and thrives in well-being without disease.

Be free of unfavorable adverse conditions by integrating circumstances into
    the path.

8.

Free the mind of fixated cherishing by casting out the form aggregate as
    food.

Disperse the self-fixater by separating out body and mind.

Liberate fear in its own ground by inspecting the fearful one.

Obstacles will arise as glory by tossing away fixation on the body as self.

9.

Chasing conditions will pacify obstacles in emptiness.

Grabbing hold of malignant spirits will disperse frightening objects.

Knowing everything as mind will liberate fixation in its own ground.

Letting go at will and surrendering [will ensure] no one can carry you off.

10.

Whenever someone rests evenly in the meaning of phenomena's nature,

devil hordes can't stand it and display various apparitions at that time.

Outer, inner, and secret; in actuality, visions, and dreams;

in various forms, they say offensive words and make predictions.

11.

When the mind becomes distrustful, self-fixation emerges from objects.

Once the inner demons of your mind are tamed, the outer demons vanish in
    emptiness.

If unbearability and inability occur, equalize and trample them.

If fear and trepidation occur, focus intently on these thoughts.

12.

When apparitions become too great, don't persist; take a break.

Regret, wrong views, doubts, weariness with Dharma,

disease, suffering, congested constituents, and scattered practice—

as these signs of resistance and obstacles occur, exert effort in practice.

13.

Extreme measures for major resistance liberate hopes and fears naturally.

Mahayana's overwhelming brilliance resolves happiness and sorrow.

Putting the stars under darkness collapses the false structure of samsara and
    nirvana.

Smiting pestilence directly in haunted places destroys gods and demons as
    illusions.

14.

If the apparitions become too vicious, put pressure on the gods and demons.

If they continue to provoke, practice crazy vanquishing conduct.

If apparitions still manifest, delight in illness and be happy to die.

Hold them by the hook of compassion that benefits all.

15.

Know how the times and signs of success occur in actuality, visionary
    experience, and dreams,

arising to oneself outwardly, inwardly, and secretly.

If you rest in single-pointed meditative stability within emptiness,
no doubt the delusion of samsara and nirvana will be distinguished.

16.

If there are no signs of uprising in the preliminaries, lose the anticipation of
    uprising.
If there are no signs of suppressing in the main practice, cast behind anger
    and desire.
If there is no evidence of success at the conclusion, lose the anticipation of
    evidence.
The hopes and fears of a desiring mind are devils, which the wise reject.

17.

Helpers and harmers are subdued by gentle and harsh conduct.
Make aspirations to establish them in enlightenment through various means.
If you wish to attain omniscient buddhahood for yourself and others,
rely on this path of emancipation, fortunate ones.

18.

This conceptual thinking, a long-standing habit difficult to relinquish,
is the single cause that produces the variety of suffering in existence.
Here in this charnel ground of assembled aggregates and elements of the
    support and supported,
sever the various agitating thoughts and memories in this fluctuating place.

19.

The yogin who has actualized the empowerment and introduction
should sever until this devil of conceptual thinking is severed.
Phenomena's nature primordially possesses incidental stains.
View, meditation, and conduct conquer them in realizing the ground, path,
    and result.

20.

When phenomena's nature is ascertained, harmful thoughts abound.

Thoughts about various knowable objective appearances come and go.

Without the support of realization and the experiences of meditation,

engaging circumstances without the ability to equalize by trampling upon
them is to revert.

21.

Cut the trunk of thought-provocation with the ax of view, meditation, and
conduct,

and all the leaves of mental factors and concepts will wither on their own.

Just as the warm rays of sunlight overcome all humidity and gloom,

the dawning of timeless awareness removes flaws, and you traverse the stages
and paths.

22.

With emptiness, compassion, and the awakening mind, [some] realize
intrinsic nonexistence,

or can transform and relinquish through antidotes, or know how to make
offerings.

Devils and spirits cannot lead you to the lower realms.

Conquer the devil of afflictions that leads you to produce suffering.

23.

The place is this haunted ground of your body where channels and elements
converge,

where the spirits of affliction abide in the manner of inhabitants in a habitat.

Realization of timeless awareness appears as expanding light rays;

keep severing until the dark gloom of ignorance is illuminated.

24.

Whenever afflictions arise, grasp them through antidotes
of view, meditation, and conduct, and conquer the devils.
Just as unsuitable food will reactivate old toxins,
the condition of practicing will raise afflictions of attraction and aversion.

25.

Unless one has attained forbearance in Dharma, circumstances on the path
  terrify.
Regret, doubts, wrong views, and annoyance with Dharma will surface.
When afflictions arise, push back with methods and wisdom.
Emptiness, transformation, offerings, and realization are supreme remedies.

26.

Not stranded in the net of existence, an unbearable ocean of afflictions,
the best conquer it by equalizing in timeless awareness, the supreme
  measure.
With faith, compassion, realization, and the vital points of instruction,
yogins sever as a means of attaining emancipation.

27.

Intense sickness, suffering, and torment are everyone's devils;
if suchness is not realized, they rob the life force of attaining freedom.
The support that produces all happiness and sadness, faults and qualities,
  samsara and nirvana,
is this place of the aggregate of four elements, afflictions, winds, phlegm, and
  bile.

28.

When sickness and suffering arise in body, speech, and mind,
you are tormented by discordant adverse conditions.

The support for sickness and suffering and every fault and problem
is body and mind; when those two are separated, it is liberation.

29.
Snakes cannot bear a threatening finger pointed at them.
Sickness spirits cannot bear your meditation on emptiness, and run away.
Whenever you are pained by intense sickness and *duḥkha*,
you revert if you lose confidence, become discouraged, and give up.

30.
Vigor increases with mental heroism, experience, and realization.
The arsenal of sharpened view and conduct conquers the devil hordes.
The profound integration of methods and wisdom pacifies sickness and
    suffering.
Flawless good qualities grow full like the waxing moon.

31.
With the confidence of realization, the force of experience, much study,
courage, daring, heroics, bravado, and vanquishing conduct,
sever the devils of various worldly disharmonies such as
sickness, demons, spirits, defilement, the eight concerns, attraction, and
    aversion.

32.
Sever in the places that give rise to afflictions, such as your homeland,
populated places, country, monastery, or residence.
For a long or short time, during personal time, or until awakening:
practice as long as it takes for pleasure and pain, faults and adverse
    conditions to arise.

33.

Integrate sickness, spirits, defilement of violation, eight concerns, pleasure
and pain,
and so forth, by meditating on their lack of intrinsic nature and timely
knowledge.
As sickness, suffering, and thinking become more blatant than before,
various outer and inner discordant adverse conditions and obstacles occur.

34.

You may doubt cause and effect, the instructions, and the spiritual mentor.
You may fear circumstances and feel weary on the path of Dharma.
How can this appearing-yet-nonexistent devil harm you?
Defeat this unreal delusion of an enemy with a mental antidote.

35.

When this devil of attraction and aversion, the afflictions of existence, is
terminated,
the coffers of all good qualities open, the source of all joy and well-being.
Recognize dreams through accumulation, purification, actions, habits, and
intentionality.
When you've grasped dreams, refine, increase, and then meditate on lucid
clarity.

36.

Drawing up the winds and consciousness is the path of transference.
Lucid clarity arising from subtle and coarse melting sequences is
intermediate-state practice.
Disease and various mental problems occur when gods and demons are
agitated.
The remedial forces are emptiness, giving in charity, and meditating in
equanimity.

37.

Karmic causes and conditions of afflictive emotions produce sickness.

Resolve it by means of vital winds, yogic exercises, and visualizations.

Congested constituents, *duḥkha*, loss of focus, and lethargy are mental
problems.

Conquer them with methods and interdependence, and wind disease by
yogic exercise visualizations.

38.

Boundless devotion, vast compassion, and taking on adversity

become the enhancement of all good qualities.

Whoever grasps this supreme Object Severance, the victors' intent,

finds the path of freedom and vast, immeasurable qualities.

39.

Profound and vast, this precious holy Dharma that benefits everyone
everywhere

is especially elevated in adherents, is compatible with all tenets, and dispels
conditions.

Uphold this priceless precious teaching with devotion,

like someone who has found a gem and cherishes it.

40.

Through the brief arrangement of this *Heart Essence of Profound Meaning*

distilled from the vast ocean of the many profound Severance sources,

may all migrators reach the culmination of Object Severance, fully realize its
meaning,

and gain the supreme Mother Perfection of Wisdom in the pure realm of
phenomena.

2

The Big General Guide to Severance

The Big General Guide to the Profound Meaning from the Profound Heart Essence Meaning of Severing Evil[32]

Golden like the Jambu River, resplendent in cross-legged posture,
smiling, elegant, holding a sword, scripture, rosary, and lotus,
fully adorned by the major and minor marks, bejeweled in thousands of
　　varieties:
I bow to Lady Perfect Wisdom, Mother of Victors, with one face and four
　　arms.

The essential extract of the stainless intent of the precepts of the Sage's
　　speech,
the teachings of the adept lineage of transcendent Severance of Evil Object,
the profound meaning of the gurus' instructions, vast nectar of their speech,
is thoroughly presented here. May it benefit migrators like rain on the fields.

This is the esoteric instruction on Severance of Evil Objects. It is drawn from the ocean-like noble sayings [of the Buddha] and the open treasury of the precious Collections.[33] Outwardly, it is the combined intent of the extensive, middling, and condensed versions of the Perfection of Wisdom. Inwardly, it clearly presents the subject matter of the four precious tantra classes.[34] It faithfully reflects the oral instructions of all the adepts and realized masters. This is the supreme elixir of the speech of Lady Labdrön, Ḍākinī of Timeless Awareness.

In this there are many systems: the two lineages of precepts and experience, the father and the mother lineages, the transmitted precepts, the hidden treasures, and so forth. Here, however, the intentions of all of them will be unified as one, and their subject matters combined together. This will present a version that does not contradict any other Severance system and is thus exalted over the others.

Homage

> Intention of the transcendent perfection precepts,
> personal instructions of the adepts,
> esoteric instructions of Severing Evil Object,
> called Heart Essence of Profound Meaning.
> Homage to the guru and Mother of the Victors.[35]

This presents what is called *homage* to the sole path traversed by all the buddhas of the three times, the teaching that includes the intentions of the entire Mantra Vehicle and [the Mahayana path of] characteristics, the method by which one achieves buddhahood in a single lifetime, the teaching through which the result arises in actuality and is not established at a later time, and the instructions for a path of precious qualities that is unmatched by any other.

Eulogy

> 1. *Dharmakāya free of elaboration, unutterable, unthinkable,*
>   *unimaginable realm of space;*
> *saṃbhogakāya fully possessing major and minor marks;*
> *nirmāṇakāya as anything to tame anyone for their benefit:*

I bow down to your consummated aspirations, emptiness, and
compassion.

The primary cause is in the mindstream of all sentient beings: the indwelling of the sugatas' intention (i.e., buddha nature). Based on that, the contributing condition at the time of the path is taking bliss-emptiness and clarity-emptiness into one's experience during meditative equipoise. The subsequent attainment in post-meditation is to consummate love, compassion, and aspiration. Thereby, at the time of the result, the three kāyas, endowed with five awarenesses and four awakened activities, enact the welfare of others. The actions of dharmakāya are taught in the Middle Way:

> Homage to the perfectly pure nonbeing equaling space.
> Homage to the wholly wordless and inexpressible.
> Homage to the omnipresent in past and future.
> Homage to the emptiness of absolutely everything.[36]

The actions of the form bodies (*rūpakāya*) are presented in the *Verse Summary* [*on the Perfection of Wisdom*]:

> Among the people, a cleverly conjured person
> has no thought to please others, but takes action
> and is seen displaying various miracles,
> though without a body, mind, or name.[37]

The actions of both kāyas are taught in *The Way of the Bodhisattva*:

> A wish-fulfilling gem and a magical tree
> completely fulfill hopes just as desired.
> Just so, the Victor's kāyas manifest
> through the aspirations of those to be trained.[38]

The Promise to Explain

2. *Mahayana Dharma overcomes the four devils,*
   neither inhibits nor indulges samsara and nirvana, the perfections' meaning,
   and makes adverse conditions the path; the Lady Mother's approach:
   I write the meaning of Severance instructions that befriend adversity.

Adversity includes devils, elemental spirits, adverse conditions, obstacles, and so forth. They are relative reality without essence and are easily eliminated because they are unstable. According to the Mahayana Dharma they are insubstantial and can be overcome. The [*Perfection of Wisdom in*] *One Hundred Thousand Lines* explains:

> If there were such a thing as an unchanging objective phenomenon that was constant, a permanent and steady form, then this Mahayana would be unable to overcome the world with its gods and humans and demigods. However, since form is impermanent, unstable, and inconstant, there are no unchanging objective phenomena. Therefore, this Mahayana is able to overcome the world with its gods, humans, demigods, and *gandharvas*.[39]

There is no reason to deny or affirm samsara and nirvana. Cyclic existence and the transcendence of misery, sentient beings and buddhas, five poisons and timeless awareness, conceptual thinking and the nature of phenomena, and so on—all dualistic phenomena such as happy/sad, high/low, good/bad—need not be adopted or discarded, denied or affirmed, accepted or rejected. All those things that would be adopted, and so forth, are not established in ultimate reality since they are empty. For example, even if there are white clouds in the center of the sky, they will dissipate, and the sky will again be empty. Also, when dark [clouds] dissipate, the sky becomes empty. The lack of realization of that inseparability causes obscuration by incidental stains. As it says in the *One Hundred Thousand*:

> [Regard] form itself as empty of form,
> feeling as empty of feeling . . . (and so on).[40]

How might that be realized? It is realized through practicing this Object Severance, which contains the meaning of the Perfection of Wisdom. As for integrating adverse conditions on the path, since all causes of the inability to attain omniscient buddhahood come from obstructions and adverse conditions, one must integrate those adverse conditions. [Sever them like] drying out completely in water, handing over a sick person to demons, consigning an escort to the enemy, and desiring what is disagreeable as an ally. This Severance instruction is the system condoned by the Lady Mother. Disagreeable conditions are those that we normally try to eliminate, such as malignant spirits, obstructors, enemies, demons, adverse circumstances, obstacles, sickness, suffering, and so forth. [In this system] these are held to be allies or supports for attaining awakening. That is because the primary causes—bad karma, negativities, and obscurations—are purified; the contributing conditions of obstructions on the path are dispelled; realization is enhanced; and the result is the creation of buddha qualities. It is stated in the [*Verse Summary*] sutra:

> Give up even your life for Dharma's sake and ever strive in the
>   yoga.
> You should know that these are the signs of not turning back.[41]

Those are all revealed in this profound Severance instruction of the *Heart Essence*. It states that it is written in order to benefit all. Inwardly, the view is decisively severed (or resolved), meditation goals are finally severed, adopting or discarding in conduct is severed, and hopes and fears about results are severed. Outwardly, aggravating enemies are severed, harmful obstructors are severed, objects of attraction and aversion are severed, and all adverse conditions are severed. Therefore, it is called Severance.

THE MAIN BODY OF THE TEXT

The Master's Characteristics

3ab. *[The master should be] realized in the words and meanings, well adorned with loving-kindness, endowed with eight skills; their personal benefit completed, emptiness and compassion accomplished, and skilled in correcting faults.*

The master who teaches this esoteric instruction must be endowed with these eight characteristics

1. Skill in casting out the body as food after definitely distinguishing samsara and nirvana through the view.
2. Skill in maintaining undistracted attention after knowing mental non-action in meditation.
3. Skill in methods that achieve others' welfare while maintaining the conduct of equalizing whatever is encountered.
4. Skill in the accumulation of merit on a relative level after understanding that sacred pledge is not to be rejected or accepted, nor denied or affirmed.
5. Skill in applying the practice of *opening the sky door* (see glossary) after realizing that in desiring the result, it was there all along, spontaneously present.
6. Skill in discerning the boundary of samsara and nirvana once the meaning of the tenets' inseparable appearance-emptiness is actualized.

7. Skill in teaching the supporting instructions of the written guides without adopting or discarding.
8. Skill in the instructions of the expository red guides for *carrying flesh carrying blood*, which are enhancements of the practice.[42]

One who possesses these eight skills may explain [these teachings].

Examining the Disciple

3cd *[The disciple should] have faith, diligence, devotion, armor, and*
  fortitude;
desire protection from fear; aspire to higher status; and hope to gain
  omniscience.
Having received supreme empowerment, they become a vessel for
  hearing the profound.[43]

The disciple who practices this teaching
has great faith, diligence, wisdom,
great courage, and resilience;
has little pride, stinginess, deceit,
envy, desire, and attachment;
is devoted to the guru and afraid of birth and death;
is a precious golden vessel.
Additionally, a suffering individual
afflicted by sickness and spirits,
who is close to death, or a leper,
abandoned by the examiner or doctor,
[who] at the time of death, abandons superstitions
from astrologers, fortune tellers, or clairvoyants,
should be known as a vessel for this teaching.
Also, a person with faith

who fears death, is deeply devoted,
and listens to whatever truth is spoken,
is known as a vessel to hear this teaching.

Thus it is said. An individual possessed of the following three greats should take up the practice: great determined disposition, great daring to sacrifice their life, and great heart of Severance. You should explain this instruction to one who has these qualities.

Introduction at the Beginning

4ab. *[To one who] becomes a vessel for hearing the profound through receiving supreme empowerment,*
introduce the seeking mind itself through the path of accumulation and purification.

In order to make the disciple's mindstream a worthy vessel for hearing this teaching, you should open the door to the Dharma through the torma empowerment. Then, in order for [the disciples] to engage the special blessings, they should receive the transmission for refuge and supplications. They should exert effort in gathering the accumulations and purifying obscurations while supplicating the guru, yidams, and ḍākinīs. The culmination of all practice is meditation; the culmination of all meditation is to seek the mind. Meditation occurs based on resolving conceptual thought, by which the mind is sought. Once those have been done, the master should introduce the meditation of opening the sky door with a support or without one. That should be learned directly from the guru.

It is imperative to give the introduction of the preliminaries in that way. If [a practitioner] arrives [at the place to practice] Severance without having that introduction and commences giving their body, it will become a condition for obstacles, since that is the criterion for conjuring gods and demons.

If practitioners are properly introduced, even if no other Severance instruction is presented, they will be able to remain in haunted retreats. Perfectly complete [the introduction] and then teach the Severance instructions.

If you follow the teaching system of the transcendent perfections (i.e., Mahayana), it is unnecessary to confer even the torma empowerment, because empowerment conferrals are not discussed in the long, middle, or short [Perfection of Wisdom sutras]. If you adhere to the Secret Mantra Vehicle, just conferring the torma empowerment does not open the Dharma door, since that does not include all ten empowerments: the seven vase empowerments and the three sublime empowerments.[44] Therefore, of the two characteristics of the Secret Mantra Vehicle, there is no difference [from the perfection system] in terms of the ultimate view, but there *is* a difference in the relative reality that operates through methods. Although the Severance view espouses the perspective of the perfections, the meditation, conduct, sacred pledge, results, empowerment, and introduction to mind belong to the Secret Mantra perspective. You must follow the Secret Mantra for those.

Now, when there is a worthy recipient, if there is no empowerment conferral, no meditation on creation phase deities during the *sādhana*, no recitation of the essence mantra, and no meditation on the vital winds (*rlung*; Skt. *prāna*) in the completion phase, and if the conduct contradicts sacred pledge, the supreme and common results will not occur.[45] On the occasion of the introduction, when there is nonconceptual meditation, you must not consign work to the three doors [of body, speech, and mind]. Physical postures, sudden jumping up, clenching fists above the head, or joining palms at the heart are all putting your body to work, which will cause distraction and prevent meditation from occurring. Just sit cross-legged and rest in equipoise. Through giving up physical exertion, your body will be at ease. A comfortable body makes a comfortable mind. If your mind is happy, meditation will arise naturally. Sitting cross-legged and resting in equipoise are the vital points of the body. If you wonder whether that makes any difference, whether that is [not also] physical activity—don't think that way. There is a different degree of effort involved in standing compared to sitting. In your speech, reciting "*ah*" is putting your voice to work, so it causes a distraction that prevents meditation. Rest your voice in a state without expression or utterance. Then intrinsic awareness will proceed to nonconceptual space. Mentally, meditating on "*ah*" and causing light to emanate and return is consigning work to the mind, creating distraction and preventing meditation. Rest mentation in a state without memories or thoughts. That alone is meditation. In *The Great Bundle of Precepts*, [Machik says]:

> Place the body however is comfortable,
> and with no thought, do no thinking.
> No object of thought will be found.
> Rest mind without memory or thought.[46]

Is not so-called "meditation" (*sgom*) beyond any knowable object and thus free of the mentality of conceptual consideration—unutterable, unthinkable, and inexpressible? If it is, then doing the previously mentioned physical postures, recitations, and emanations [of light] will prevent that [experience]. Though they are required acts, they are unnecessary. Since the body is pervaded by the mind, there is no need to centralize [everything] into that one mind. That pervasion does not pervade an actual thing. It is pervasion by a non-thing. That non-thing is nothing that can be centralized as one. It would be redundant to centralize it. Whatever is pervaded, it is fine just to let it vanish on its own. As when clouds vanish in the sky, there is no need to gather them up and then make them disappear; they will vanish wherever they are.

In general, mind's essence is not a thing. It makes no sense to meditate on syllables or lights or rainbows, turning nonexistence into existence. To make a *nonthing* into a thing is perverse. Since the mode of being of the innate disposition is empty, it is sufficient to introduce emptiness. But you might say, "There is no fault in doing the introduction with *ah* and light emanating and returning, and then introducing nonthing based on that." Yes, there *is* a problem. To introduce nonthingness, you don't need to introduce it based on a thing. It is enough to introduce [the fact that] there is absolutely nothing to depend on as a support with regard to nothingness. If you say, "But that is unacceptable to produce [something," the correct response is that] it is sufficient to make the introduction based on that nonarising alone. To call nonseeing a path is to be close to traversing the path. In meditation, not to meditate is excellent. In the view, to have nothing to view is excellent. In conduct, to be free of rejecting and accepting is righteous. In sacred pledge, not to keep the rules is excellent. And as for the result, if there is no hope or fear, it will be obtained. So it is said.

If you [think that you] must generate some thing in meditation, the truth is that it is untenable to create a support that is insupportable. In bringing about the understanding of a *nonthing*, it is said that you needn't rely on a support. Therefore, this introduction in the opening the sky door practice is a suitable fast track for the very sinful if they are guided in the transference of consciousness. The one called Dakpo Rongé Kyemé Gayen[47] held that, outwardly, one should understand according to the [Buddha's] word, and inwardly, one should understand through the four great tantra classes of Secret Mantra. That is the position of the great practitioner of Severance.

Now some people say that once the mind pervades the body, it exists, or once it is separated [from the body], it exists. They are wrong, since mind is not a real thing. You might think that therefore it cannot pervade [something], but there is no contradiction. There are scriptural citations, logical reasons, and examples [in support of this position]. From the *Hevajra Tantra*:

> Great awareness resides in the body,
> precluding all concepts.
> It is the pervader of all things,
> residing in the body, [yet] not produced from it.[48]

From the [*Verse Summary*] sutra:

> For example, as clouds in space abide without an abode,
> nonabiding is abiding; this the Victor spoke of as abiding.[49]

Logically, from top to bottom, whether something is helpful or harmful, it is the mind that has the experience of happiness or sadness. For example, though the sound of a drum is not an actual thing, the condition of the drum's skin determines the pervading sound.

Outwardly, Severing Gods and Demons

The person who severs

4cd. *Fortunate ones should adhere to this path of the victorious ones*
in order to sever the lack of realization, false realization, partial
realization, and doubts.

A person who takes into practice this instruction on Severance may have four faults: they may lack realization, have false realization, have partial realization, or harbor doubts. Any of these individual types might take up the practice. A person who lacks realization does not realize nonself inwardly, nonexistent demons externally, and nonexistent adverse conditions in between. A person with false realization is one who, inwardly, realizes that since there is a self, it can truly be harmed; outwardly, realizes that since there are demons, harm-doers are real; and in between, realizes that since adverse conditions exist, obstacles are real. A person with only partial realization is one who knows that there is no self that is afraid, but does not understand that fear itself is empty; who knows that there is no reason to fear demons, but does not understand that the object of fear is empty; and who realizes that there is no object of fear or one who fears, but does not realize that mere sickness and obstacles are not truly existent. A doubtful person wonders whether the existence of demons is true or not. Since all of those [misunderstandings] should be severed, practice Severance. Furthermore, in order to dispel obstructions when they occur in all practice on the path, practice Severance. If view, meditation, and conduct do not develop, practice Severance to enhance them.

At first, when a person goes to a haunted place to do spiritual practice but cannot follow through, the reason is that they were previously lost on the path of distraction. Second, once the inner frightened person encounters the conditions of the outer frightening object and takes up the practice, resolution will come [like] drying out in water. Third, one who is inwardly timid and unable to suppress will come to distinguish phenomena by trampling upon [the conditions]. It is said that having such mental confidence is what differentiates the confusion of samsara and nirvana.

The devils that are severed

5ab. *The devils are the afflictions, divine child, aggregates, and death lord.*
The special four are tangible, intangible, exaltation, and inflation.

The defining characteristic of any devil (*bdud*; Skt. *māra*) is that it interrupts spiritual practice. The categories are the devil of afflictive emotions, the devil of the divine child, the devil of the aggregates, and the devil of the death lord. The devil of afflictive emotions is the five toxic emotions that interfere with the practice of virtue. The divine child is the exaltation, pride, haughtiness, and arrogance that arise when good qualities develop inwardly, because those cause obstacles to the evolution of those very qualities. The devil of the aggregates is the aging, sickness, and decline of the body. The devil of the death lord is what causes the interruption of the remaining life based on the condition of death. Lady Machik taught four more:

> Devils are classified as four:
> tangible devil and intangible devil,
> the devil of exaltation, and the devil of inflation.
> [All are included in the devil of inflation.][50]

The tangible devil is fire, water, poison, weapons, wild animals, precipices, and so forth—anything that appears as an object to the senses. Severing that devil is difficult on the [Mahayana] paths of accumulation and application, which are mundane paths where one has not yet gained the stages of a bodhisattva. At that time the support of the body is powerful, but the supported mind has not gained control. Sickness, suffering, and so forth occur against one's will. Since one has not gained miraculous abilities and omniscience, one is obstructed by the four elements. That is the tangible (literally, "sense-obstructing") devil, so it is difficult to sever. Once the stages are gained on the path of seeing and onward, [one proceeds to] the supramundane paths. Still, one must train on the path until one arrives at the level of a buddha. Even though one still practices hardships on the path, sickness and suffering are not experienced. They merely appear as hardships, so there is no fatigue or weariness. Examples are Sadāprarudita donating his body and Guru Nāropa leaping into a fire and an abyss. It is said that attaining the stages entails freedom from five fears. At that time, it is possible to sever the tangible devil.

The intangible devil is the external devil of gods and demons and the internal devil of afflictive emotions, sickness, suffering, and so forth, whether subtle or rough, which are felt and experienced as mental objects. Regarding those, a person who possesses the antidotes, even if they have not attained the stages, may still sever them at the time of the paths of accumulation or application.

The devil of exaltation is when someone takes up the practice of the instructions for Severance and, based on that, the external gods, demons, and devils do not affect them, and sickness and suffering are pacified.

Consequently, they think, "Now abilities and blessings arise through this practice. Material goods will accumulate and good luck will increase. Fame and renown will spread. Vast outer and inner qualities will develop." Once they harbor such hopes, desires, joy, and exaltation, they set their sights on the benefits and results. In the practice of Severance, this is the devil of having exaltation. Therefore, practice without exaltation over the benefits of Severance. Moreover, you must even be without desire or hope for buddhahood.

The devil of inflation occurs when you go to a haunted place—such as a graveyard, empty valley, or remote highland—and yet no evidence of success arises.[51] Why is that? You are inflated by thinking, "I have the deity and guru to watch over me, the Three Jewels to protect me, and the heroes and ḍākinīs to stand guard." You have the confidence of thinking, "I have this profound instruction on Severance." You have the arrogance of thinking, "I have an excellent experiential practice of mahāmudrā, which means internally, gods and demons don't exist." You have the notion, "If obstacles from gods and demons do occur, it is enough to donate my body. If I'm able to give it away, they can't carry me away, they can't eat me, and they will turn away and leave. It is sufficient to act in that way." In the practice of Severance, this is the devil of inflation.

Therefore, when you are about to go practice, don't say, "Guru and Jewels, please guard me. Please protect me. Please pacify obstacles." Don't say, "Please bless me so that sickness and adverse conditions will not arise." Don't say, "Please bless me with pacifying devils, spirits, demons, malignant spirits, and obstructors." What should you say? There is no contradiction with having gone for refuge to the Three Jewels at first. There are, however, different systems of supplication. Here, you pray, "Bless me that adverse conditions and obstacles are taken as the path. Bless me to equalize happiness and sadness. Bless me to abandon self-fixation on the body." Then go on your way.

Once you arrive at a haunted place, the blessings of the guru and Three Jewels, the protection of the heroes and ḍākinīs, and your meditation on mahāmudrā won't work. Do not be inflated by thinking that you can handle it because you have the Severance instructions. Do not harbor confidence and arrogance. There is no refuge, no protector, no confidante, no friend, no relative, no support, no backup, and no reinforcement. All alone, rest and remain there. Whatever apparitional and vicious things occur, think without inflation: "I have no safe refuge or reinforcement. I can't fight, or escape, or be cautious. You all can come whenever you want. You have the power; do whatever you like."

Moreover, when one is still a beginner, there is no problem even if the four devils do occur. If there is no tangible or intangible devil, then since there is no object to sever, there's no reason to go for Severance. The practice won't be enhanced later and the good qualities won't arise. If there's no thought about qualities to exalt, there won't be anyone to go for Severance. For example, if there's no thought of the fruits of harvest, there won't be anyone to cultivate crops. If there's no concern for the profits of commerce, there won't be anyone to do business. Just so, if there's no inflation from having the practice and instructions, you can't go do Severance in a haunted place, just as a warrior can't go to battle without weapons. Therefore, at first, don't discard the four devils that are to be discarded. It is said to be a lesser problem if they arise. It's like the medicine that eliminates the four kinds of disease; you discard the medicine when the disease is cured. Unless you have mastered Severance, don't discard exaltation and inflation. Those two can be eliminated later on.

How the devils are severed: Where to sever

5cd. *In charnel grounds, desolate valleys, temples, lone trees, deserted*
      houses, and so forth:
      sleep in places where your mind is anxious and afraid.

It is very important to find a haunted power place to practice Severance. Places where subterranean malignant spirits live, such as springs with nine, seven, five, or three sources, or one. In those places live nāgas that are out-caste, brahmin caste, nobility caste, royal caste, and low caste, respectively. Minor nāgas live near springs of disrupted or circling waters where the sun does not shine. Pestilent spirits stay at lakesides and in waterfalls, lone trees, bushes, meadows, and unclean waters. Earth lords live near boulders that are shaped in the likenesses of tigers, snakes, toads, and pigs. The earth lords, great nāgas, and pestilent spirits live by cliffsides in the shapes of tortoises, scorpions, bears, yaks, water oxen, camels, or buffalo. Red rock faces, mountain spurs, and fissures that look like upright humans, monkey faces, swords, and blood daggers are the abodes of *tsen* spirits. If they are black, the devils live there. Oath-breakers, female *sen* spirits, and *theurang* live under overhangs and in dark caves, crevices, rock fissures, and hollows. Single, empty, dilapidated houses; abandoned nomad camps; desolate ruins; and streets and shops are the hungry-ghost abode of male and female knife ghosts and *serak* ghosts, who move in space. Graveyards, places where Dharma is taught, corpse pits, crematoriums, places where people have died, and battle grounds where warriors have been killed are the dwelling places of *mamo* mothers, death lords, life-force masters, and devils. Temples, stupas, storerooms, crumbling homes, crumbling monasteries, meditation centers, and remote retreats are all places for king spirits, custodian spirits, and *pekar* spirits.

In short, many abodes are described, but the point is to practice Severance in places where you yourself are afraid and apprehensive—places that induce an experience of fear. These are the auspicious places where you can sever mental superimpositions, ascertain your own mind, and take emptiness into experience—where a yogin can clearly discern and differentiate conflicted samsara and nirvana.

You might think that you must go to stay only in those places, or that it is inappropriate to remain in your own home. Although demons are not actually established as existent in those places, you have the idea that demons won't be caught at home and that you must go out to conjure them. Then again, in this Severance there is both the severance of objective demons and the severance of the subjective mind. Though you must go to a big demon place, those demons are not the adversaries, nor are they to blame. Those demons are also not produced from that area. There is no hope that the demons will grant spiritual powers. So then why go to that haunted ground and that big demon place? Objectively there are no demons, but subjectively there *is* fixation on demons and on a self, with self-cherishing that must be severed. That, and in order to ascertain the lack of true existence, is why you go to a haunted place. Based on external scary conditions, the inner consciousness that is frightened is [exposed and can be] thoroughly investigated.

Through doing that, progress is made on the path. Your view, meditation, and conduct will be enhanced. By trampling upon whatever is unbearable (*mi phod pa*) and equalizing any inability (*mi nus pa*), the obstructions of the path will be dispelled and qualities will arise.

There are six objects that are unbearable: fire, water, poison, weapons, dogs, and precipices. Since they are life-threatening, they are unbearable. This was presented previously in the section on the tangible devil. Fear and apprehension of gods and demons feels unbearable—turn it around by giving up self-fixation. Disgust with the five elixirs[52] feels unbearable—know that they are sacred substances by recalling their benefits, and cultivate their equality through the confidence of that realization. Shame between brothers and sisters makes being naked, and so forth, feel unbearable—thoroughly cut through the one who feels shame by knowing that the six sense groups are not truly existent. Value judgments, criticism, exposed faults, and unpleasant words feel unbearable—equalize fear and apprehension by knowing that all sounds are empty. You need wealth and possessions, so you are attached to them, and giving them away feels unbearable. Practice giving through knowing that all apparent existence is illusory. Since everything is understood as your mind, fearlessly trample upon the unbearable.

When to sever

> 6ab. *At night, the terrifying gods and demons gather and concepts arise. This is the time to sever doubts, dispel obstructions, and enhance progress.*

The best time to go practice Severance is at night under cover of darkness. In the daytime, no matter where you are, you won't be afraid. If you arrive with companions, no matter when and where you sleep, you won't be afraid. If you are not afraid, qualities won't arise because there is nothing to sever in your Severance practice. For example, it is like brandishing a sword in space—it makes no difference whether it cuts or not. If you do not experience fear and trepidation inwardly, there is no difference in arriving [at a special place] or not; because if you try to sever only the one who is fearful, there will be nothing to sever when there is no fear. For example, though domestic or wild animals wander in wild places, and jackals roam in graveyards, they don't develop any of the qualities of Severance practice. And don't think that being free of the fearful one and feared object is only the desirable outcome of Severance practice, just because it is a sign of [successfully] cutting through. That is not the case. Someone who is fearless from the start without practicing Severance, and a fearful person who has practiced Severance but has become fearless through ascertaining the emptiness of the frightened subject and frightening objects are not the same. Therefore, do the practice when you feel afraid and apprehensive, when doubts have arisen, and to dispel obstructions and enhance your practice.

As for the manner of going: Don't go with hatred and an adversarial mind. Don't go in high spirits with arrogance. Don't go with haughtiness and boastfulness. Don't go with pride and lofty goals. Don't go for gain and honor. Go with the motivation of the great faith of true renunciation.

The preliminaries: Going for refuge and arousing the awakening mind

6cd. *Those who desire omniscience go for refuge and supplicate.*
Having supreme awakening mind is the path for all migrators to gain
freedom.

When you embrace refuge and the awakening mind, whatever you do will become a spiritual path. Whatever you do will benefit migrators. Therefore, before going to practice Severance in a haunted retreat, go for refuge and arouse the awakening mind:

> For the sake of all sentient beings, I will take up the practice instructions of this profound path of Severance, which is the Buddha's word, the intent of the Perfection of Wisdom, the path along which all buddhas of the three times have passed, and the practice of all the guru adepts. I shall inspire realization in all sentient beings who lack it. I shall liberate all who are not liberated. I shall cause all who have not attained perfect awakening to attain it. In order to do that, from this evening on I will take up the practice of this Severance of Evil Object. Gurus with the word transmission, yidams with the host of mandala deities, heroes and ḍākinīs—all of you, please grant your blessings. From this evening on, bless me that adverse conditions and obstacles rise up on the path. Bless me to experience the equal taste of happiness and suffering. Bless me to abandon fixating on the body as the self. Bless me to consummate Object Severance. Please bless me so that all sentient beings will attain perfect buddhahood based on this path.

Once you have said that, proceed on your way. Some Severance practitioners do a supplication such as this: "I go for refuge to the Buddha. I go for refuge to the Dharma. I go for refuge to the Sangha. I rely on the

Buddha. I rely on the Dharma. I rely on the Sangha. Whether I am in an empty valley, a mountain ravine, a dark cave, a crevice, a precipice, or out in the open—wherever I am, please guard me. Please protect me. Please pacify conditions and obstacles."

This is a big mistake. It is unsuitable because it contradicts the customary intent of Severance. [To supplicate like this] is to go for refuge from fear without abandoning the attitude of fixation on a self. To go for refuge to the Three Jewels will prevent obstacles from arising, which is not the instruction of Severance. It states in *Heart of the Sun Sutra*:

> Whosoever goes to the Buddha for refuge
> cannot be killed by ten million devils.
> Even if their discipline has waned and their mind is unsettled,
> they are certain to transcend to the other side.[53]

It says in the *Sacred Victory Banner Sutra*:

> Monks, if you stay in hermitages, charnel grounds, under trees, in the open, or on the outskirts of town . . . and have gone for refuge to the Three Jewels, fear, suffering, and hair-raising experiences will not occur.[54]

But with just that [reassurance], if you are still fearful and have not abandoned an attitude of self-fixation, it would be better not to go to a haunted place. That kind of Severance practitioner is a "great meditator" (*sgom chen*) who desires food but is fearful, like a fox slinking around a human corpse. It is said of those great meditators who practice like that, "With the butchered corpse in their right hand they clean up the stains with their left."

The main part: releasing self-fixation from the object

7. The resident [practitioner] is lent to the devil, and the ground [master]
   and guest mix as one.
   The escort is entrusted to the enemy, and you are fearless, free in a
   secure stronghold.
   The patient is entrusted to demons and thrives in well-being without
   disease.
   Be free of unfavorable adverse conditions by integrating
   circumstances onto the path.

Once you have arrived at that haunted place, take up the practice by meditating like this:

Since beginningless cyclic existence I have grasped body, speech, and mind as a self, and cherished them. In the short term, demons and spirits and obstructors caused harm and sickness and suffering that afflicted me. In the long term, I have cycled through the three realms and wandered among the six classes of beings. All of that has self-fixation to blame. Now, this body's primary cause is the previous karmic actions that have produced it. The contributing condition is my parents' desire, which gave rise to it and resulted in me obtaining a human body with freedoms and endowments. I have the complete five sense doors, the complete five internal organs, and the complete set of five aggregates and sense fields: this is my beautiful, clean form aggregate—my attractive, cherished, valuable, necessary, and desirable body.

In general, I give away this body as ransom for all sentient beings of the six kinds. In particular, I give it as ransom for my kind parents. Even more specifically, I give it to you gods and demons to consume. Those who come from afar, eat it cold. Those not far, eat it cooked.

I do not have even a sesame seed's worth of attachment. Whoever wants it, take it away. I let this body go like spit and snot without any attachment. I let it go like throwing away a leprous corpse. I let it go like expelling feces. I let it go without self-fixation like dirt and stone. You demons, spirits, and obstructors contend for it—eat the flesh, drink the blood, swallow the innards, gnaw the bones, and carry off the sense organs—consume it all without leaving a tiny morsel. This objective material body you all may eat. This emptiness of mind is not a material thing. I don't need to cling to it with self-fixation and cherishing as if it is me. Now there is nothing to preserve or protect. There is no need to cherish or care for the body.

With these thoughts, rest and relax into that state. Many Severance practitioners say, "I don't need this aggregate of the impure body, this bag of pus and blood, this glob of snot. I don't need it. Whoever wants it, take it away." There are four inappropriate faults in that approach. (1) Fundamentally, in the practice of generosity, if you give something impure, it will not result in the perfect accumulation of merit. (2) It is inappropriate to give the demons something you yourself don't want, because they also won't want it. (3) Inviting demons to carry away the body is a way to assuage your fears, [which is why you said it]. (4) Since you said the body is a bundle of impurities, the demons will be turned off and they won't want it. Since those [attitudes] cater to your hopes, they are inappropriate. The [correct] practice is to lend the resident to the devil, to entrust the escort to the adversary, and to consign the nurse to the demon, [as follows].

The resident [practitioner] is lent to the devil, and the ground [master] and guest mix as one. That is, in going to that haunted place, say to the local ground master, "I have come to donate my body here; you do whatever you like." With that, you must do away with self-fixation. In addition to not harming you, that ground master will help you. The ground master protects against danger from others and becomes a guardian for the practitioner. But don't hope for that to happen, because that is the devil of inflation. For instance, in whatever country you may travel, you come as a guest of its residents. You don't say to them, "Please guard me, please protect me, pay attention to me."

The escort is entrusted to the enemy means not to cling to the idea of an enemy, because doing that and being careful transfers the harm to you. Without being apprehensive, if you just let them be, not only will they not harm you, they will even protect you against harm from others, like an escort. Whatever harmful demons are there, do not regard them as demonic. Don't be apprehensive, just stay there and spend the night. Say, "I won't harm or condemn you; I just came to give my body. Whether you eat it or not is up to you." By saying that, the enemy will cause no harm to you and even guard you against harm from others.

The patient is entrusted to demons applies to when you are standing guard at a patient's pillow[55] or ensuring the well-being of a child. If there is any demon who harms small children or sick people staying in some place, take the child or patient and go there. If you can't do that, call the harmful demon to you and give it the child or patient. Meditate that it joyfully eats them. By doing that, since there is no greater enemy to the small child or patient than a demon, when you give them to the demon it is pleased and will carry the patient's karmic retribution and debt. The demon will believe it decisively and won't inflict harm. It will even guard against the harm of others.

Those are the instructions for integrating conditions into the path. For example, if you extract the essence of deadly poison, it alleviates all head-aches, pestilent spirits, and harm from nāgas, and afterward the effect of poison will not be felt. As it states in *Another Bundle*:

> The sickness, the patient, and the demon:
> these three are nondual.
> Rest in a state of emptiness.
> Chop up your body and offer it as a feast.

Hide concepts as treasure in the nature of phenomena.
And, moreover, do that many times.
Don't give rise to joy if you get better.[56]

Casting out the form aggregate as food

8. *Free the mind of fixated cherishing by casting out the form aggregate*
   as food.
   Disperse the self-fixater by separating out body and mind.
   Liberate fear in its own ground by inspecting the fearful one.
   Obstacles will arise as glory by tossing away fixation on the body
   as self.

When you arrive at the haunted place, lie down without hesitation. To cast out the form aggregate as food, you must relinquish all aggregates, constituents, and sense bases (Skt. *skandha, dhātu, āyatana*) that you hold as part of yourself and throw them out as food for gods and demons, inviting them to take what they like. Become free of the attitude of fixated cherishing. Once body and mind are separated, send out the body as a gift. Resting your mind in the state of emptiness will disperse the one who is fixated on the self and on cherishing as, for example, a human corpse in a graveyard that does not cling to a self because the body and mind have parted.

Liberate fear in its own ground by inspecting the fearful one. Whenever you feel afraid, look for the location of the fearful one from your head to your soles. Is it in the flesh or the blood? Is it outside or inside? Look: is it square or round or triangular or spherical or pointy? Look for its shape. What color is it? Is it white, black, blue, green, gray, or what? If fear is part of the body, it is inert matter. If fear is in the mind, that is already known to be empty. So now where is the fear? Think about what there is to be afraid of. If you search in this way, since the fearful one is not found, all dread and anxiety will be self-liberated. The answer is that all adverse conditions, obstacles, sickness, and suffering are due to the existence of self-fixation. When you are free of self-fixation, those [conditions] are no different from stones, and there is no reason to fear them. From *Another Bundle*:

> Rest the body in the way of a corpse.
> Regard it in the way of being ownerless.
> Sometimes, rest with the five sense organs hollow
> like a dried-up human head.[57]

With just that realization, devils arise as glory and obstacles arise as spiritual powers.

Befriending adverse conditions

> 9. *Chasing conditions will pacify obstacles in emptiness.*
> *Grabbing hold of malignant spirits will disperse frightening objects.[58]*
> *Knowing everything as mind will liberate fixation in its own ground.*
> *Letting go at will and surrendering [will ensure] no one can carry you off.*

Whatever adverse conditions, obstacles, and apparitions occur, follow these four vital points: chase (or confront) conditions, grab spirits, know that everything is mind, and let go at will and surrender. Practice these four. **Chasing conditions** is going and staying in whatever place is frightening, going in the evening or whatever time is scary, and staying near whatever is frightening, such as statues, corpses, or bushes. **Grabbing malignant spirits**—whether they appear in actuality, in a dream, in visionary experience, or as embodiments seen with the eyes—means to hold them with your hands and grab them, saying, "As you are my relative, please take a seat." Don't send them off. If this occurs as a visionary experience, increase the clarity even more. If this occurs in a dream, go back to sleep and request [the spirit] to come back. If it occurs by invitation, say "Hey, here I am, please come here." **Meditating on everything as mind** means that whatever pleasant or unpleasant feelings occur—whether you give the body to demons or protect it, whether you meditate on existence or nonexistence, whether [you experience] fear and trembling or joy and cheer, or feel carefree without fear—all of them are the apparitions of mind, the patterns of mentation, the emanating and gathering of thought, the shifting array of awareness, and solely created by conceptual mind. The point is that they don't have even a hair's tip of true existence. **Letting go at will and surrendering** is to let the body go and send it off without any sense of caring, self-fixating, cherishing, grieving, attachment, or clinging. If you do that, no one can carry it off, and no one will desire it. It is like a grown-up [teasingly] begging for the food that a young child is eating. They keep requesting it as long as the child is reluctant to give it up, but when the child finally consents, the grown-up doesn't want it.

Signs of uprising

10. *Whenever someone rests evenly in the meaning of phenomena's nature,*
    devil hordes can't stand it and display various apparitions at that time.
    Outer, inner, and secret; in actuality, visions, and dreams;
    in various forms, they say offensive words and make predictions.

[This verse addresses] the signs of malignant spirits rising up. There are three parts of this: reasons for uprisings or their absence, signs of uprising, and displays of devils' ridicule.

Reasons for uprisings or their absence

Once you have arrived in the haunted place, if you fall asleep while doing the practice, [whatever abilities the spirits have][59] will cause an uprising.

In the best case, an uprising will occur within one day, middling in five or seven days, and the least after ten days. The reason for an absence of uprising, a weak uprising, or a belated uprising is that the spirits' power is weak and cannot rise up. When the yogin's ability is great, the spirits are overwhelmed and cannot rise up. Alternatively, when the spirits are very dull and the yogin's ability is weak, there's no uprising, or the duration of the Severance practice is too short so there's no uprising. There are many possibilities and you should know which one it is.

A lack of uprising when the individual's ability is weak [could mean that] a beggar is secretly staying there, a farmer is guarding their field, a merchant is traveling by at night, a nomad is searching for their lost cow, or a thief is coming to steal. In any of those cases, you will have no ability to raise a spirit. If you don't harm that demon and ask it for refuge, even if you sleep in that place where it is, it won't rise up. If, after arriving at that place, your fear does not grow after a few days, it will be easy to raise the lesser malignant spirits. Lesser malignant spirits have lesser apparitions, and suppressing them is easy, but bringing them under control has little benefit. If at first fearlessness and joy arise, but after a while you become more and more afraid and the experience of displeasure grows, it indicates that it is a strong spirit, and raising it will be difficult. It is fierce. Suppressing that strong apparition will be difficult, but if it is suppressed there will be great benefit. Furthermore, upper spirits are easy to raise but lower spirits are difficult. In shrine rooms, empty houses, and so forth, fearful apparitions are big but easy to suppress. In springs, lakes, and such, first there are pleasant small apparitions, but suppressing them is hard.

Yogins who have the confidence of the view, māntrikas who meditate on deity yoga, people who have been harmed by demonic spirits, and those whose minds harbor doubts may experience uprising in one day. There are also cases where the uprising, the suppression, and the evidence of success all occur in a single day. And there are even cases where the apparition that arises at dusk is successfully terminated at dawn. Or the apparition rises up early in the evening and is terminated later that evening. There are many types. For the most part, three days each are usually required.

Signs of uprisings

This has three parts: outward signs of god-demon uprisings, inner signs of uprisings as conceptual thinking, and in-between signs of uprising as sickness.

(1) Outward signs of god-demon uprisings: Once you arrive at that haunted place, separate the body and mind. The body is freely and completely thrown out. The mind is without dread, without apprehension, without concepts, and without inflation; consciousness is intrinsically non-existent. Within that state, rest at ease, loose and relaxed. With that blessing, the unbearable brilliance of phenomena's nature, the unbearable power of emptiness, and the yogin's unbearable practice cause various apparitions to arise. For the most part, the spirits manifest in various unpleasant visible forms. They emanate as tigers and lions that make a show of devouring. They emanate as dogs and wolves that make a show of biting. They emanate as buffalo and yaks that act as if they are charging and goring. They emanate as snakes, bears, scorpions, and all kinds of fearsome creatures that appear to terrify and frighten. They emanate as enemies, men and women carrying various weapons, who make a show of striking, beating, and binding you. They threaten to fight and suppress you, entrap you in avalanches, turn you upside down, and move you from your seat. They emanate as mothers, sisters, and beautiful women who display expressions of desire, smiling and seductive. They emanate as fathers, brothers, and friends crying, lamenting, and roaring with intensely unpleasant sounds. They emanate as khenpos and lopöns to tell you that your Dharma is all wrong, that it is an aberrant path. They say that without a body, this lifetime of yours will end today. They say that now in seven days you will die. They say that once you die, you will be born in the Incessant Hell. They call to

you with disembodied sounds and leave you trembling. They make sounds of "strike" and "kill" in your ears. These experiences occur in actuality at best, in visions on average, and in dreams at the least.

Average apparitions emanate as blazing fire; being swept away by floods, trapped in rock slides, squeezed in crevices, and crushed by boulders; the advent of earthquakes and whole ground movements, shaken and stirred; thundering, booming, and roaring sounds; thoughts of being beaten, as if someone is really there; thinking that a face is coming closer; fists beating on your back; being pulled by your clothes or hair; nerves being pummeled by rocks and stones; being called by name; and so forth.

The lesser apparitions include your body hairs horripilating, feeling prickly fear, and various unpleasant smells arising to the nose, such as of garlic, burning, and vultures. In dreams as well, the devils manifest terrifying appearances, such as that of you entering a doorless house, you tumbling into the opening of a chasm or great crevice, water sweeping you away, your house crumbling, and a bridge over a big river shaking and nearly falling. In short, various apparitions will manifest in dreams that cause discursive thinking and doubt. At those times, the best response is to be without fear in the dream. Whatever frightful thing arises in a dream is a devil's test, so when you awake, don't evaluate whether it was a good or a bad dream; just rest in your practice without fear or anxiety. That way, pleasant feelings will vanish, you will be content and at ease, and you will feel cozy and comfortable. Concepts about apparitions will be pacified and various new experiences will arise.

When apparitions occur, even if you can't apply the antidote at that time, focus on the antidote in their aftermath: that there is no terror, no anxiety, no concepts, and no inflation, and even fear is not existent—just rest relaxed in consciousness's own nature. Thereby, devils will dawn as glory, conditions will arise as allies, and obstacles will occur as spiritual powers. Those apparitions might arise at other times if you are practicing the Dharma, but mostly they occur when doing Severance.

(2) Inner signs of uprisings as conceptual thought: These occur in your mind stream: congested constituents, heart-wind sickness, joylessness, senseless suffering, sadness, desiring to leave, desiring companionship, scattered consciousness that gets carried away, anger, unease, really not wanting to practice all the Severance instructions, various thoughts arising, and strong afflictions occurring. Continue practicing as before, knowing that all these are mental apparitions, drawings in space, mere reflections of conceptual thought, and mentally constructed. Therefore, they are unborn and liberated in their own place. Don't mind; they are empty. Pay no attention; they are false. Know that the movement of thought is not real and will disappear and liberate automatically.

(3) In-between signs of uprising as sickness: Your body may develop gout (*shu thor*), swellings (*skrangs 'bur*), quivering (*sha 'phrig*) or trembling skin (*sha 'gul*), cysts (*glang shu me dbal*), cow-lick,[60] carbuncles (*lhog pa*), chronic pain (*gzer nad*), and so forth—occurring in variety and sporadically.[61] Don't be happy or unhappy whether they occur or not. Do not entertain even a dust mote of fear or apprehension: relax into a baseless and rootless state and think, "Whatever happens, let it happen; whatever comes, let it come; wherever it goes, let it go."

Displays of devils' ridicule

This can occur while practicing Severance or at other times. There are sixteen ridicules of the devils and others. Those sixteen are four ridicules of excellence, four ridicules to incite fear, four ridicules to sow doubt, and four apparition ridicules.

(1–4) *Ridicules of excellence*: [You will hear words like] "Since you have gathered the accumulations for many eons, just this year you will become a buddha in the buddha realm called such-and-such, you will have such-and-such a name, you will have this many disciples, and perform this much awakened activity." These words will please you and uplift your mind, making you proud and arrogant and haughty. They say, "Now that you will be a buddha, why keep practicing generosity and upholding morality?" And "Now you don't need to meditate. Give up all this striving and endeavoring on the path." This turns your mind from virtue. They say, "Now you have attained the result. At this time it is enough just to enjoy yourself. Engage in desire, anger, and stupidity as you like." Then you engage in misdeeds. They say, "These are my authentic prophecies, be pleased and happy and delighted." You are uplifted by such praise. "Teach, explain, and proclaim widely to others." They will say such things.

(5–8) *Ridicules to incite fear*: They say, "I am the butcher that killed seven generations of your ancestors, and I will also eat you." They say, "I am the one who shortens the life of all your gurus and their lineage. I am the one who takes away their life force." They say, "Our yidam tramples you underfoot, grabs your Dharma protector by the neck, and carries off your gods and guards, leaving nothing of value. What can you do about it?" They emanate as your own deity, saying, "I cannot protect you. Go for refuge in that other one." This causes fear, alarm, and terror; degrades your courage; and causes trembling and horripilation.

(9–12) *Ridicules to sow doubt*: Emanating as your yidam, they say, "Your deity is wrong. Your mantra is mistaken. Even if you practice for an eon, you will not accomplish it." Thus, doubts are sown. They emanate as your guru and say, "Child, your master's teaching is erroneous. I practiced that and was reborn in hell for many eons. Now you should abandon your view, meditation, and conduct and take up any other practice but this." They say, "If you practice this Dharma of yours, you will be reborn in hell for an eon." They say, "Your Dharma of devotion to the guru, emptiness, compassion, and so forth is not the authentic path. Give it up." These cause doubt and uncertainty, a conflicted mind, suspicion, and discursive thinking.

(13–16) *Ridicules by apparitions*: This makes you think that your heart has been pulled out raw, your inner organs have been gouged out, and your body has been chopped to pieces. You think that the flesh of your body is being devoured by wild animals, cannibals, and harm-doers, or that your body is on fire, or the ground you are sitting on cracks and you fall into it and are reborn in hell, and so forth.

These sixteen ridicules of the devils happen when you are engaged in Severance, but they can also occur during other practices. According to the approach of Secret Mantra, they are considered experiential appearances at the time of the initial congested constituents caused by the channels and vital winds. Inwardly, one experiences ridicule just so, but outwardly there is actually nothing at all real. There is an inner experience, but it's like last night's dream. The assertion of an Object Severance practitioner, [on the other hand,] is that it is the lingering warmth of the inner yogin's meditative absorption (Skt. *samādhi*). It is held to be the awakening of the experiences of spiritual practice. No matter which of those two assertions you follow, you should do four things: cast out the body as food, separate the mind from the body, investigate the one who is afraid, and give up fixating on the body as the self. When apparitions occur, apply them directly to your practice. Holding them to be real, conceptualizing or regarding them as problems, will make them obstacles. In essence they are fallacious, hollow, and insignificant. Since they have no core, don't mentally attribute permanence, validity, or reality to them. Don't think about them. Rest in a state without reference or valid existence.[62]

Causes of reverting

11. *When the mind becomes distrustful, self-fixation emerges from objects.*
    Once the inner demons of your mind are tamed, the outer demons
        vanish in emptiness.
    If unbearability and inability occur, equalize and trample them.
    If fear and trepidation occur, focus intently on these thoughts.

There are four causes of reverting in Severance: distrust arising in the mind, self-appearance arising as demons, inability to bear the practice, and fear and trepidation.

When the mind becomes distrustful is when you don't understand that mind is empty because you did not receive the introduction to mind in the preliminaries. You don't realize that samsara and nirvana are in your mind because you haven't listened to many teachings. You can't go to a haunted place because you don't have the confidence of experience and realization. You can't cast out the body as food because you have not relinquished fixating on the body as the self. You can't integrate adverse conditions because the Severance characteristic of fortitude is weak. You give up Severance because your hardiness and forbearance are meager. And you don't reach the culmination of Severance because your laziness and distraction are great. Those seven are the reasons for being unable to go to practice Severance in the first place, the conditions for turning back in the middle, and the obstructions to achieving success in the end. If you interrupt Severance practice and are too busy to go to the haunted place, don't prepare a bed there, construct stone cairns, or leave excrement.

Self-appearance arising as demons means that the inner demons summon the outer demons. Though there are no external demons to experience, there is an internal attitude that fixates on demons. When you go to practice Severance and stay in a haunted retreat, any external circumstance brings up the concept "demon." If [you hear] "meet" you think it's a demon. If you hear "come," if a wall disintegrates, stones and earth clumps roll down, fissures crush, boulders crumble, tree branches and plants move in the wind, or wolves, foxes, and monkeys move around, you think there are demons. That is what is called self-appearance arising as demons. For example, someone may not have tasted sugar, molasses, or honey in their mouth, but subjectively, due to some chronic disease, as soon as they eat those three sweets they taste bitterness. That is due to their own internal problems. In the practice of Severance, you must not let appearance become demonic appearance.

Unable to suppress due to not bearing is like being unable to bear giving up worldly food, unable to bear practicing the Dharma, and so forth. At the time of Severance, it is first hard to bear going to a haunted ground, hard to bear blending [with circumstances], hard to bear giving up your body and life, and hard to bear staying until final evidence of success. As it states in *Another Bundle*:

> Parting from happiness is unbearable;
> experiencing misery is unbearable;
> going to haunted places is unbearable;
> and sickness, demons, and so forth,
> though unbearable, must be suppressed.[63]

Fear and trepidation occur when staying in haunted retreats. Fright, trepidation, fear, panic, dread, and terror will come. Once you have become fearless, you need to stick it out. Even if fear, and so on, do not arise, there is no reason to feel superior, no reason to rejoice, no reason to think it very amazing. When those things occur, do not leave until severing is accomplished. Once you are frightened of them and there is resistance, the severing will fail, and again [you might want to] leave. Within half a month, obstacles like pains and upset stomach will occur. The best practitioners stay there within the state of realizing the view, the middling rest in an intellectually concocted view, and the least, if they develop endurance and antidotes, let it go with the thought "though I sicken, though I die." To wrap it all up, you must have the ability to give. If you focus intently and trample upon them, the unreal demons will vanish within the emptiness of mind itself. There is no cause for fear, no concern. Within that state, the fearful one will be liberated without concern. At that time, don't engage in pushback or extreme measures, and so on. Take up the practice of methods described previously. If none of the methods work to suppress, then practice pushback and extreme measures as explained below. Don't react to insignificant conditions. Don't act right at the start. When nothing at all suppresses them, then take action.

Signs of resistance

12. *When apparitions become too great, don't persist; take a break.*
    Regret, wrong views, doubts, weariness with Dharma,
    disease, suffering, congested constituents, and scattered practice—
    as these signs of resistance and obstacles occur, exert effort in practice.

External signs arise as apparitions in waking time, in visionary experiences, as visible objects, or in dreams. They may be too intensely fierce to tolerate and no kind of technique will help. When those occur, sit with your big cushion and say, "I will sit here until the great ocean of cyclic existence runs dry. Fierce apparition, you yourself please come by any time of day or night. If I can't stay, I am weak. If you can't come, you are weak. If I can't give, I am weak. If you can't eat, you are weak. You don't need to remain a mere apparition. Come for real and gobble up the food; that is fine indeed. As for escape, there is no escape. As for protection, there is no protection. As for shelter, there is no shelter. As for dispute, there is no dispute. Do whatever you do, that's just fine." Say that many times out loud and mentally.

Internal signs arise in the mind when you have come to practice Severance but then you regret it; or at first you think you won't come; or you think timidly that it was the guru who imposed this kind of practice; or you wonder whether this will make you a buddha or not; or you think that any instructions on pushing back that you were taught will bring no benefit, and whatever you do will not help and "they" will win. You have no trust, you regard the methods perversely, you are beset by doubts about

Dharma, you are fed up with practice, you have no desire to do Severance, you are afraid to go practice Severance, you wish to go elsewhere, you pine for companions, you are unhappy, your mind drifts away carried by the wind, your awareness floats away, you can't shake the fear, in the daytime there's no time before sunset, at nighttime there's no time before sunrise, at noon your consciousness sinks and roams, shadows lengthen in the gathering gloom, awareness soars and is carried off, dust rises and you cower in fear, you feel chilled, your head and body hairs stand on end, you think that humans or demons, and so on, are agitated and a battle is coming, you think they have been summoned and are coming to fight and that they are coming to eat you. You cannot call out, you cannot spit, your seat is irritating, sleep won't come, you break out in cold sweats, consciousness is cast down, and your powers of awareness are fractured. These are all signs of being overwhelmed by gods and demons.

At those times, utter *phaṭ* [and know that] whatever appears is an apparition of awareness, whatever arises is a conceptual pattern, and whatever occurs is the phantasmagoria of your own mind. Say, "You demons who rise up as my enemies in apparent existence, you don't scare me. Eight gods above, take my upper body. Eight nāgas below, take my lower body. Eighteen captains, take my entrails. Eight classes of gods and *sinpo* spirits, take my vital organs. All gods and demons of apparent existence, take my five sense organs. I don't have even one iota of ownership over this old guise. I don't have even a dust mote of attachment." Body is not real, mind is emptiness, conceptual thought is resolved—rest relaxed in that state. If just that can occur, then pushing back, extreme measures, and any other methods are unnecessary. Just that is sufficient. So it is said.

Secret signs arising in the body occur as intense illness, swellings, acute pains, abscesses, eczema, erysipelas, cow-lick, fearful reactions to every little condition, frantic consciousness and agitated heart, meaningless mental upset, perspiring, constant craving, dysentery, vomiting, and so forth. Don't cling to and cherish the body. Always hold the attitude of giving it away.

Harmful spirits may occur: human bodies with the heads of lions, tigers, bears, yaks, wolves, pigs, or snakes. Meditate that some eat your body from the head down, some eat it from the feet up, some eat the sense organs, some eat the vital organs and entrails, some flay the skin, some eat the flesh, some drink the blood, and some gnaw the bones. Meditate that they consume the body without leaving a single morsel of flesh, drop of blood, or tuft of hair. Their appetites are appeased and they each want to go home to their own places. Those who really want to stay surround you and remain.

That is called the pure offering of the body aggregate, the accumulation of merit that is built on the ground of apparent existence, the generosity with threefold purity, the communal feast of suchness, and the banquet of a great being. Even if you were to fall to hell, there is nothing more powerful to be done. Think, "Now, come what may." This applies not only to the times of practicing Severance, but to all times. It is the ultimate accumulation of merit, the supreme dispensation of generosity, and the principal ritual to reverse adverse conditions.

Extreme measures if there is resistance

13. *Extreme measures for major resistance liberate hopes and fears
     naturally.
     Mahayana's overwhelming brilliance resolves happiness and sorrow.
     Putting the stars under darkness collapses the false structure of
     samsara and nirvana.
     Smiting pestilence directly in haunted places destroys gods and
     demons as illusions.*[64]

Extreme measures for major resistance: When you first arrive at a haunted retreat to practice the instructions on severing methods, if there are no uprisings, follow the previous explanations on conjuring techniques.[65] If there is minor resistance, follow the explanations from the signs of resistance. But if nothing is helpful and major resistance occurs, then resort to the extreme measures. In terms of meaning, this is [known as] the "extreme measures for major resistance." In terms of practice, this means to come down directly on the pestilent spirit. The necessity is that the **Mahayana Dharma overwhelms them with brilliance.** It is like [the sun] **putting the stars under darkness.** Practice like this.

There are three parts to the practice: externally, extreme measures for gods and demons; in the middle, extreme measures for the aggregates; and internally, extreme measures for self-fixation.

Externally, extreme measures for gods and demons

[Go where there are] gods, nāgas, devils, *tsen* spirits, and so on—whether they are formerly harmful gods and demons, or those that were not severed in the practice of Severance, or those that were raised by other conditions, and so forth. Also go where there are major apparitions of pestilent spirits from the haunted places of others that are extremely savage and difficult to sever by any means. Go there and practice Severance. To **smite directly** on the pestilent spirit is like applying moxibustion directly on a diseased area. When a doctor applies moxibustion, once the [hot needle] finds the particular point, it is said to hit the sick spot and sickness disappears. Similarly, if you sleep on the [geomantic] neck of that haunted place, the gods and demons cannot bear it and quickly rise up. At that point, a great meditator arouses total confidence, the signs of experiential realization, perfect confidence of fortitude, and stays the course. That [demon] will find no opportunity and will flee. For example, it is like a dog that enters the opening of a cave. When it tries to turn back, it suddenly turns but hesitates, becomes alarmed, and escapes. The intellectual's approach is like wanting to turn back, but in the system of Severance the idea is to draw out the demon spirits from the object. Therefore, this Severance comes down directly on the spirits. As such, it is the excellent way to cure leprosy.

In the middle, extreme measures for the aggregates

Once you have arrived at a place with major apparitions that are difficult to sever, take a black rope and, making a knot, put it around your neck (or waist). If you are at a temple, put the other end of the rope in the hands of a statue. If there is a tree trunk, tie it there. [If there is a rock, boulder, or bush, tie it there.]⁶⁶ If you are in a meadow or a wide plain, plant a stake in the middle of it and tie it there. If you are at a water spring, tie the end of the rope to a river rock. In that [state], cast out [the body] and give it to any gods and demons who live there.

Internally, practice extreme measures for self-fixation

The body is an aggregate of inert matter. However it was made, it will not transcend death. It will not stay forever on Earth. No one will escape with their life. In time, the body will be cast off anyway, so now, while they desire it and you have the power to donate it, why not give it away? Then say out loud:

> In general, I offer the body as ransom for the six kinds of migra-
> tors. In particular, I give it up for the sake of my kind parents. More
> particularly, I give it up for the sake of you gods and demons. Eigh-
> teen great chief malignant spirits, fifteen great malignant spirits of
> children, eight classes of gods and *sin* spirits of apparent existence,
> death lords, *mamos*, nāga devils, nāga *tsen* spirits, king *pekar* spirits,
> harm-doers, *sinpo* spirits, malignant spirits and obstructors, male
> and female knife ghosts, earth lords, and local lords—great, fierce,
> pestilent gods and demons of apparent existence from the top of
> existence down to the bottom of the *narak* hells—all of you, come
> here! I, by the name of so-and-so, give to you this whole body, a col-
> lection of the four elements that is the nature of flesh and blood:

a net of veins and ligaments, head and limbs, flesh, blood, sense organs, innards, vital organs, marrow, fat, bone, brain, thirty-three constituents, life, breath, and life force. Upper devil kings, take my upper jaw; lower devil queens, take my lower jaw; male spirits who like the torso, take my torso; female spirits who like the lower body, take my lower body; *pekar* spirits who like the heart, take my heart; nāgas and earth lords who like the veins and sinews, take my veins and sinews; male and female knife ghosts who like the flesh and blood, take my flesh and blood; *serak* spirits and oath-breakers who like the corium and skin, take them. I give to anyone whatever they like. Partake with satisfaction. Joyfully consume. Accept it and be pleased. If I can't give it, I am weak. If you can't eat it, you are weak. At the very best, you can all throw me to hell and never let me escape. Next best would be to shorten my life and, this evening, eat well so that in the morning I cannot go anywhere. At the least, send me leprosy, send me tumors, send me ascites, send me grime disease (*dre[g] nad*), send me heart-wind sickness, send me congested constituents, send me the insanity of king [spirit] sickness, or send me pestilent diphtheria.[67] Send me death or no death; kill me or don't kill me.

Regarding meditation on the visualization, invoke all the spirits, headed by the gods and demons that have initiated obstacles and caused harm, to come before you. Meditate on them all as not being bad or wild, and each having their own variety of body. Meditate that your own body is an ordinary aggregate, youthful and beautiful, fat and white. Meditate that all the gods and demons of apparent existence—primarily the bull-headed [death lord], snake-headed scorpions, pig-headed *yakṣa*,[68] and bear-headed harm-doers—chop up this body into hundreds and thousands of pieces and consume it. All of them get equal portions. Meditate that each of the gods and demons gets an excellent abundance of food and drink equal to what their individual hands or bodies [can handle]. Practice such generosity. Stay on your bed in an empty, clear state of awareness without fixation.

Through holding this in your mindstream, any kind of sickness, evil spirit, and obstacle cannot affect you. First of all, the blessing of truth will liberate the actions of gods and demons that initiate obstacles.[69] Second, the meditation on compassion will arouse the notion in their minds of parents and children. Third, the meditative absorption on giving away the body will bring satisfaction to their minds. Fourth, yogins who realize the view and act in such a way within a state of emptiness will turn their minds away from attachment to the fixation on the reality of gods and demons. Fifth, the blessings of making aspiration prayers will free the minds of gods and demons from thoughts of attraction and aversion and the afflictive emotions.

In the past, the eighteen great malignant spirits headed by Tashi Tseringma came to see Jetsun Milarepa with the intent to cause obstacles, but Jetsun donated his body to them. Through mastering the view of fearless confidence, he pacified the obstacles and brought the [spirits] under control.[70] [Machik's] son Gyalwa Döndrup was targeted with magic spells by many *bandhes* (Buddhist or Bön mendicants), but by hiding beneath the bandhes' torma table [and eating their offerings], the spells could not harm him, and in fact were turned back [on the perpetrators].[71] There are many such instances.

Also, there is a type of god-demon that, if they acted that way, would be unbearable, or else would come in homage or to display apparitions. They would cry and moan, lament and call, howl, utter terribly bad language, and display various forms and so forth, either in actuality, in experiential appearances, or in dreams. But whatever comes, it is sufficient to put it directly into practice. Do not hold it as real, but know that it is like an illusion and a dream. It states in the sutra:

> Even if you see various miraculous emanations clearly displayed,
> they have no body, no mind, and even no name.[72]

Whether in experiential appearance, visionary appearance, or dreams, there is nothing beyond magical appearance. If the sky falls from above, water gushes from the ground below, mountains crumble from behind, cliffs crack in front, or any kind of apparitional obstacles arise, rather than saying, "please guard me, please protect me" a hundred times, it is better to say once, "kill me, eat me, take me." Rather than summoning a hundred god-protectors, it is better to let a thousand god-demons eat. Rest your mind on the nature of phenomena. Then everything will be self-liberated.

Even if you're scratched by wild dogs from behind, pecked by birds in front, flanked by fierce devil hordes on your right and left—rest your mind, relaxed without fear. Then everything will be self-liberated.

Even if a nine-headed black devil rides on your neck, ready to cut your throat and extract your heart, saying, "Right now I will kill you and cast away every morsel of meat and drop of blood," still, rest your mind unwavering on the nature of phenomena. Then, even one claw will not touch you, let alone kill you.

Even if [an apparition] tears down the door curtain, sharpens a knife, and thrusts in a copper pot, saying, "After I slaughter you, I will boil you in this copper pot," rest your awareness in the emptiness of nonexistence. Not even a needle will touch you.

Even if an evil man lays out a rope on the ground and ties a noose around your neck, saying, "I'm going to rope you in and drag you away," rest your mind softly upon fearlessness. You won't be dragged even one step. Again, whatever apparitional obstacles occur, rather than saying, "please guard me, please protect me" a hundred times, it is better to say "kill me, eat me, take me" just once. Rather than summoning a hundred god-protectors, it is better to let a thousand god-demons eat. Rather than tie a hundred protection cords on your body, it is better to rejoice in sickness and delight in death.

Even if an army of devils, messengers of the death lord, and millions of armed men surround you saying, "Your death will be marked on the devil's notched death-stick, the *tsen* spirit's wager will be brought down on you, the death lord's scythe will fall on you," rest your mind lightly in a state that is baseless and rootless. Rather than an army of millions of devils and death lords, there is not a single being near you. There is not even a footprint left by a passing individual. If you think that the gift could not have been eaten by you yourself and hold that conceit, that isn't the case. In fact, all of that is delusion, the apparitions of mind, created by intellect. It is the emanation of discursive thought, the conscious creation of awareness, no different from drawings in space, the moon reflected in water, and water mirages. One cannot attribute meaning to appearances.

You need not cling to the validity of everything. You need not have doubts. You need not entertain concepts. Has anyone ever been poked by a rabbit's horn? Or killed by a barren woman's child? Who has sustained harm from an illusory person? Who has been swept away by a water mirage? Who has been overshadowed by a swamp lion? Has anyone ever been struck by the black lord carrying a cudgel, standing day and night at the doorway of the shrine room? None of those things can possibly be true. Wise ones who understand that cannot be harmed by devil armies. As it states in the sutra:

> If sentient beings equal to the [sands of the] Ganges
> were all hypothetically to become devils,
> even emanating again as many as their body hairs,
> they all could not cause obstacles to the wise.[73]

Some Severance practitioners go for Severance and as soon as there is an uprising, they engage extreme measures and pushback. They do not understand their own degree of warmth (i.e., progress) in Severance. It is not necessary to use extreme measures and pushback as soon as there is an uprising. That mainly depends on the kind of god or demon, the style of the apparition, and the time of the Severance practitioner. If you encounter a wrathful, fierce god or demon, then use extreme measures. If it is gentle, there is no need. If it is a big apparition, do it; if it is small, then don't. After finishing Severance, if no matter what you do [the apparitions, etc.] are not severed, do it. No need to do it right from the start. Some Severance practitioners say, "To remain unsevered, to leave the Severance undone, and to waste the project without evidence of success is perverse." [But Machik's] son Gyalwa Döndrup said, "It depends on the individual. A realized Severance practitioner who goes to practice Severance, who realizes nonself and realizes that there are no demons out there, may interrupt the process. If they have mentally forsaken fixating on the body as a self, and they leave the Severance process and postpone Severance without evidence of success, they will not experience reversion or obstacles. All of that is mentally created." He said, "But now, if you are thinking of a way to turn back once you leave off the Severance process, that is a major pushback on oneself."[74] Those were the instructions on extreme measures for major resistance.

Mahayana's overwhelming brilliance: Externally, don't pay attention to or engage mentally in the obstacles of devils or whatever kinds of subtle or coarse discursive thoughts arise internally, such as attraction and aversion, happiness and sadness, pleasing and displeasing, and so on. They are all overwhelmed by the brilliance of the Mahayana view.

Putting the stars under darkness[75] makes them unable to rise up. For example, anything in the sky—such as the moon and constellations—is overwhelmed by the brilliance of the light of the rising sun. All the great stars are put under darkness and are of no consequence. Just so, the yogin who realizes the view is like the sun, and does not attend to or mentally engage in the external obstacles of devils or the internal eight concerns of attraction, aversion, and so forth. All those subtle or coarse discursive thoughts are like the constellations; they cannot show up because they are overwhelmed by splendor.[76]

Smiting pestilence directly in haunted places: Outside, the palace of the nāgas is pestilent (or powerful), but more pestilent is the mind itself with the realized view. Once you cling to pestilence by thinking of the nāgas' palace, then that pestilence will appear. But in reality, there is no cause of pestilence. It is provisional. It is a notion. It is a fabricated phenomenon. It can be destroyed. It can be conquered. You can burn it. You can sever it. But mind itself with the realized view is not combustible, not severable. Nothing has the ability to conquer it. It is the same with the pestilence of the devils' city outside: the emptiness of the realized mind itself is more pestilent. The devil's city is provisional, and so forth, as above. This is the case also for the palace of the death lords, the citadel of the devils, the gathering place of *mamo*s, the treasury of king spirits, and the fort of the *tsen* spirits. With the confidence of realization, you will have no fear or trepidation toward those places. That is what's called *smiting pestilence directly with pestilence*, and it is said to collapse the false structure of the provisional. It resolves discursive thinking and releases self-fixation from the object, since it is a teaching that holds gods and demons to be illusory. For example, wherever paupers go, they have no enemies, since they have no wealth. Since a Severance practitioner has no fixation on a self, no demons will come.

Actual extreme measures

14. *If the apparitions become too vicious, put pressure on the gods and demons.*
    If they continue to provoke, practice crazy vanquishing conduct.
    If apparitions still manifest, delight in illness and be happy to die.
    Hold them by the hook of compassion that benefits all.

In general, the system of Severance does not endanger the gods and demons, nor start a rivalry with them, nor inflict harm on them. The practitioner remains humble and accepts defeat, and whatever happiness or suffering occurs, still hopes to eventually give their body. In any case, if [the body] is not taken, just saying "please take this" won't help because they will not listen. Sometimes you must blend [your consciousness] with the corpse and engage in crazy vanquishing conduct. Dampa [Sangyé] said, "Sometimes, if you do not exaggerate awareness, a subtle yoga will not subdue the place."[77]

Crazy vanquishing conduct is cutting down tree pestilence, overturning earth pestilence, splitting cliff pestilence, digging earth pestilence, cutting bushes, disturbing water springs, and so forth.[78] If you do those things, apparitions will manifest even though there was no harm inflicted previously, since now there is a reason to manifest. Therefore, apply yourself and say, "You did not cause harm, but I am not beyond dying eventually. Even though you always guard and protect me, my life force has not been captured. Ultimately, if I do not reverse my karmic acts that made me hellbound, all the gods and demons may try but cannot change that fate. There is not even a chance to extend or shorten life by two or three days. Let me die this evening." Saying that, engage in harsh conduct.

Do not destroy the places that contain sacred images and palaces and then go back home. Face up to it and stay in that place. No matter what apparitions occur in dreams, just wake up. Do not muse over them, just rest naturally in the nature of phenomena. Change your mind and grasp the antidote like a drawn bow—don't miss the moment.

And that's not all. [When engaging in a project where you need to] cut down tree pestilence, smash cliff and boulder pestilence, repair the earth in earth pestilence, or build a monastery—initially, do not cut trees or break stones. First practice Severance two or three times there to begin to tame the wild land of that haunted place. Then you may cut the trees and break the stones, and so forth, to do repairs. It is not right to work on repairs and such without first taming the area with Severance. This is said to be a very important instruction called "If your head fits, the whole body will fit." If you do this, the bad karma and negative actions of those gods and demons will be purified, and they will make aspirations for the gathering of disciples. Whatever gentle or harsh conduct you enact, meditate on the benefits for the gods and demons and hold them with emptiness and compassion. Thereby, your path and that of others will not go wrong, but will only be a genuine path.

Evidence of successful severing

15. *Know how the times and signs of success occur in actuality, visionary experience, and dreams,*
    arising to oneself outwardly, inwardly, and secretly.
    If you rest in single-pointed meditative stability within emptiness,
    no doubt the delusion of samsara and nirvana will be distinguished.

The three measures of success are by time, by signs, and by culmination. The first is that if there are no obstacles for three, five, seven, or more days, then that is evidence of success. The measure of success by signs has three parts: signs of success regarding outer gods and demons, signs of inner qualities arising in the mindstream, and signs of gaining control over the gods and demons.

Signs of success regarding outer gods and demons are: the subsiding of physical illness; the clearing up of all mental [conditions] of heart-wind, congested constituents, and suffering; the subsiding of all comings and goings of conceptual thought; and the pacification of all harsh experiential appearances, visionary appearances, dreams, and apparitions. [The resulting] happy mind is at ease, becoming joyous and bright, cheerful and buoyant.

Signs of inner qualities arising in the mindstream are: delighting in places such as haunted retreats and having a deep desire to stay there, becoming engrossed in generosity and loving it, having a deep desire to do virtuous activity more than previously, unprecedented experiential realization, and the arising of meditative absorption. Appearances have become irrelevant and unreal, and a special compassion is born for those beings who do not realize that; an extraordinary devotion to the guru arises; all conditions arise as supports for the practice of virtue; and there is no fear or apprehension over adverse conditions. Those are all evidence of success. The best is to persist until you have all of those signs, but at the least until some appropriate evidence of success or some part of these signs occur. Hold your ground, engender fortitude and determination, and remain in residence. Take up the practice without turning back, even if it kills you. At that time, if evidence of success does not occur, do not be unhappy. If it does occur, don't be happy. Abandon hopes and fears; discard them without concern, and let go. If there is hope or fear, that itself is a devil, so cast it out. Even if this appearance appears as a duality, if you know it is unreal and have no clinging, it becomes the path.

Signs of gaining control over gods and demons occur to the yogin in actuality, in visionary experience, or in dreams according to greater, middling, or lesser degree of warmth in the practice. Gods and demons bring you food and drink, welcome you, bow respectfully, present riches and offerings, do prostrations and circumambulations, request teachings, offer you their life-force mantras, and grant you the common spiritual powers. In that case, you should bestow refuge and awakening mind, provide rules for food, and establish them on the path of virtue. It states in the *Appendices*:

> Spiritual powers arise from nāgas and devils.
> *Tsen* and king spirits will act as patrons.
> Food and wealth accrue from *mamo*s and ḍākinīs.
> Fame spreads by gods and demons of apparent existence.[79]

The ultimate evidence of success: Severance practitioners might recover from illness, pacify malignant spirits, and cure leprosy in the short term and leave it at that. You might think that you have achieved the result that you needed, and henceforth do not sustain Severance and virtuous activity. That is an insignificant result of the conduct, and is not sufficient.

You must maintain the practice until you become a buddha who achieves the two purposes [of helping yourself and others]. Don't have a desirous attitude. Don't meditate thinking it is sufficient that a few good results arise momentarily. Don't be so easily satisfied. Don't imagine that you are finished. Train energetically in the practice until the supreme qualities arise. Keep practicing until you realize the equality of samsara and nirvana.

Again, whether in actuality, in visionary experience, or in dreams and so forth, when big apparitions manifest and initiate obstacles, no matter how pestilent the gods and demons are, the Severance practitioner must have great fortitude. A great responsibility rests directly on the circumstances, and by arousing some energy (*bla tshan*) and sticking with it, it is not feasible to fail at suppressing them. It is impossible not to bring them under control. For example, when a cannon meets a castle, the cannon wins. When an ax meets a tree, the ax wins. When a hammer meets rock, the hammer wins. When fire meets dry wood, the fire wins. Just so, when the ultimate truth meets the conventional, the ultimate wins. When nonentity and entities meet, nonentity wins. When a Severance practitioner and demons meet, the practitioner wins. That is the nature of it.

At that time, whatever dualistic apparitions manifest—faults and qualities, obstacles and spiritual powers—keep your mind neither high nor low. Don't be discouraged by adverse circumstances. Don't be encouraged by favorable conditions. With your mind like a tuft of cotton, don't let it float away. Like a bird's feather in the sky, don't let it slip away. Like rubble on the road, don't get caught up in it. Add your attachment to spirits to your self-fixation and throw them out. No matter what afflicts body and mind that is difficult to take up on the path, the perpetrator is the mind itself. And that is not a thing. It is a nonthing, and it is empty. Remember that and rest relaxed. Do not pay attention to appearances, calculating whether they exist or not. Don't examine whether your mind is happy or sad. Don't get involved in the attraction and aversion of the six sense groups that don't truly exist.

Abandon the attitude of hope and fear

16. *If there are no signs of uprising in the preliminaries, lose the*
    anticipation of uprising.
    If there are no signs of suppressing in the main practice, cast behind
    anger and desire.
    If there is no evidence of success at the conclusion, lose the
    anticipation of evidence.
    The hopes and fears of a desiring mind are devils, which the wise
    reject.

What if the required signs of raising gods and demons in the preliminary practice do not occur, the required signs of suppressing in the main part don't happen, and the required evidence of success in the conclusion doesn't develop? If there is no uprising in the preliminary, there is nothing to suppress in the main part. That is like having nothing to clean if there are no stains. If there is no suppression in the main part, there will be no evidence of success. That is like not overpowering when there is no enemy to subdue. If you do not sever whatever is difficult to sever, and your followers don't sever it, even if obstacles don't affect you personally, obstacles will come to your entourage. In the end, harm could even reach your animal herds.

In that severing, whether your followers sever or not, everything depends on whether self-fixation is mentally abandoned or not. Once self-fixation is resolved, it is fine if the followers do not sever because there is no problem with being a follower. Therefore, if you want an uprising during the preliminaries, that is the devil of hope and fear, so think that even if there is no uprising, it is all right. And if you desire to push back in the main part, that is also the devil of hope and fear, so think that even if there is no suppression, then there simply is no suppression. In the conclusion, if you desire some evidence of successful termination, that is also the devil of hope and fear, so think that even if evidence of success does not come, then it does not come.

Now, don't think that if evidence of success does come, you should rejoice. Again, most practitioners of Severance wish for a conjuring of gods and demons at first, wish for a suppression in the middle, and wish for some evidence of success at the end. They desire the demons to be defeated and themselves to be victorious. They want to distinguish themselves as special. That is the big devil of unsuccessful severing. Therefore, the Severance approach by a person of the best capability endowed with instructions is that if they perform Severance in a haunted retreat, they do not desire signs of uprising at first, signs of suppressing in the middle, and signs of success in the end, but if they do happen, then that is the nature of it. Do not hope for them to come, be happy if they occur, or develop pride, arrogance, and self-aggrandizement at their occurrence. It states in the *Appendices*:

> Renouncing things [while] believing in emptiness:
> when there is no regard even of mere emptiness,
> let alone fixation on [existent] things,
> is a pitiful lack of realization.[80]

Dedicate the virtue of practice to awakening

17ab. *Helpers and harmers are subdued by gentle and harsh conduct.*
Make aspirations to establish them in enlightenment through various
means.

Evidence of success has arisen in experience. At the completion of Severance, you should make aspiration prayers for the benefit of oneself and all others:

> Gods and demons first manifested fierce apparitions to me and
> inflicted harm, but later showed respect and deference, benefit-
> ting me. With gentle conduct I gave them my body and with harsh

conduct inflicted harm. Through these various means, I placed gods and demons on the path to awakening. Based on these roots of virtue, may the bad thoughts in the minds of all you gods and demons, and all the fierce practices and harsh afflictions, be pacified. May you come to possess love, compassion, and the mind of awakening. Initially you tried to harm us and inflict injury, and later were respectful and honored us. Based on that virtuous root, as in the case of King Maitrībala and the five yakṣa cannibals,[81] first may [love, compassion, and the awakening mind] arise in my assembled entourage. May all negativity and the habitual patterns of unvirtuous cause and effect instantly be refined and purified, and may you quickly attain precious all-knowing buddhahood. I myself, the yogin, have given my body in generosity and with a loving mind nurtured the gods and demons. Based on the roots of that virtue, may I thoroughly complete the transcendent perfection of generosity like King Candraprabha or Prince Gedön.[82] Ultimately, may I and all others quickly attain the precious state of a buddha possessed of the two purposes.

Since that dedication is for the sake of the outer gods and demons, it is a hundred times more powerful than the welfare of human migrators. These were the instructions on outwardly severing gods and demons.

Inwardly, Thoroughly Investigate Mind Itself

17cd *If you wish to attain omniscient buddhahood for yourself and others, rely on this path of emancipation, fortunate ones.*

A person who has faith and diligence, who would accomplish perfect buddhahood in one lifetime, and who desires to liberate themselves and all others from the ocean of suffering of cyclic existence—that is the person who practices Severance.

18ab. *This conceptual thinking, a long-standing habit difficult to relinquish,*
  is the single cause that produces the variety of suffering in existence.

Conceptual thinking is difficult to relinquish because it has become a conditioned habitual pattern over the course of the long duration since beginningless time. It produces all the suffering of cyclic existence and the lower realms. It is this devil that must be severed.

18cd. *Here in this charnel ground of assembled aggregates and elements of*
  the support and supported,
  sever the various agitating thoughts and memories in this fluctuating place.

The inner place, the support, is the charnel ground where all the aggregates, elements, and sense fields are assembled. That which is supported is one's awareness in which various thoughts and memories arise. This haunted place where the likes of jackals, predators, and vultures of six types prowl is where to sever. The outer place is taught in the [*Perfection of Wisdom in*] *One Hundred Thousand Lines*:

> Those who wish to learn the Perfection of Wisdom, should stay in mountain caves, earthen caverns, rugged mountains, empty huts, graveyards, mountain ravines, and unsheltered places.[83]

19ab. *The yogin who has actualized the empowerment and introduction*
  should sever until this devil of conceptual thinking is severed.

A person who was previously made a worthy recipient through empowerment, and then properly received the introduction through opening the sky door, should practice severing. The shortest time [to practice] is a mere moment. The middling is to sever until death. The longest time is to sever until one reaches enlightenment. In short, you must sever until discursive thinking is cut off. It states in *Another Bundle*:

> In fact, there is no object to sever.
> When the severer is liberated,
> that is taught as the unmistaken evidence of success.[84]

> 19cd. *Phenomena's nature primordially possesses incidental stains.*
> *View, meditation, and conduct conquer them in realizing the ground,*
> *path, and result.*

There is both an aspect of totally pure realization and an aspect of impure stains in the mindstreams of sentient beings. It states in *Ornament of the Sutras*:

> Timeless awareness and obscuration:
> those two are with and without stains.
> Like the water element, gold, and the sky,
> [stains can be] purified, therefore purity holds.[85]

The pure aspect of realization is ascertained by the ground, path, and result. The stained aspect of not realizing is conquered by view, meditation, and conduct. This has three parts: the abiding nature of the ground, how to meditate on the path, and how results arise.

The abiding nature of the ground

The essence of what is called "ground" (*gzhi*) is that it pervades everything as the cause. It has the ability to generate conditions on the path—good, bad, and middling—which result in superior, inferior, and intermediate results. The categories of the ground are as follows: if realized, it is the ground or cause that produces the transcendence of misery, or buddhahood. If not realized, it is the ground or cause that produces cyclic existence and bad rebirths. The function of the ground is the ability to produce all the happiness and suffering of both cyclic existence and its transcendence. Analogies for the ground are that it is like wool, iron, or grain: although no result at all is established [in the thing itself], if it is processed, it is possible for something [functional] to arise. Some people say, "Mind is primordially buddha, the five poisons are timeless awareness, and conceptual thinking is the nature of phenomena." If you make an effort, [the ground] is the cause that makes it possible for those things to occur, but it is not the actual thing itself. If it were, all sentient beings would be liberated effortlessly. But since that is not the case, great, middling, and meager effort leads to the best, middling, and lesser liberation. It says in *Ornament of the Sutras*:

> If somehow there were no afflictions,
> all embodied beings would become liberated.
> If somehow there were no total purity,
> even effort would yield no results.[86]

Some people say, "[The ground] is not only the cause of buddhahood, it is actual buddhahood itself." As it states in the [*Hevajra*] *Tantra*:

> There is not a single sentient being
> who is not a buddha.[87]

Also in a sutra:

> Once ignorance arises, for however long it exists, for that long timeless awareness also lasts, once it arises.[88]

Does that clarify it? But those are citations in terms of the expedient meaning. It is clarified in this statement from the root [*Hevajra*] *Tantra*:

> Sentient beings are buddhas.
> But they are obscured by incidental stains.
> When those are resolved, they are buddhas.[89]

Therefore, at the time there is the causal wool, anything can be made from it, such as woolen cloth, yarn, or felt of whatever color. Some people say, "At the time of the ground, the sentient being is the result. That is also called the cause of buddhahood."

How to meditate on the path

View, meditation, and conduct conquer them. The path has three parts: resolving through the view, familiarizing through meditation, and practicing through the conduct.

Resolving through the view

Resolving through the view itself has three parts: the essence of the view, the categories of view, and how to practice the view.

(1) The essence of the view is that the phenomenal nature of the object is empty and the subjective mind itself is empty. The two blend as one in the essence of emptiness.

(2) There are three categories of the view: the view that arises from hearing, the view that arises from contemplation, and the view that arises from meditation.

The view that arises from hearing means that although you might think that what's called the view based on hearing the Mahayana teachings would not be the real emptiness, [one *does*] gain a good understanding of the general meaning.

The view that arises from contemplation means that, while you might think that if you investigate through reasoning and examine through contemplation, more is not worthwhile, yet it is still a good understanding of investigation.

The view that arises from meditation means that through undistracted practice, experience that is not theoretical understanding or mental fabrication actually arises in your being. These three [categories] are like the example of India's betel nuts, [which are made into] *pani* and such: hearing with the ears about such things or seeing their form with the eyes, [is quite different from] tasting them in the mouth. Therefore, just the general understanding that comes from the view that is heard with the ears or examined by contemplation is not enough. Through merging that inseparably with mind, you must experience and relate to it in the manner of no experience.

(3) How to practice the view has three parts: viewed object, viewer, and how to view.

The viewed object is emptiness. As it says in the *Heart Sutra*:

Carefully view, perfectly and correctly, the emptiness of inherent existence of the five aggregates also.[90]

The viewer is one's awareness that arises as anything at all if not examined. If examined, this nonthing is the viewer. How to view is by entering a state with no mental fixation on anything at all, with no reference to any object at all.

Familiarizing through meditation

Familiarizing through meditation has three parts: meditating in equipoise, maintaining in subsequent attainment, and blending in integral unity.

(1) Meditating in equipoise: When discursive thinking has been released from calculation, logic has been discarded, consciousness has been uplifted, and thoughts have disappeared in basic space, mind is naturally totally pure, resting relaxed in equipoise free of all elaborated characteristics. At that time, a meditation object is nonexistent, a meditator is nonexistent, and the result of meditation is nonexistent. In meditative equipoise, all phenomena are realized to be like the center of space. Enter that state. At that time, incidental discursive thinking will pop up, but it is like water and waves or the sky and clouds—recognize it as emptiness, and rest in the state devoid of inherent existence. Whatever thoughts and memories arise, be certain that they are mind's apparitions, that mind is empty, and that emptiness is the dharmakāya. Regardless of whether or not it is explained in the Kangyur, Tengyur, scriptures, sutras, and tantras; whether or not it is taught by the gurus; whether or not it is realized that way by individuals—the fundamental character of reality is forever and always so.

(2) Maintaining in subsequent attainment: During subsequent attainment in post-meditation, know that all phenomena appear but are not true, like the sixteen examples of illusion.[91] Mind is a mere sequence, a mere awareness, a mere movement, a mere memory. The problem is clinging to the validity, the permanence, or the reality of this suddenly-arising consciousness. Therefore, know that it is insubstantial, untrue, and unreal. This conceptual thinking is considered [something to be] abandoned by both śrāvakas and pratyekabuddhas, refuted by the Cittamātrins, destroyed by Pāramitā proponents, transformed by Secret Mantrins, and asserted as essential emptiness by proponents of Madhyamaka. The position of Object Severance practitioners is not to abandon or refute or destroy or transform [this conceptual thinking], but to rest within a state of its intrinsic nonexistence and know that its timeless emptiness is timeless emptiness. If one knows this intrinsic nature, it is more sublime than all abandonment and transformation.

(3) Blending in integral unity: When equipoise and subsequent attainment are united, whatever memories and thoughts arise, know them to

be unified appearance and emptiness, inseparable bliss and emptiness, unfixed clarity and emptiness, and nondual thought and emptiness. This is called "the essential meaning of the abiding nature," and all buddhas of the three times have become buddhas based on realizing just that. Although that is how it is, we don't recognize it due to the existence of obscurations caused by bad habitual patterns in the all-ground (*kun gzhi*); objective conditions, such as not being introduced to it by a guru; and subjective conditions, such as not putting it into practice. It is primordially abiding yet not recognized; coemergently remaining yet of unseen face; forever allied yet not identified. It is like our own face that is so close to our two eyes for so long, and yet it is not seen unless there is a mirror. The guru's introduction is like the mirror, and one's practice is like the eyes: when those two come together, one sees the nature of phenomena, like one's own face. Both must be present.

Practicing through the conduct

There are three [levels of] vows with ten features [each]. The defining characteristic of the śrāvaka vows is to do virtue as an antidote that guards against the four root downfalls and associated [transgressions]. The essence is to turn away from causing harm and its basis. The divisions are the eight types [of individuals] who have vows of personal liberation (*prātimokṣa*): male and female fully ordained monastics, male and female novice monastics, male and female ordained laypersons, postulant nuns, and temporary renunciates. The locale for taking the vows is before an abbot and venerable monastics. The support is men and women of the three continents with functional sex organs who have previously gone for refuge.[92] The ceremony is taken authentically by those with an attitude of definite renunciation, and is obtained through the derivation of language. The observances are to turn back from injuring others and its basis, and abandon hurting sentient beings. The duration is for the rest of the current life. The circumstances for losing them are stated in the *Abhidharma*:

> Cutting off the roots and the passing of night,
> returning the training and passing away,
> and if two sex organs develop,
> the personal vows of liberation are lost.[93]

The results in the short term are to obtain the citadels of gods and humans and ultimately, the result of being an arhat.

The defining characteristic of the bodhisattva vows is the virtuous attitude that desires perfect buddhahood for the sake of others. The essence is having the concurrent mental antidote that benefits others. The divisions are the essential two [kinds of awakening mind]: aspirational and engaging. The trainings are the twenty vows. The support [is beings] who know how to speak and understand the meaning, which can occur in nāgas and animals as well. The locale is before a guru who upholds the vows and is skilled in the ceremony in which they are found. The ceremony is taken authentically by those with an attitude of desiring perfect buddhahood for the sake of others and is obtained through the derivation of language. The observance is the impartial benefit that covers both the short and long term, through knowing that all beings were once your parents. The duration is until attaining the essence of awakening. The circumstances by which they are lost are not desiring perfect buddhahood and mentally abandoning mother sentient beings. The result of keeping the vows is to obtain the eleventh stage of a buddha possessed of the two purposes.

The defining characteristic of the Mantrayāna vows of an awareness holder is not to transgress the sacred pledges made while learning the Vajrayāna trainings. The essence is to follow up on accomplishing the sacred pledges that were sworn before the vajra master. The divisions are the fourteen root downfalls and the eight major branch [transgressions]. The locale is an empowerment conferral from a vajra master at the time the vows are taken. The ceremony is during the prelude (*sta gon*) when the vows of the five families are received. The observances are to regard all sentient beings as gods and goddesses and to make offerings and worship them. The duration is that those vows remain until the essence of awakening. The circumstances of losing them are to not reject what should be rejected and not accept what should be accepted. The result of keeping them is to obtain the state of Vajradhara, the thirteenth stage of a buddha possessed of two purposes.[94]

In this way, do not deny the relative and do not deny the ultimate. Within the integral unity of appearance and emptiness, engage in offerings, mandalas, flour tormas, water tormas, prostrations, circumambulations, liturgies, and sutra recitation—all conduct done from within [the state of knowing] the unreal appearances of conditioned phenomena.

How results arise

Through practicing the view, meditation, and conduct one attains buddhahood, the essence of the three kāyas and five awarenesses. Then, by means of the eight common spiritual powers, eight qualities of mastery, and four kinds of awakened activity, one enacts the welfare of beings.

To explain the three kāyas: At the time of resting in equipoise, you become certain that mind itself is completely devoid of shape, color, and so forth. That empty, clear transparency is the cause of the arising of the dharmakāya. You become habituated through sustaining that without distraction, and at the time of culmination, mind is naturally totally pure and free of the temporary incidental stains. From that, the manifest result of nondual dharmakāya arises.

In the realm of emptiness, the bliss aspect and clarity aspect are unimpeded. The integral unity of clarity and emptiness arises: that is the cause of sambhogakāya. You become habituated through sustaining that without distraction, and from its culmination, at the time of the ultimate result, the perfected saṃbhogakāya arises in forms with colors, faces, hands, ornaments, and attributes.

During subsequent attainment, in the state of [knowing] unreality, performing unimpeded deeds while understanding their nonexistence is the cause of nirmāṇakāya arising. You become habituated through sustaining that without distraction, and from its culmination, at the time of the ultimate result, the nirmāṇakāya that emanates as anything at all arises. Those three kāyas are all essentially the real buddha.

Though this is precisely the buddha since time out of mind, the problem is that we folks don't know how to handle that fact. Therefore, buddhas and sentient beings appear as two even though in essence they are one. That is mind's unique apparition. For example, though the fingers are essentially one thing, when they are extended, we call it a palm, and when they are contracted, we call it a fist. In ascertaining through words, the uttered sound is "buddhas" who arrive to train whomever is to be trained in whatever way works. In accord with that function, those are *symbolic buddhas*. However, those are not *actual buddhas*. As an object of the devoted mind, they occur based on aspirations and compassion. Therefore, they represent just a reflection. Similarly, to the mind of one to be trained, it is possible [for buddhas] to appear, but these are like the faces in a mirror; they are just the reflections of the buddhas. Like our actual face, that nondual dharmakāya is one's own mind itself, uncontrived—this is the real buddha. Well then, you might wonder why it is necessary to label these [reflections] as buddhas. It needs to be presented that way in order to lead those to be trained who are of lesser intellectual capacity and are attached to real things and bring them to the genuine path. It states in the *Diamond Cutter Sutra*:

> Whoever sees me as form,
> whoever hears me as sound,
> has entered a mistaken path.

Those people do not see me.
Buddhas are the dharmakāya;
the guides are unconditioned.[95]

And in the [Perfection of Wisdom in] Eight Thousand Lines:

Child of good family, tathāgatas should be viewed as dharmakāya.
They should not be viewed as rūpakāya.[96]

In the [Perfection of Wisdom in] One Hundred Thousand Lines:

So-called "buddha, buddha" is not observable.[97]

Thus, to practice Dharma is to abandon cyclic existence. With realization, Dharma is also abandoned. When one has become completely relaxed in the falling away of intellect and the exhaustion of phenomena, that is to be a buddha. For example, all sickness can be cured by medicine. If the medicine isn't absorbed and goes to the sickness, then when the potency of the sickness subsides, the potency of the medicine also subsides. When the sickness is cured, it is assumed that both the sickness and the medicine are gone. In general, to become enlightened one needs to practice the Dharma. At the point of awakening, once free of the mind that fixates on the Dharma, one realizes there is no Dharma, and that is buddhahood. It is like the depletion of fuel and the [simultaneous] dying out of fire. Therefore, in subsequent knowledge, train the mind in [knowing all phenomena to be] like dreams and illusions.

Signs of uprising

20ab. *When phenomena's nature is ascertained, harmful thoughts abound.*
Thoughts about various knowable objective appearances come and go.

Practicing as before, the signs of uprising are the occurrence of various concepts, the occurrence of various afflictive emotions, fear, discontent, scattered consciousness, an agitated mind, second thoughts, doubt, uncertainty, intrigue, disgust, trepidation, longing to leave, irritation, suffering, multiple foci, random ideas, mental joy and sorrow, and various highs and lows. Since it is a time when conceptual thinking and its antidotes are struggling, a variety of happiness and sadness occurs. For example, when you capture an enemy during a battle, you both may sustain wounds. It states in the *Sutra*:

> The precious Dharma is rare but constant troubles are many.[98]

It is like taking medicine for sickness: it cures the sickness, but then there is the sickness of the medicine.

Causes of reverting

20cd *Without the support of realization and the experiences of meditation,*
engaging circumstances without the ability to equalize by trampling
upon them is to revert.

Reverting comes from [not] severing the basis with realization, not attaining stability in meditation, and being unable to equalize and trample upon [circumstances] in the conduct. Lacking the reinforcement of realization, having meager confidence of experience, and having little power of conduct create the causes of reverting. The problem is being lost in the antidote's impasse, not pursuing the object, and not immediately pouncing on circumstances. As it says in *Another Bundle*:

> Without knowing that occurring circumstances are allies,
> having a lofty but mistaken view,
> not internalizing the instructions,

and having no confidence of understanding,
just hearing the words is not definite resolution.
Think about that, noble child.[99]

Pushing back

21ab. *Cut the trunk of thought-provocation with the ax of view, meditation,*
and conduct,
and all the leaves of mental factors and concepts will wither on their own.

There is pushback of the view, pushback of the meditation, and pushback
of the conduct.

Pushing back with the view

This is just the introduction by the guru. It is what makes the lack of
understanding become understanding, makes unknowing become knowing, makes unawareness become awareness, and makes lack of realization become realization. Later, sustaining that personally is important.
Mere understanding doesn't help—you must become habituated, well-
acquainted, attain stability, stay directly with it, expand upon it, make it
enduring, and become totally clear. Gain confidence in dispelling obstructions and enhancing practices. At that time, whatever arises to your mental
perception, whatever is remembered, whatever appears, whatever moves—
resolve definitely that it is your own mind. Decide that mind is without
birth or cessation. Decide that the unborn is the dharmakāya. Decide
that though dharmakāya cannot be identified, whether it is thinkable or
unthinkable, it does not transcend emptiness. Whether [thoughts] move
or do not move, emanate or do not emanate, what is recalled and whatever arises is emptiness. Wherever a bird flies, it does not get beyond the
sky. Wherever a fish swims, it does not get beyond the water. Rest with the

thought that whatever arises in the yogin's mind does not transcend emptiness. Whether thoughts proliferate or not, reabsorb or not, fixate or not, emanate or not, exist or not, stop or not—rest in their self-dissipation and self-liberation. It states in the *One Hundred Thousand*:

> Conceptual thinking is neither fettered nor liberated.[100]

Pushing back with meditation

When meditating, relax into a state of nonrecollection without being mindful of anything: virtue and vice, happiness and sadness, or samsara and nirvana. Abruptly let go in nonfixation. Let go in loose nondistraction.[101] Rest without hopes and fears. Rest without calculation. Rest [knowing that] wherever you've gone is fine. If you don't understand that this appearance is of no concern, no matter what you do, it will be the cause of clinging. If you know there is no concern, there is no need to block appearances. Know them as false. Understand that they are of no concern. If you realize nonbeing, it is sufficient to remain unattached. No need to accomplish emptiness; it is enough to let it be in its own mode. If you let it rest in its own mode, you won't need to meditate on emptiness. Discursive thinking will subside from within. Even without blocking appearances, if there is no attachment to their reality, you won't accumulate the actions based on attraction and aversion that result in bad karma, be tainted by negative habitual patterns, or be uncontrollably born in the places of worldly existence. It is like the rotten roots of a poisonous tree, the inanimate human corpses of a graveyard, or the clay images in a temple—even if there were a faculty, there is no ability to cause harm. Machik said:

> Fixation is the devil. Effort is the disease. Fear is the demon. Resting is the foundation. Not doing is the path. Not accomplishing is the result. Whatever arises is a friend. Buddha is mind. Mind itself is space.[102]

In this kind of view and meditation, it is not enough to have a mere understanding of mental objects, [because] when you merely encounter intense circumstances, you will remain in an ordinary mental state. When circumstances arise, in order to take on that adversity directly, you must blend mind and Dharma. And even just blending is not enough: if you have not trained the energy (*rtsal ma 'byongs*), nondissipating qualities won't arise impartially. Therefore, when encountering various circumstances, you have to train the energy without partiality. If that has not been trained, you need to equalize through conduct.

Pushing back with conduct

At that time, fear, terror, trepidation, disgust, and so on, make you unable to engage the conduct. When that produces the thought that you can't bear it and can't equalize [the circumstances], intensify your awareness directly in the view. Cast it out in a state of fearlessness. If you are afraid, cast it out directly in the immediacy of fear. If you feel ashamed, cast it out in the immediacy of shame. If you are disgusted, cast it out in the immediacy of disgust. Blend with the circumstances by equalizing and trampling upon [that feeling of being] unable to bear them. Disrupt the normal order. Give up hypocritical behavior. Leave the crowds and take up practice. When you feel terror, trepidation, unbearability, and inability, look at who is the agent of that inability and where it abides. Look for its essence. Look for its form and its color. Look for the location and cause of that inability. Then pursue it like a dagger or an arrow. Follow it far [with] awareness. Act like an old woman pointing a finger, and investigate whatever it is you can't bear, can't do, and is hard to get rid of. Collapse the false structure. Get to the bottom of it and leave it instantly. Let go in its lack of true existence. Release into its nonbeing. This is the instruction for collapsing the innermost falsehood of conventional reality. It is the method of severing the roots of discursive thinking. It is the teaching for distinguishing the boundary between samsara and nirvana. It is the esoteric instruction on pushing back conceptual thinking. In *The Great Bundle of Precepts*, [Machik] says:

> The yoga that brings together view and conduct
> is like the weapons carried by warriors.
> And as all enemy hosts are vanquished,
> devils are vanquished in the space without inflation.[103]

Evidence of success

21cd *Just as the warm rays of sunlight overcome all humidity and gloom,*
the dawning of timeless awareness removes flaws, and you traverse
the stages and paths.

There is both short-term and ultimate evidence of success. In the short term, the degree of attachment, aversion, and the eight concerns lessens; subtle or coarse discursive thinking doesn't cause harm; any adverse conditions become supports for engaging in virtue; fixating on the reality of appearance is reversed; unprecedented experiential realization arises; boundless compassion is born for sentient beings who lack realization; a special devotion to the guru who has taught Object Severance arises; and there is no acceptance-rejection or affirming-negating of whatever phenomena arise on the path. The ultimate evidence of success is the automatic traversal of the five paths, the successive achievement of the ten stages, the arising of the ten signs and eight qualities, the attainment of the eight great accomplishments, and the achievement of the four actions. It states in *The Great Bundle of Precepts*:

> Body, speech, and mind purified
> are designated as the resultant three kāyas.
> Samsara is liberated in its own ground;

apart from that, nirvana is not achieved.

If nothing at all is engaged in the mind,

habitual patterns don't arise; levels and paths are completed.[104]

Karma and Afflictions

The person who severs

22ab. *With emptiness, compassion, and the awakening mind, [some] realize*
intrinsic nonexistence,

or can transform and relinquish through antidotes, or know how to
make offerings.

An individual who has entered the door of Object Severance is a yogin who desires to obtain omniscient buddhahood for everyone. There are six attitudes. The best [individuals] realize that afflictions are by nature nonexistent and self-liberated. They are fully matured by emptiness and compassion, and they overcome [the afflictions] through brilliance. The middling, by skillful means, can transform afflictions into timeless awareness. They accomplish the benefit and welfare of others with the mind of awakening. The least know how to make offerings to the sugatas. They can relinquish through antidotes and sever with that. It says in the *[Eight Common] Appendices*:

> Don't be attached to appearance; meditate on emptiness.
> Don't take pleasure in competition; stay alone.[105]

The devils that are severed

22cd. *Devils and spirits cannot lead you to the lower realms.*
Conquer the devil of afflictions that leads you to produce suffering.

The devils of attraction and aversion, the demons of the three poisons, the malignant spirits of the five poisons, the harm-doers of the root afflictions of the six consciousness groups, the elemental spirits of the twenty secondary afflictions, the flesh-eaters of the 84,000 afflictions, the *sinpo* spirits, and the ḍākinīs who always reside in the charnel ground of your body, speech, and mind cause obstacles to virtue, obstruct emancipation, and steal the life force of meditative concentration. Although the worldly devils and elemental spirits, and so forth, rise up as fierce enemies, they cannot make you roam through the three realms or wander in the places of the six kinds of beings, nor can they cast you down to the lower realms. This devil of afflictive emotion casts you into the ocean of suffering in cyclic existence. It states in the *Way of the Bodhisattva*:

> If somehow the gods and demigods
> all rose up as my enemies,
> they could not lead me into the fire
> and consign me to unremitting hell.

> Yet this mighty foe of my afflictions
> will throw me down in a single instant
> to where even the Supreme Mountain
> would burn without any ash remaining.[106]

The majority of Severance practitioners mainly try to vanquish the external devil of gods and demons. The internal devil of attraction and aversion is not severed. If it is severed, attraction and aversion must subside naturally. Afflictions must be allowed to self-liberate. By not letting that happen, some Severance practitioners resort to taking on consorts, drinking beer, and engaging in crude behavior. If you think that resorting to consorts and beer is done without attachment, there *is* attachment—which is exactly why they do those things. If there weren't, they would not resort to them. For as long as there is desire and craving, it follows that there is attachment and clinging. For example, if you eat garlic, you can't get rid of the garlic smell. If you take medicine, that smell also remains. If you take medicine and garlic, the smell comes up. Carrying that smell is a sign of having consumed those ingredients. Therefore, it stands as a connection between cause and effect.

There are four kinds of Severance practitioners: Severance practitioners who have severed externally but not internally, Severance practitioners who have severed the devils but not their own superstitions, Severance practitioners who have cured leprosy but have not cured the afflictive emotions, and Severance practitioners who have not gathered the causes but have gathered the results. Severance [practices] such as these, [which only tame demons,[107]] are not right. What is called "Object Severance" is a general Dharma term that has been applied to a specific [practice]. There are vast implications. It applies to all dualistic phenomena, such as attraction and aversion, the eight concerns, happiness and sadness, accepting and rejecting, denying and affirming, hopes and fears, and so on. It states in *The Appendices*:

> Many vanquish demons and devils,
> but few vanquish their own self-fixation.
> There are many who cure leprosy,
> but just few who cure the afflictions.
> Many alleviate sickness,
> but giving up samsara is barely possible.[108]

The method of severing [the devils] has three parts: where to sever, when to sever, and through what means.

How the devils are severed

Where to sever

> 23ab. *The place is this haunted ground of your body where channels and*
> *elements converge,*
> *where the spirits of affliction abide in the manner of inhabitants in a*
> *habitat.*

In the haunted ground of the body consisting of the four elements, the support habitat is the abode of jackals of the five aggregates, vultures of the five elements, and wild animals of the channels, constituents, and sense fields. The supported inhabitants are the gods and demons of the five toxic afflictive emotions. It states in *The Appendices*:

> If you wish to accomplish perfect buddhahood,
> go to an isolated place and take up practice.
> Stay in a haunted place and maintain awareness,
> relax into nondistraction—liberation is assured.[109]

When to sever

> 23cd. *Realization of timeless awareness appears as expanding light rays;*
> *keep severing until the dark gloom of ignorance is illuminated.*

Once you have entered the door of this Dharma, keep severing until the sublime timeless awareness of realization arises. When afflictive emotions arise in your mindstream, sever them using the antidotes of Severance. It states in *The Appendices*:

The arising of afflictions and discursive thinking,

the experience of attraction or aversion, happiness or sadness:

that itself is the devil; take up the path.

At that time, use the Severance antidotes.[110]

Through what means

24ab. *Whenever afflictions arise, grasp them through antidotes*
of view, meditation, and conduct, and conquer the devils.

When afflictive emotions arise in your mindstream, rest in the view of emptiness. Enter into forgetfulness through meditation. Equalize them through conduct. Watch where desire, anger, stupidity, pride, or jealousy come from in the first place, where they abide in the meantime, and where they go in the end. What is their essence? What is their form? What is their color? Looking at those, you see there is nothing that could be established, nothing to see, and nothing to identify. Rest in that state. From *Another Bundle*:

Buddha: what's called "buddha" is taught

as the means of liberation from samsara.

Once you realize the meaning of no acceptance or rejection,

rest in the state of great equanimity.[111]

Entering into forgetfulness through meditation refers to the sudden arising of afflictions. When you suddenly become aware of them, do not prolong their continuity. Don't expand or lengthen or clarify them; just forget them. Let them dissipate, self-destruct, and move away. Don't ponder them, don't let them proliferate, don't recollect them, and don't let them re-arise. Let them go like striking a sword into water without leaving a trace. Leave them like a bird's flight in the sky without tracks. Let them evaporate like snow falling on fire. Let them release themselves like the coils of a snake. It states in *The Appendices*:

Whatever good or bad thoughts arise in your mind,
the esoteric instruction is to not hold on to them.
Resting without contrivance assures their release.
Let mental fixation disappear.[112]

Equalizing through conduct means to understand the meaning of *severance* as cutting attraction and aversion and cutting afflictions. Whatever occurs—happiness or sadness, high or low, joy or sorrow, or the eight worldly concerns—equalize it. Push it down. Take up the practice on the path. Cut through with the instructions. [As it is said in Machik's] miscellaneous sayings:[113]

What's the use of wealth and knowledge
if there's nothing in the time of need?
What's the use of profound instructions
if they're not helpful when adverse circumstances arise?

Signs of uprising

24cd *Just as unsuitable food will reactivate old toxins,*
the condition of practicing will raise afflictions of attraction and
aversion.

In this example, for some people who have internal toxins and eat unsuitable food, or have swallowed a decoction that concentrates the sickness, the sign that [the toxins] have been consolidated is that the concealed toxins within the channels rise up and the person gets sick. Similarly, by your practice of the view, meditation, and conduct, the hidden and latent afflictions rise up and become manifestly clear, arising quite blatantly. Outwardly, they cause you to have greater attachment to possessions than before. Inwardly, you feel stronger desire and craving than before. Likewise, anger, stupidity, pride, jealousy, and greed become more pronounced than before. Your mindstream worsens, your interest shortens, and you have thoughts about your master that are worse than before. These are the early indications that afflictions are about to subside and that your desire for negative actions is running out. For [another] example, in order to extract the flaws and enhance the luster of gold, black vitriol[114] is applied. The stains rise up, and for a moment the gold seems to go bad, but that is the portent of changing into fine gold.

Causes of reverting

25ab. *Unless one has attained forbearance in Dharma, circumstances on the path terrify.*
   Regret, doubts, wrong views, and annoyance with Dharma will surface.

Causes of reverting are hardships of the path, irritation with asceticism, sealing the retreat cell, fear of isolation, discouragement when the experiential realizations and signs of accomplishment don't happen in a timely fashion, fear of accomplishment and practice, renouncing the Dharma, being skeptical of the instructions, not believing the guru, and thinking, "Now I guess the Dharma is just not working." From *The [Eight Common] Appendices*:

> Danger is great if the view is wrong.
> Enemies rise up if sacred pledge is damaged.
> Obstruction is harmful if your mind is deluded.
> Poison is produced by concepts of self-fixation.[115]

Pushing back

25cd. *When afflictions arise, push back with methods and wisdom.*
   Emptiness, transformation, offerings, and realization are supreme remedies.

There are three ways to push back on afflictive emotions: vanquishing them through emptiness, transforming them on the path through methods, and making imaginary offerings.

Vanquishing afflictive emotions through emptiness

Outwardly, if the enjoyment of desirables is not informed by emptiness—even if sanctified substances are consumed and sutra [recitation], aspiration prayers, dedications, and the yoga of food are performed— if, inwardly, they are enjoyed with thoughts of attachment and craving, the result will be worthless because there is clinging. With inner desires of the mind—even for one who is an appropriate support for obtaining the supreme empowerment and is worthy of the supportive [practices of fierce inner heat] due to knowing the descent, holding, reversing, and spreading of vital essence—if you do not abandon the desirous mind internally, the result will be worthless. That dissipating bliss is not the genuine path because it lacks the realization of undissipating emptiness. Regarding aggression, even if you have the ability to liberate through [wrathful] direct action (*mngon spyod*), if it is not informed by emptiness, the result will be worthless because emptiness has [not] been liberated in the realm of phenomena.[116] Regarding stupidity, even if you have the ability of lucid dreaming and refining and increasing dreams, [which can purify stupidity,] if the realm of phenomena does not become lucid clarity, you will accumulate the habitual patterns of fully ripened delusion, which will be worthless because a dream is doubly delusional. It states in the sutra:

> Those mentally attached to cyclic existence will ever cycle;
> they don't truly realize the phenomenal nature of *me* and *mine*.[117]

And in the words of Master Nāgārjuna:

Those for whom emptiness is possible,
for them everything is possible.[118]

Therefore, emptiness conquers all afflictions. However strong your five toxic emotions, however hard they are to relinquish, piercing your meditative stability and hindering virtuous practice—gain clarity and let them get worse than before, let them become evident, and let them be curtailed. Let them burn like fire, blow like the wind, and stabilize like the earth, such that nobody could interfere. Meditate like that and look nakedly at their essence. You need not *apply* emptiness: it was always empty. Extend that experience longer. It will become no-thing. Rest relaxed in that state. It becomes self-pacified and self-liberated. For example, it is like conquering poison with poison or conquering the enemy with the enemy. It says in the tantra:

Existence binds the world,
existence itself purifies existence.[119]

And in *The Great Bundle of Precepts*:

Just as burns by fire are treated by fumigation
and wounds are bled with moxibustion,
repeated severing and pushback are the point of instruction.
Make the circumstances carry the load.[120]

Transforming afflictive emotions on the path through methods

The object of reliance in transforming afflictive emotions is the authentic female [or male] consort, the one who relies is the qualified male [or female] consort, and the manner of relying is to possess the vital points of methods. Through that reliance, desire becomes empty bliss, dissipating [bliss] becomes undissipating [bliss], and attachment is realized as the nature of phenomena. This is the perspective from all the explanations in the tantras about appropriate reliance [on consort practice].

Imaginary offerings

If the antidotes work, that is fine. If not, purify the desire in your mind-stream and control the four ecstasies of descent. You [should] not choose the objects [of your offerings] with regard to whether they are high or low, but give away your body in generosity to all lepers, beggars, and beings of the lower realms. At that juncture, imagine the yidam deities and make offerings to those higher beings. Think of those lower beings as guests. For yourself, gather the accumulations and purify obscurations. Engage in those meditations. It states in the *Kālacakra Tantra*:

> Giving horses and cattle, the merit is a thousandfold.
> Giving children and spouses, it is a hundred thousandfold.
> Giving one's body, it becomes ten millionfold.
> Giving the Dharma, [the merit] becomes incalculable.[121]

Similarly, with regard to anger and hatred, those to be liberated are the particular objects of the six realms. That which liberates is the individual who has particular mastery of emptiness and compassion. The manner of liberating is the particular technique used by the practitioner who has attained the spiritual power of methods. That which is accomplished is the necessary birth in the realm of the victors [from whence] they can enact the long-term benefit of beings, not [just] the immediate needs that would please them, which are of no benefit. It states in the *Collection on the Stages*:

> In doing whatever benefits and pleases,
> do what helps, even if it becomes suffering.
> Don't create unhelpful pleasure.[122]

Evidence of success

26ab. *Not stranded in the net of existence, an unbearable ocean of*
afflictions,
the best conquer it by equalizing in timeless awareness, the supreme
measure.

The evidence (or measure) of successful severance of afflictions is, in the best cases, to completely transform the basis of afflictions, along with the seeds of habitual patterns, into timeless awareness. The middling is to pacify the subtle and concealed [afflictions]. The least is to eliminate the actual causes of blatant [afflictions]. At the very least, the afflictive emotions will do no harm, will diminish, and are easy to suppress with antidotes if they arise, and the mind and the antidote are not overpowered by those afflictions. It states in a treatise:

> The result of listening [to the Dharma] is pacifying and taming;
> the meditation sign is the diminishing of afflictions.[123]

The Result: Severing Sickness and Suffering

The person who severs

26cd. *With faith, compassion, realization, and the vital points of instruction,*
yogins sever as a means of attaining emancipation.

The person who practices severing sickness and suffering is endowed with four dispositions. With faith in the Dharma, they take suffering onto the path. With love and compassion, they can take on suffering for the sake of others. With the vital points of the instructions, they know the methods for integrating sickness and suffering on the path. With the realization of phenomena's nature, they understand that sickness and suffering are empty. Endowed with those four factors, they sever.

The devils that are severed

27ab. *Intense sickness, suffering, and torment are everyone's devils;*
if suchness is not realized, they rob the life force of attaining freedom.

When you are experiencing physical sickness and intense mental suffering, they are devils if you don't realize the nature of phenomena and see the meaning of mind itself. In the short term, they rob the body's life force. Ultimately, they rob the life force of freedom. Therefore, they are the devils that you must sever.

The place to sever

27cd. *The support that produces all happiness and sadness, faults and*
qualities, samsara and nirvana,
is this place of the aggregate of four elements, afflictions, winds,
phlegm, and bile.

Within this body reside the causes that create all samsara and nirvana—channels, vital winds, seed syllables, vital essence, and good or bad thoughts—that depend upon it. The essence of the body itself is the thirty-two constituents, such as flesh and blood, and the aggregates of the four elements, winds, phlegm, and bile. Since that is its essence, that is the place to sever.

The time to sever

28ab. *When sickness and suffering arise in body, speech, and mind,*
you are tormented by discordant adverse conditions.

When the sickness of heat and cold arise in the body, the sickness of the winds arise in the speech, and the sickness of discursive thinking arises in the mind—sever them.

Through what means

28cd. *The support for sickness and suffering and every fault and problem is body and mind; when those two are separated, it is liberation.*

When sickness occurs in the body and suffering in the mind, imagine that the essence of this mind is the letter *ah*. Send it out through the cranial aperture and blend it in the emptiness of space. This material body is like the empty house of a dead owner that has no one to be the caretaker. Rest fully in that state. The material body and the aware mind have been divided in two. The body's caretaking does not fall to the mind. The mind's mastery does not fall to the body. Rest without any mental engagement whatsoever in the great pervasiveness of awareness. Rest carefree. Rest relaxed. Rest any time. Rest well wherever you've gone. There is no cause of sickness or dying in this sky-like empty mind. There is no one to get sick or die in this earth-like inert body. [Tell the mind,] "You, incidental conceptual thinking, if you have a cause of sickness, then let there be sickness. If you have a cause of death, then let there be death." With that, rest relaxed within the nonthing-ness of mind and stay on your bed. There is no purposeful meditation at all in resting in nonbeing in this way. Not to meditate is precisely the ultimate meditation. If you do that, you will recover from sickness. But don't hope for recovery or be happy if you do recover. [Machik says in] *The Great Bundle*:

Just as a lion on the empty snow peaks
has no fear or apprehension,
if you happen to be happy without inflation,
sickness and spirits cannot harm you.[124]

Signs of uprising

29ab. *Snakes cannot bear a threatening finger pointed at them.*
Sickness spirits cannot bear your meditation on emptiness, and run away.

The outcastes of Mön point their fingers in the nest of poisonous snakes and if they say, "Here there are poisonous snakes," the snakes can't bear it. If there is no antivenom (*rtsi ma ghi*), they will attack.[125] If there is, that snake will die or flee to another area. Similarly, the yogin practicing vanquishing conduct focuses on a visualization of sickness. The malignant spirit that produced the sickness cannot bear it and rises up, and the disease gets even worse. But if the yogin possesses the antivenom of realizing emptiness, that sickness will subside. From Mother [Machik's] personal advice:

> If, meditating, the sickness persists,
> it may be an uprising, so make an effort.
> For instance, as when eliciting fire through friction,
> it only happens after a long time of intense work.[126]

Causes of reverting

29cd. *Whenever you are pained by intense sickness and* duḥkha,
you revert if you lose confidence, become discouraged, and give up.

When intense sickness and suffering (duḥkha) arise, you experience a loss of confidence, mental heroism recedes, your strength of will is broken, doubts about the method eat away at you, and you don't believe the instructions. At that time, nothing at all helps, no matter what you do or don't do. You think that nothing will improve, and so you abandon efforts in the practice and revert. As it states in [*The Way of the Bodhisattva*]:

Can the disheartened, abandoning exertion,
even find freedom from this deficiency?
But those who strive with proud resolve
are hard to vanquish even by [something] big.[127]

Pushing back

30ab. *Vigor increases with mental heroism, experience, and realization.*
The arsenal of sharpened view and conduct conquers the devil hordes.

There are three ways of pushing back: the view of realizing phenomena's nature, the meditation of profound visualization, and the conduct of auspicious methods.

The view involves the triad of sickness, patient, and spirit; the triad of mind, adverse conditions, and suffering; the triad of body, speech, and mind; and the triad of methods, visualization, and interdependence. Look at the empty essence of everything. From *The Great Bundle*:

If nothing at all is taken into experience,
that itself is taking into experience.
Experience is mind-made knowledge.
In the genuine meaning, there is nothing to experience.[128]

The meditation of profound visualization regarding sickness and suffering is to meditate on clarifying the realization of phenomena's nature. It will arise through not finding the sought-for sick person and as a result of emptiness. The meditation to enhance experience and realization is to contemplate sickness and suffering and take up practice, by which a special experiential realization will arise—like looking for a lost needle and finding a turquoise. That is meditation with favorable conditions for attaining emancipation: the one that will purify obscurations, that will sever on the path, and that will establish you in emancipation. From the miscellaneous experiential teachings:

> Sickness and suffering are most kind.
> Devils and obstructing spirits are most kind.
> Circumstances and obstacles are most kind.
> They bring the fortunate to the Dharma.

The conduct of auspicious methods is when that visualization gathers the external and internal accumulations of merit and purifies what is to be discarded, eliminating the obscurations of the path. Once the accumulation of merit is complete, you will attain emancipation. From a miscellaneous saying:

> This practice of integrating happiness and sadness on the path—
> when obscurations are eliminated, you will see me.

Evidence of success

30cd *The profound integration of methods and wisdom pacifies sickness and suffering.*
Flawless good qualities grow full like the waxing moon.

Success is evident when physical sickness and mental suffering are pacified. Special experiences and realizations arise. Henceforth, you are joyful when sickness occurs, thinking that it is sufficient to rest directly in the practice and that good qualities will accrue. You experience joy and good cheer. You have a heartfelt desire to laugh, dance, and sing. But, although that occurs, maintain equilibrium of the experience without attachment and clinging. A worldly person regards these [experiences as] hindrances or faults or adverse circumstances. According to this teaching, they are the manner in which experience arises, the forerunner of good qualities, and the enhancement of virtuous activity. You need not seek elsewhere for methods to clear up or abandon any highs or lows of awareness. Whatever appears, whatever arises, all of it is arising to yourself alone. Even though things appear as problems, by being absolutely sure that they are your own mind, they will dissipate and liberate on their own. From [Machik's] miscellaneous sayings:

> Iron ore is the nature of iron,
> but if it's not melted, iron doesn't appear.
> Faults are actually qualities,
> but if not realized, they don't arise.

Secretly Severing All Adverse Conditions

The intermediate state of birth and death: The person who severs

31ab. *With the confidence of realization, the force of experience, much study,*
courage, daring, heroics, bravado, and vanquishing conduct,

The person who severs all adverse conditions in the daytime must be one who is endowed with eight characteristics: the courage of realization, the force of experience, many Severance instructions, great courage in Severance, great daring in giving away their body and life, great bravado of the view, great bravery of awareness, and great vanquishing conduct of Severance. From [Machik's *Eight Common*] *Appendices*:

> First, seek with great courage.
> In the middle, forsake self-fixation.
> Finally, it is crucial to be free of inflation.
> If you have those three, you are a Severance practitioner.[129]

The devils that are severed

31cd. *sever the devils of various worldly disharmonies such as*
sickness, demons, spirits, defilement, the eight concerns, attraction, and
aversion.

Contagious disease, pestilent sickness, leprosy, widows, bastards, vow-breakers or the unvowed, defilements, attraction/aversion, the eight concerns, [verbal] abuse, people's disparagements, and so forth—in short, all things that are in disharmony with the world should be severed. From *The Great Bundle of Precepts*:

> Fearing unreal demons,
> hoping for unseen gods,
> formless five poisons, and so on:
> sever all mental objects of hope and fear.[130]

Where to sever

32ab. *Sever in the places that give rise to afflictions, such as your homeland,*
populated places, country, monastery, or residence.

To practice Severance, a place with many adverse conditions is preferable to a place where all harmonious conditions come together. That's because in a place of many adverse conditions, equalizing them enhances virtuous practice and makes good qualities arise. Therefore, populated regions are good places to practice Severance. Populated regions are more pestilent than water springs, lone trees, and mountains because the demons of attraction and aversion, eight concerns, happiness and sadness, and conflict dwell there and make you ever roam in cyclic existence. You can also practice Severance impartially throughout the countryside. That is more pestilent than boulders, meadows, and bushes, because the demons of happiness and sorrow, loves and hates, and likes and dislikes dwell there and kidnap you when you're under the influence of this life. Practice Severance in the place of your birth. Your birthplace is more pestilent than valley caves, cliff caves, or empty valleys, because the demons of your bloodline, arrogant reputation, and status dwell there and kidnap you when you're under the power of afflictive emotions. Practice Severance in monasteries and Dharma centers. Monastic centers are more pestilent than mountain ravines, empty houses, high rocky cliffs, and snowy hermitages because the demons of envy, rivalry, criticism, and attraction and aversion dwell there, erasing your sacred pledges and vows. Practice Severance in proximity to your guru. Being in the presence of your guru is more pestilent than shrine rooms, isolated places, and graveyards because the demons who mislead you with wrong view, criticism, paltry devotion, and familiarity dwell there, obstructing your attainment of freedom. Practice Severance in your own residence. It is more pestilent than the open road, four-way intersections, and main streets, because at your residence the demons of laziness, peaceful equanimity, comfortable Dharma, the inability to meditate, the inability to sit, and avoidance of the cushion dwell there, hindering the practice of virtue, experiential practice, fortitude, determination, and retreat practice. Therefore, take up the practice without falling under the power of those adverse conditions and you will distinguish yourself as a formidable Dharma practitioner, a warrior of practice, and a separator of samsara and nirvana.

When to sever

32cd. *For a long or short time, during personal time, or until awakening: practice as long as it takes for pleasure and pain, faults and adverse conditions to arise.*

The longest time [to practice Severance] is until you attain awakening. The intermediate time is for the duration of your life. The shortest time is for one week. The straightforward duration is to keep practicing as long as pleasure, pain, faults, and adverse conditions arise.

Through what means

33ab. *Integrate sickness, spirits, defilement of violation, eight concerns,*
   pleasure and pain,
   and so forth, by meditating on their lack of intrinsic nature and timely
   knowledge.

Previously you cycled in the three realms, wandered in the six places of beings, and experienced various kinds of *duḥkha*. Why is that? It is because the timeless awareness of realization did not arise. And what is the reason for timeless awareness not arising? It is your involvement in rejecting and accepting, denying and affirming, and falling into hopes and fears about all the phenomena that appear and resound, such as their faults and qualities, pleasure and pain, and so forth. In short, the culprit is your failure to equalize. For example, hungry ghosts search for food for entire eons but don't find it; the culprit is the anguish of their desire.

There are three methods to engage this: severing sickness and spirits, severing impurity and violation defilement, and severing the eight concerns and pleasure/pain.

Severing sickness and spirits

(1) Severing spirits concerns [the following problematic] times: Hindrance years, hindrance months, hindrance planets, bad stars, bad directions, the five demons, devil severance, hopes and desires, fourth-removed unfavorable signs (*bzhi gshed*), seventh-removed corner unfavorable signs (*bdun zur*),

multiples of nine (*dgu mig*), tomb signs (*dur mig*), bad divinations (*mo ngan*), bad astrological calculations (*rtsi ngan*), and bad dreams.[131] Furthermore, there are the times of ceremonies involving crossed-thread rituals (*mdos*) and Bön rituals, longevity rituals, torma exorcisms, charms (*gto*) and hurling magic weapons (*zor 'phen*), empowerment rituals, accomplishment rituals, feast accumulations, making proclamations, attaching protectors, the [divination] turtle (*rus sbal*), daggers (*phur ba*) and such, and changing names and bodies. All of those are concepts of conventional delusion. [By contrast,] in this Dharma tradition, you bring down pestilence directly on pestilence, bring down devils directly on devils, drop down directly on concepts, go directly into fears, and go directly to dread. Thereby, the protection or antidote works by itself. For example, when one is bitten by a mad dog, the mad dog's own canines are given as medicine. It says in *The [Eight Common] Appendices*:

> Fixation is the devil.
> Effort is the disease.
> Fear is the demon.
> The body is the corpse to cast out as food.
> The caster is mind: rest at ease.[132]

Once there was a Severance practitioner whose brother was an astrologer who told him, "This year, all the bad hindrances, corpse activation, multiples of nines, and tomb signs will impact you. Be careful in your activities. Apply yourself to the rituals [to pacify hindrances]." The practitioner burnt a corpse atop a dog, removed the ceiling from a black place, and slept in a bad area.[133] No obstacles whatsoever came up. He said he had never had a better year for the increase of virtuous activity.

All of that concerned the beneficial result of realizing the view of emptiness, reversing fixation on the veritable existence of appearance, and mentally forsaking self-fixation. To one who has genuinely abandoned self-fixation, obstacles and such cannot penetrate in the least; leprosy, sickness, and spirits are cured; gods and demons come under control; the timeless awareness of realization arises; supreme spiritual powers are gained; and so forth. There are many benefits and stories about this.

If there are harmful demons and magic spells cast by *bandhe*s, lie under their torma table, take the torma, and eat it. Stay inside the hiding place of their practice house and meditate on emptiness. Upon their mandala, meditate on their guardians butchering your body and eating it. Rest in the emptiness of yourself, the bandhe, and the incited demons (*rbad 'dre*). If you think someone is practicing magic, don't think about how to fix it, and so on—don't mentally engage it at all; it's not important. Forget about it. Let it wander off. Let it vanish. Let it go. Wherever it goes, that's fine. Separate body and mind. Cast out the corpse as food. Rest in the emptiness of mind itself. In doing that, first of all, apparitions will come. In the middle, by your resting without inflation or fear, the apparitions will subside and cannot possibly return. Finally, once they are turned away, the imprecator will leave their bed and go. So it is said.

Even if they send a cursing object (*mtu gtad*), if the source of the curse is severed, it will stay in its place. If the source is not severed, one should sleep in the places where great nāgas and pestilent spirits reside until there is evidence of success. When that severs them, then go. [Success] is the turning back of that cursing demon upon those who sent it. It is the fall of the god's heart on the devil, [changing it to good]. If, in generating the gods, they arise as demons or if, suddenly, new demons threaten, terminate them. If king spirits threaten, stay in a place with demons, such as shrine rooms, stupas, and temples. If *tsen* spirits or devils threaten, stay in red or black cliffsides or mountain ledges and gorges. If female spirits and oath-breakers threaten, stay in hillside caves or cave cracks. If *mamos* threaten, stay in graveyards, retreat houses, isolated places, corpse pits, and in empty residences. If pestilent spirts and *sin* spirits of earth or rock threaten, stay in bushes, boulders, meadows, and water groves. If *pekar* spirits, *gongpo* spirits, or male or female knife ghosts threaten, stay in empty houses, mountain valleys, ruined mounds, and crowds of men and women. Wherever you stay, practice as before. That will bring any interference to the yogin under control. The [spirits] will become Dharma protectors. From *The Great Bundle of Precepts*:

> Just as burns by fire are treated
> by applying incense from that very fire,
> and wounds are bled with moxibustion,
> repeated severing and pushback are the vital points of instruction.[134]

(2) To sever sickness, when you come in contact with houses or bedding that have been exposed to bad infectious diseases, such as carbuncles, intestinal infections, and smallpox, say *phaṭ* and relinquish attachment to your body and arouse heroic confidence in your mind. Separate the mind and body and meditate on the emptiness of infectious disease.

When you arrive there, don't avoid the sick person's pillow; mingle with the patient and their food and eat from the same plate. Sniff the odors and vapors of the disease and swallow so that they completely enter inside the central channel. Meditate on how they have become empty and dissipated. Have no concern or fear. If you get sick yourself, for an intestinal infection [involving] diarrhea, recycle your washing water and drink it. For smallpox, take the tip [of the pustule] and swallow it. For carbuncles, suck them from the top. For fevers, drink your own urine. The residue of whatever disease you have becomes its antidote. Like that, even eating the flesh of a dead person becomes an antidote.

Severing defilement and impurities

If violation defilement touches you from lepers, butchers, cripples, pledge-violators, the vowless, the sinful, fishers, hunters, butchers, grudge-holders, widows, bastards, and so forth, mingle with their bedding and eat their leftovers. That is the supreme [method of] washing and cleansing—it is the immaculate purification. For example, after you eat garlic, you don't notice the smell of garlic. Just so, each person's own antidote becomes effective.

Furthermore, if you have to handle a corpse, stay near a hearth of the vengeful or grudge-holders, wear unclean clothing, sleep in unclean houses and beds, eat food from an unclean vessel, eat unclean food, stay with acquaintances who have been defiled by violation, share dishes, or get involved in polluting actions—don't be overly concerned. Integrate [those experiences] on the path with the three equalizers: vanquish the things that you fixate on as truly existent through emptiness, vanquish attachment to self-fixation through contrary meditation, and vanquish superstitious thinking about cleanliness and uncleanliness.

Vanquish the things that you fixate on as truly existent through emptiness: all phenomena—including the outer environment and inner inhabitants, samsara and nirvana, and the six types of beings—have been empty since forever. They are neither clean nor unclean, fragrant nor foul, repulsive nor attractive, pleasant nor unpleasant. Although phenomena appear in these dualities, it is our own conceptual thinking that labels them so. In fact, there is not even an atom of true existence that can be established. It is like the twelve examples of illusion that are elucidated in the teachings of all the canonical scriptures, treatises, sutras, and tantras. That [emptiness] is established by esoteric instructions and experienced through reason. Whether it is realized or not, understood or not, primordial emptiness is a nonthing. Think along those terms.

Vanquish attachment to self-fixation through contrary meditation: Subjectively, this consciousness that fixates on clean and unclean, if left unexamined and unanalyzed, manifests as repulsion or fear toward appearances. Yet when examined and analyzed, it is conceptual thinking that creates this nonthing. In fact, there is not even an atom of an entity or true existent. What is the one who is repulsed and what is the object of repulsion? What is clean or unclean? What is pure or impure? And where is the agent who fixates on repulsion and uncleanliness? Who is it? How is it? In contemplating these thoughts, look vividly at the nonthingness of appearances. Completely jump into emptiness. Meditate in the immediacy of nonbeing.

Vanquish superstitious thinking about cleanliness and uncleanliness by equalizing: Equalizing defeats fear, trepidation, repulsion, and whatever is undoable for the same reasons as before. In the state of those two [above-mentioned categories], trample them and chase after them. To equalize, think, "You, the one who is repulsed, take this!" Then, if there is unclean food, gulp it down. If there is an unclean drink, guzzle it. If there is an unclean place and bedding, sleep in them. If there are unclean clothes, don them with gusto. If there are leprous corpses and infectious diseases, go to them straightaway without hesitation. If there are lepers and sinful people, mingle with them.

There is no difference between clean and unclean in this mind of emptiness, just as to the sky there is no difference between incense and a rotting corpse. The body, an aggregated collection of the four elements, is itself a heap of unclean substances. It is the embodiment, a leather bag, an essence, so it is devoid of clean and unclean. Pouring water into water does not soak it. Adding fire to fire does not burn it. Smearing coal with black stuff does not blacken it. Just so, even if you pour unclean substance into unclean substance, it does not become clean and it does not become unclean. Therefore, in both shunning and mingling, there is nothing to be designated by concepts—there is not the least bit of difference in their meanings. By realizing such things, much conceptual thinking and attraction/aversion is destroyed and equalized. The realization of the nature of phenomena will follow automatically. [Machik] states in *The Great Bundle of Precepts*:

> Carry the load of appearing conditions.
> It's crucial to put the load on circumstances.
> If you don't carry the load of all phenomena,
> the remedy of peace and happiness cannot liberate you.[135]

Severing the eight concerns and pleasure/pain

It is more important to sever the devil that harms the internal mind than to sever the devil that harms the external body. From the experiential teachings:[136]

Once the demon devil enters within, this outer severing won't work.

Severing the eight concerns and pleasure/pain has three parts: what adverse conditions to sever, which antidotes to use, and what benefits will accrue for the Dharma practitioner.

(1) What adverse conditions to sever: Sever all the conditions that worldly people try to be rid of: loss, disgrace, infamy, slander, value judgement, others' criticism, malicious insults, having little interest, having little respect, being undervalued, having little honor, receiving undeserved accusations, receiving everyone's scorn, unhappiness, displeasure, and so on.

(2) Which antidotes to use is threefold: don't evaluate the liability when meditating on karma; since sins and obscurations are purifying, don't see them as something to be eliminated; and since it is [a matter of] cause and effect, don't discredit [others] for having wrong views.

Don't evaluate the liability when meditating on karma [means that] whatever undesirable adverse conditions you encounter, they are a sign that you previously accumulated bad karmic actions in response to adverse conditions and that you did not accumulate the causes for experiencing favorable conditions. Nothing befalls those without the [specific] karma, because bad karma is never ever inconsequential. Do not return the evil of others, quarrel, fight, or seek revenge. It states in a sutra:

The actions of living beings
are not lost even after a hundred eons.

Once done, when the time comes,
the fruit will ripen.[137]

Since sins and obscurations are purifying, don't see them as something to be eliminated. In this life, disagreeable adverse conditions and
your degree of experience in [using them as] fodder through body, speech,
and mind purifies previous bad karma and obscurations. Subsequently,
all the karma that would have led to birth in bad existences is exhausted
and purified. Look on that favorably. See it as indispensable. Regard it with
great appreciation. Thereby, the results of your hardships for the sake of
the Dharma—such as [experiencing] fatigue, heat and cold, drinking
[only] water, constructing cairns, sitting on a single seat, confessing, and
so forth—will swiftly come to pass. In all the life stories of previous adepts,
[they became accomplished] only from engaging in hardships, not from
sitting around in comfort and leisure. It says in a sutra:

Even experiencing suffering in a dream can exhaust previous bad
karma.[138]

Previously created adverse conditions occur in this life as a result of not
resolving them [earlier]. Therefore, view them as supports [to your prac-
tice]. Some see them as hindrances and obstacles, and take steps to be rid
of them. That just shows their meager knowledge of the Dharma.

Since [adverse conditions] are the result of cause and effect, don't
blame others. Nobody can prevent the results [that occur due to] causes
created previously, because they are the one who accomplished them. It
is not reasonable to accuse others, to falsely attribute faults, or to lay the
blame on anyone else. It states in a sutra:

The total ripening of previous actions cannot be assigned to anyone [else].[139]

And in a treatise:

> Suffering comes from unvirtuous actions.
> "How can I escape that for sure?"
> It is right to consider only this
> at all times, day and night.[140]

For example, when your face appears reflected in a mirror, whatever nice or flawed aspect appears, it is not the mirror's fault. It is the fault of your own visage. Likewise, whatever happiness or sadness you experience is the fault of previous causes. Therefore, you must abandon them at the time when you created the cause. At the time of the results, don't hold them as enemies, don't regard them as faults, and don't see them as misfortune. Meditate on karma, integrate it on the path, generate tolerance, and rejoice.

(3) What benefits accrue: If you understand in the [above-mentioned] way, all the faults of the path arise as qualities. All misfortune arises as glory. All devils come as gods. All hindrances and obstacles come as spiritual powers. That is the reason why what were once adverse circumstances are now seen as a cause for joy. It says in [Machik's] *Great Bundle of Precepts*:

> Even though white is not established in butter,
> recognizing butter confirms white.
> Once butter is just recognized,
> there's no need to establish white elsewhere.
> Similarly, when you recognize your own mind,
> there's no need to establish buddha elsewhere.[141]

Signs of uprising

33cd. *As sickness, suffering, and thinking become more blatant than before,*
various outer and inner discordant adverse conditions and obstacles
occur.

Hidden propensities from bad karma, negative actions, and obscurations rise up when you do the practice. The signs of their uprising are physical sickness, mental suffering, and more blatant discursive thinking. Outwardly, all adverse conditions and discordant obstacles rise up. Inwardly, congested constituents, heart-wind, lice infestation (*shig nad*), or other conditions occur. For example, [these signs] are like the smells that rise up when cleansing with carbonate of soda and campion.

Causes of reverting

34ab. *You may doubt cause and effect, the instructions, and the spiritual mentor.*
You may fear circumstances and feel weary on the path of Dharma.

When you practice the Dharma without knowing the signs of bad karma that rise up through your practice, [you will experience] many adverse circumstances, many sicknesses and sufferings, people's enmity, less loving-kindness, and sadness. When you practice the Dharma, you should reasonably improve, but by practicing the Dharma you [might actually] worsen. Depending on your degree of effort in virtuous practice, you've become unwilling to take action. Other people seem to be well and happy though they performed evil deeds, so you wonder whether karmic cause and effect is untrue. You wonder if the guru who taught the instructions, and the Dharma that was taught, and all the explanations derived from those instructions are untrue. While doing your practice, the amount of effort you put into virtuous deeds seems to cause unfavorable adverse conditions to increase, so you think you cannot take action, and you become consumed by doubts about cause and effect. A perverse view of the guru and instructions arises. Since the adverse conditions on the path discourage you, you don't understand the meaning of the final extinction of virtue and vice. This is a lack of recognition of the signs of uprising, and it is a cause for devils to enter. As it says in the sutra:

> Those who newly enter a vehicle are small-minded.
> Whoever does not appreciate this rare precious jewel
> is the devils' delight on whom to inflict with obstacles.[142]

Pushing back

34cd. *How can this appearing-yet-nonexistent devil harm you?*
Defeat this unreal delusion of an enemy with a mental antidote.

Do not love and crave gain, fame, renown, praise, respect, devotion, high esteem, greatness, and so forth. That temporary joy and all superficial happiness is just the experience of joy felt by worldly people. At the time of death, you must abandon everything and leave, with nothing to accompany you. If you are attached to all those things, it will hinder your emancipation and create the causes of cyclic existence. Based on that, others will accumulate much obscuration, and your own merit will be depleted. Transgressive views and unfavorable conditions will rise up. Once you have gone over to attraction and aversion, obscurations will accumulate. The value of experience won't be equalized and qualities won't arise. It states in *The Way of the Bodhisattva*:

> Though we be rich in worldly goods,
> Delighting in our wealth for many years,
> Despoiled and stripped as though by thieves,
> We must go naked and with empty hands.[143]

Thus, all mundane appearances are delusory appearances, the mind's apparitions, the play of illusion, and the happiness of a single nap. In the long term, all of it is unreliable, unhappy, unreal, and empty. To be attached to that is to totally delude yourself. As Nāgārjuna said in his *Letter to a Friend*:

> You who know the world, take gain and loss,
> Or bliss and pain, or kind words and abuse,
> Or praise and blame—these eight mundane concerns—
> Make them the same, and don't disturb your mind.[144]

So, rather than practicing Severance with demons that may or may not exist, it makes more sense to practice Severance with attraction, aversion, and the eight concerns. Internally, even though you may have no concept that fixates on demons, that is no different from saying "demons are untrue." That can cause the downfall of contradicting the skillful methods. Even though you realize that there is no virtue or vice, when you say that virtue/vice and cause/effect are not true without differentiating them, you are making a choice about what to reject or accept from within the state of their unreality. While making those choices, don't allow attraction and aversion. Whatever appears, make the definite determination that it is the mind. And when you meditate on that mind, do not mentally engage in any [thinking about] existence and nonexistence, being and nonbeing, or samsara and nirvana. Rest relaxed in mindlessness. Abruptly let go in nonfixation. Rest in loose nondistraction. Drive away [any notion that] something is difficult to equalize or that taking up the path is difficult. Equalize their value. Train the energy by getting on top of it. Take on the load and do the practice.

Evidence of success

35ab. *When this devil of attraction and aversion—the afflictions of*
existence—is terminated,
the coffers of all good qualities open, the source of all joy and well-being.

Signs of terminating the aforementioned devils of rejection and acceptance
are that without making a distinction for even a moment between worldly
likes and dislikes, there is no need to reject or accept, deny or affirm; attraction and aversion and the eight worldly concerns subside from within; the
conditions of the six consciousness groups apprehending the sense objects
do no harm; and you are not sullied by external attraction and aversion,
even when sitting in the assembly. It is like mixing dust and mercury. Ultimately, the things to be rejected, such as the eight concerns and attraction/
aversion, are all exhausted and the special experience and realization that
are to be obtained are born. Immeasurable good qualities arise. Gods and
gurus are pleased. The benefit of both yourself and others is achieved. You
become a support for homage by all the world with its gods, and a fitting
recipient of offerings. It says in [Machik's] *Great Bundle of Precepts*:

> The supreme Severance is to be without hopes and fears,
> free of extremes of both rejecting and accepting.
> When dualistic fixation is decisively cut off,
> you definitely reach the state of a buddha.[145]

Severing in the intermediate state of dream

35cd. *Recognize dreams through accumulation, purification, actions, habits,*
and intentionality.
When you've grasped them, refine, increase, and then meditate on
lucid clarity.

Do the dream practice with three vital points: the vital point of accumulation, purification, and supplication; the vital point of conditioning of habitual patterns in the daytime; and the vital point of intense intentionality when going to sleep.

The vital point of accumulation, purification, and supplication is to purify obscurations, which are the cause of [not] recognizing dreams; accumulate merit, which is the cause of recognition; and supplicate the guru, which is the method to grasp dreams. The vital point of daytime habitual conditioning is to think and meditate that there is not even a moment of difference between dreaming and all the daytime appearances, deeds, and activities. That habit will continue in your nighttime dreams. The vital point of intense intentionality when going to sleep is to think, from when you lie down until you fall asleep, "Tonight I will recognize my dreams no matter what." Through concentrating mindfulness with that intense intentionality, that night you will recognize your dreams with recollection. Dispel obstructions to recognition such as fear and rejection/acceptance in the dream. Enhance the practice by emanating multiple [dream images] from the one, and so forth. To master [those techniques] and change them into lucid clarity, during sleep, place your consciousness directly on meditation. When the day's meditation directly affects nighttime sleep, that is the recognition of lucid clarity.

Severing in the intermediate state of becoming at the time of death

36ab. *Drawing up the winds and consciousness is the path of transference.*
Lucid clarity arising from subtle and coarse melting sequences is
intermediate-state practice.

The best practitioner achieves stability in the intermediate state between birth and death once they have trained in the daytime practice based on the Severance instructions. The average practitioner achieves stability in the intermediate state of dreaming by practicing the instructions at night. The lesser practitioner recognizes lucid clarity, blocks the entrance to rebirth in a womb, and achieves stability in the intermediate state of becoming, based on the instructions. If the intermediate state of birth and death is not refined in the daytime, at night the intermediate state of dreaming will not be refined. If that is not refined, after you die the intermediate state of becoming will not be refined, so you should train in consciousness transference.

In general, this Object Severance is mainly a path of the Perfection of Wisdom. According to the vast scriptural sources, there are also ten paths of method. Illusory body and mahāmudrā are for the occasions of severing discursive thinking. [Practices based on] another's body and one's own body are taught for the occasions of severing the five poisons. Dream, transference, and intermediate-state practices are taught for this occasion of the time of death. Integral unity and lucid clarity practices are found throughout all the source texts. More on this should be learned from oral instructions.

Final Acts: Dispelling Outer Obstructing Gods and Demons

36cd. *Disease and various mental problems occur when gods and demons*
are agitated.
The remedial forces are emptiness, giving in charity, and meditating in
equanimity.

In general, the obstructions of malignant spirits do not affect the yogin who practices Object Severance. Nevertheless, as long as hope, fear, attraction, and aversion are not eliminated, sickness will come. When sickness occurs, since a malignant spirit will come as its support, the sickness will be sharpened by that support of the malignant spirit. For example, the force of an arrow depends on the bow; the bow's job is the arrow's action. If [sickness spirits] occur, there are two [approaches]: investigating which of three malignant spirits it is, and applying the methods of expelling sickness.

Investigating which of three bad spirits it is

Examine whether it is an upper malignant spirit, a lower malignant spirit, or an in-between malignant spirit. When upper malignant spirits, [such as] *tsen* spirits and devils, cause harm, they enter the upper body, causing sickness and pain in the head and torso. King spirits and *pekar* spirits enter the vital organs and heart, causing scattered consciousness, deep dislike, and desire for conflict. Female malignant spirits enter the channels and lower body, sickening the kidneys at the waist, blocking urine, and causing excretion of vital drops. Male and female knife ghosts enter blood and phlegm, causing sudden pains in the stomach and large intestine. The symptoms of all those are insomnia, irritability with bedding, cold sweats, goosebumps, mental prickling fear, and stretching and bending of the limbs.

Lower malignant spirits enter the entire subtle constitution, such as the flesh, blood, bones, and so forth. This causes dry leprosy, moist leprosy, and black rot. Examine the shape and color of the outer body, examine the inner veins and water, and examine the face and eyes in-between. These are explained in the instructions on [medical] examination.

In-between malignant spirits enter the skin and corium, externally causing blemished complexion and blotches and causing swellings and gout. Internally, they bring diseases of the upper stomach and liver, and diseases of tumors, ascites, and calculus stones. Quivering and numbness of the flesh occur in all cases.

Methods to expel sickness spirits

There are three methods to expel sickness spirits: rest in equanimity through the view, give away the body in meditation, and directly trample them in the conduct.

Resting in equanimity through the view

When you are sick, it's fine if you can go to a haunted place and accomplish Severance. In case you cannot, do this practice of integration on the path [by thinking] as follows: The sickness is a virtuous mentor. The malignant spirit is an emanation of the Buddha. The adverse conditions are a call to practice virtue. Suffering is the splint for sins and obscurations. The hostile enemy is the teacher of patience. Thus, in the general Mahayana tradition, you do not regard these as things to reject but to meditate on joyfully. Especially in the Object Severance tradition, whatever obstacles and apparitions of gods and demons arise, one does not make offerings to god-demons, nor beat them, rely on them, exorcise them, summon them, or ask for protection. Don't give presents [to bribe] even the huge demons, don't hope for their help, don't give puny presents to the little ones, and don't befriend or torment them. Let them be. All external obstacles are the creation of conceptual thinking. When you welcome concepts, this is your inner demons summoning outer demons. In fact, they are not truly existent. In general, thinking "demons will come" and wondering "will they harm me?" and "can I overcome them?" are occasions of inflation when you need to cut through. When in doubt, you need to sever in the immediacy of that doubt. When afraid, you must sever at the time of fear. When horrible forms are manifesting, unpleasant sounds are echoing, and rough conduct is being exhibited, even when weapons seem to rain down on you, remember that the body is just inert matter and the mind is without basis or root. Rest in that state. Be without even a scintilla of fear or trepidation. Until you have cut through the conceptual thinking that fixates on demons, do not desire to be cured of any sickness that has arisen due to malignant spirits. Until you are cured, cultivate bravado in realization, mental antidotes, and energetic practice. Try again and again to tackle whatever has not been cut, and carry the load. Thereby, Severance will be achieved.

Giving away the body in meditation

Invite all the buddhas, bodhisattvas, gurus, yidams, and ḍākinīs to appear in the space before you. Present them with your own body as the perfected four-fold offering [of outer, inner, secret, and suchness offerings]. Then call the six kinds of sentient beings before you. Imagine the yidam deity chopping up your body into a hundred or a thousand pieces and giving it to all beings. In particular, summon the gods and demons who would harm you, cut up your body into pieces, and give it to them a hundred times over. Then this body is an offering to those above, a charity to sentient beings below, and a remuneration of karmic debt to harm-doers in between. Mind is not a thing. Without fear or trepidation, think, "Come what may." Rest relaxed in your own fashion without inflation or conceptual thinking. Consciousness will be liberated in the nature of phenomena, and sickness will recover and be gone.

Directly trampling [spirits] in conduct

When any harm is done by gods and demons, no matter what haunted place the harmful malignant spirits came from, go to that place and engage in crazy vanquishing conduct, as was presented in detail previously (see page 57).

Dispelling obstructing sickness and obstacles in between

37ab. *Karmic causes and conditions of afflictive emotions produce sickness. Resolve it by means of vital winds, yogic exercises, and visualizations.*

There is the examination of disease from the elements and the method to expel it. As for the first, it is said:

Four hundred and four kinds of human disease
arise from the four elements as the cause.
The conditions are spreading, agitation, and indigestion,
essentially subsumed under heat and cold.[146]

All disease arises from the four elements as the [primary] cause. The earth [makes] phlegm, water [makes] bile, and fire [makes] wind. These [three humors] mainly come from the contributing conditions of spreading, agitation, and indigestion. The results can be subsumed into two categories: sicknesses of heat and sicknesses of cold. As for the first, a disease of the earth [element presents as] physical heaviness, foggy consciousness, sleepiness, reticence, and loss of appetite. A disease of the water element presents as shivering with cold, cold sweats, not digesting food, stomach inflammation, diarrhea, and vomiting. A disease of the fire element leads to sweating from the forehead, being irascible and spiteful, fever, dry mouth, anger, and a sluggish mind. A disease of the winds brings wandering consciousness, turbulence, confusion, random chatter, a desire to leave, toothaches, and tinnitus.

There are three methods to expel sickness: the preliminary is supplication, the main part is visualization meditation, and the conclusion is to rest with the idea of "come what may." For the first, arrange whatever feast items, offerings, and tormas you have collected. Invite all the lineage gurus, such as the Lady Mother, and so on. The best practitioners supplicate for attaining buddhahood based on this sickness. The middling supplicate to purify obscurations once sickness arises on the path. The least supplicate to quickly recover from that sickness. From [Machik's] scattered sayings:

Once the disease of elements is planted,
meditate on the guru, without distraction.
Progress through the entrance of supplication,
and you'll quickly recover; this I know.

The main practice, which is the meditation with visualization, has three parts: blending outer and inner elements as one, balancing the four elements, and applying disease directly to the disease.

Blending outer and inner elements

Whichever of the outer four elements has caused the sickness, stand right up and straighten your body [like a] lion. Place your two feet side by side. Put your two hands above your head, palms together. Hold a gentle breath (*'jam rlung*). If the sickness is on the outside of your body, visualize that the external four elements dissolve into the four elements of your body. The earth element dissolves into flesh and bone, the water element dissolves into blood and phlegm, the fire element dissolves into warmth, and the wind element dissolves into breath. In particular, they dissolve into wherever there is sickness. The outer and inner four elements are inseparably blended together, while the mind itself dissolves within space. Rest immediately in that emptiness. Then, wherever there's pain, enter beneath it and cast that body far away into nonself. Completely release the unsupported mind. When you go, you go from within space. When you stay, you stay from within space. When you sleep, you sleep from within space. When you eat, you eat from within space. Whatever you do is done from within space. Applied to each of the four elements in this way, external sickness will be cleared up.

With an internal sickness, you are sick inside your body. In that case, send these four elements out of your body and dissolve them into the four external elements. Make the flesh and bone dissolve into earth, and so forth. Then the mind vanishes like mist, and you enter that disappearance while your body lies down curled up. Quietly go to sleep from within that state. You will have recovered from the sickness when you wake up.

Balancing the four elements

In sicknesses of the four elements, the problem is that the elements are out of balance. In order to equalize them, you need to know what to increase and what to reduce. For sicknesses of heat, the problem is that fire is strong and water is weak. By meditating on water at the site of the sickness, cold is added and heat is reduced. Likewise, by meditating on fire for cold sicknesses, heat is added and cold is reduced. For wind sicknesses, meditate on earth. For earth sicknesses, meditate on wind. For sicknesses of desire, meditate on hatred. For sicknesses of hatred, meditate on desire. For diffusion [of concentration], gather it back as before. For congestion, just let it diffuse.

Applying disease directly to the disease

If you are sick from heat, you can also relieve it by using whatever you were eating and doing that caused harm [in the first place]. Putting heat in fire is a way to pacify it. For example, if you put fire-producing sunstone[147] or grass kindling or flintstone into water, afterward they cannot produce fire. Cold sicknesses will be pacified by using whatever food or activity caused it, because the way to conquer cold is in water. For example, if you put ice into water, it melts and disappears. Similarly, for a wind sickness, eating beans will expel the wind into the environment. Smearing swellings with elixir will dry them up naturally. Washing wounds with urine will ensure they do not return. Purgatives after diarrhea stop it. Blood-letting clears up infected wounds. Warmth expels the onset of fevers. For chills, submerge in water. Drink ice water for sickness of the stomach and large intestine. Likewise, with regard to fear, wandering in haunted places will banish the fearful one. For beings who cause obstacles, gifting your body aggregate to demons will make the harm vanish by itself. Eat unclean food to cure nausea. Go naked to cure shame. Equalize to cure attraction and aversion. By meditating on the equality of the eight concerns, the characteristics of dualistic fixation will be self-liberated.

In conclusion, rest with [the attitude of] "come what may." If you recover after engaging in these methods, that is good. It is the reason to practice the profound path. It is enough to benefit yourself and others. If you don't recover and die, that is also good. Once you have taken up the special practice of integrating Object Severance on the path, death is a reason to rejoice, because in ultimate reality [it means] to be awakened in the realm of perfect wisdom. That is indeed the case whether you get better or don't get better, whether you are helped or harmed, whether you recover or not, and whether you die or live. "Do whatever you like. Come what may." With those thoughts, don't be attached to anything at all. Say *phaṭ* and rest without hope and fear. A scattered saying states:

> Like the sky without hope and fear,
> rest relaxed without hope and fear.
> Like the sky without self-fixation,
> don't fixate on self, let go of clinging.[148]

Inner mental obstructions of conceptual thinking

37cd. *Congested constituents,* duḥkha, *loss of focus, and lethargy are mental problems.*
Conquer them with methods and interdependence, and wind disease by yogic exercise visualization.

There are three parts to dispelling mental obstructions: the signs of congested constituents, the problems with congested constituents, and the way to alleviate congested constituents. The signs of congested constituents also has three parts: causes of the onset of congested constituents, conditions of congested constituents arising, and signs of congested constituents.

Causes of the onset of congested constituents also has three parts: natural congested constituents, meditational congested constituents, and circumstantial congested constituents.

Signs of congested constituents: causes of the onset

The primary causes of natural congested constituents are former negative karmic actions. The contributing condition is negative conceptual thinking. Without reversal in the channels, there's no reversal of the winds. This comes from bile.[149]

Meditational congested constituents are the various problems that occur at the time of the first congested constituents. If they don't rise up on the path, obstacles will occur. If they do rise up, this opens the door to the development of good qualities.

Circumstantial congested constituents occur to angry people [as constituents that are] subsumed around enemies; for the desirous, they are subsumed around wealth; and for the faithful, they are subsumed around Dharma.

The conditions of congested constituents arising

There are three circumstances that raise congested constituents: those that are raised externally through the harm of gods and demons, those that are raised internally through the involvement of the three poisons, and those that are raised in between by discordant situations.

Those that are raised externally through the harm of gods and demons come from digging pestilent ground (i.e., ground occupied by pestilent spirits), crushing pestilent rocks, cutting down pestilent trees, splitting pestilent cliffs, disturbing pestilent waters, conveying harm to temples, harming king *pekar* spirits by desecrating donations, and disagreeing with Buddhist and Bön priests who cause demonic curses.

Those that are raised internally by involving the three poisons come from the activities of desire and sleep in a haunted place, and from getting into fights.

Those that are raised in between by discordant situations occur due to not keeping your promises, not achieving your hopes, your wishes not falling according to calculations, hearing audible unpleasant sounds, sudden panic arising, couples quarreling, sadness, and so on.

The signs of congested constituents entering

Unhappiness, constant craving, mental discomfort, a deep desire to cry, a deep desire to quarrel, a deep desire to lament, a deep desire to leave, occasional confusion, occasional unfocused verbosity, anger, short-lived enthusiasm, a bad mood, the inability to eat or talk, and awkward writing are signs of congested constituents entering.

The problems with congested constituents

The problems are that congested constituents hinder the practice of virtue in the short term, become a condition affecting the life force in the long run, and ultimately obstruct the door to emancipation.

Alleviating congested constituents

There are three methods to alleviate congested constituents: considering the cause, meditate on joy; examining the conditions, meditate with visualization; and regarding the result, integrate it on the path.

(1) Considering the cause, meditate on joy: Why are you [afflicted by] congested constituents? What purpose does that serve? You haven't committed murder, so you don't need to pay the price. You didn't steal valuables, so there's no payback. Controversy with others has not touched you.

Bad talk has not touched you. Spiteful rumors have not affected you. Your wealth has not been lost or scattered. Your vows have not been broken. Your sacred pledge has not been damaged. There's no enmity with the guru and your Dharma siblings. The guru has not passed away. Fake Dharma has not been committed. Why are your constituents congested? As a support, you have attained an able human body. The five doors of perception are whole. You've met an excellent guru. You've found the Dharma. No need for congested constituents. Lighten up. Feel joyful and bright. Let consciousness relax. Be clear. *Phaṭ* will make you happy.

(2) Examining the conditions, meditate with visualization, [as described in this verse]:

> In an isolated place, utter *phaṭ*.
> Intensely count long and short *ha*.
> Meditate on your upper body as a hollow sieve.
> Do the yoga to overcome wind sickness.

The revealed meaning of that verse is: practice!

(3) Regarding the result, integrate it on the path: Whatever comes up that is discordant—sickness and suffering, adverse conditions and obstacles, congested constituents and heart-wind [sickness], reprisals and judgements, and so on—is not something to be avoided, according to the Mahayana teachings. Regard it as something to accomplish. Make it a direct desire. Regard it as a joy, as a necessity, as indispensable, and as a great kindness. Why? For one, it purifies many negative actions of the past. Second, it enhances virtuous practice. Third, it opens the door to many good qualities. It distinguishes the strong Dharma practitioner. It dries by putting in water. It resolves all paths. It accomplishes all ultimate goals. It will be the friend and escort. All the former adepts developed qualities, realization, and accomplishment guided by obstructions and various circumstances. So be happy.

[Regarding the line about] **loss of focus** (*'byams pa*): If you are scattered due to an agitated mind and inability to pay attention, suddenly recollect and freely settle down. Bring up [that agitation] and look nakedly. Recollect clearly and completely let go. Changingly move and immovably rest. By those means, your lack of focus will be severed. If that does not sever it, let your consciousness be scattered, let it be spontaneous, let it go wherever. Send it off, and it will become exhausted in its destination and come back. For example, it is like bridling a new horse and then pulling: if you pull, you will startle the horse and fail, so just relax, as if you're staying put. When you stagnate without any aspect of bliss or clarity and begin to sink, examine that sinking thoroughly. Look at the essence. Send it on its way. Rest naturally. Rest in relaxation. By doing that, the stagnation will be released. [Machik] states in *The Great Bundle of Precepts*:

> Don't cut off sensations and thoughts after the fact.
> As lightning bolts revert to the sky,
> conceptual thinking arises and so subsides,
> like a bird flies [back] to the ship at sea.[150]

Enhancement

38ab. *Boundless devotion, vast compassion, and taking on adversity*
become the enhancement of all good qualities.

If qualities don't arise through practice on the path, you need to do enhancement practices. There are three [methods]: enhancement by supplicating the guru above, enhancement by meditating with compassion on sentient beings below, and enhancement by taking on the adversity of intense adverse circumstances in between.

Enhancement by supplicating the guru above

Though you are engaged in virtuous practice and exerting effort on the path, if you don't desire the development of qualities, that is a sign that the guru's blessings have not entered [your mindstream]. Therefore, you need to supplicate for blessings to enter. In supplicating and arousing devotion, you should recall the guru's kindness and qualities. To contemplate their qualities, think about the guru's physical emanation, the guru's speech activities, the guru's mental knowledge, and so on—qualities equal to that of a buddha. In essence, the guru is none other than a buddha. The awakened activities of all the buddhas are performed by your guru. It states in the *Vajra Tent*:

> Why am I called Vajrasattva?
> I take the form of a spiritual master.
> With a view to helping beings,
> I appear in an ordinary body.[151]

That being the case, if you don't see the guru adorned by the major and minor physical marks of a buddha and hear their speech as the melody of Brahma, it is the fault of your own impure obscurations. It's like a person with a chronic disease who tastes sugar as bitter, or a person with an eye disease who sees a white conch as yellow. Contemplate the guru's kindness:

> The guru is kinder than the Buddha; even though all the buddhas
> of the three times have come, they haven't actually appeared to me.
> There are innumerable representations made by pouring molds,
> drawing figures, and casting statues, but they do not actually teach
> me the Dharma. It is the guru who explains the full results of right
> and wrong actions, teaches the meaning of cause and effect, and
> introduces the timeless awareness inherent within me—that is the
> greatest kindness.

Therefore, meditate on your root guru above your head. Surrounding your guru, meditate on the lineage gurus and other gurus with whom you have a Dharma connection. Dissolve all the buddhas of the ten directions and three times, bodhisattvas, yidam deities, heroes, and ḍākinīs into them. Supplicate sincerely, not just paying lip service. Make loving supplication by means of intense powerful longing from the bottom of your heart, the soles of your feet, and the marrow of your bones, and request the guru's compassion to pacify obstructions and adverse conditions. Request the blessings for enhancing and improving your practice. Request the spiritual powers of perfecting the training and qualities. Afterward, dissolve the guru into yourself. Meditate on the complete blending of the guru's awakened mind with your own mind—clarity and emptiness without fixation, inseparable bliss and emptiness, and appearance and emptiness in integral unity. Rest your mind without embellishment, in a state of lightness and relaxation. When you do that, whatever practice you are doing will be enhanced.

Enhancing by meditating with compassion on the sentient beings below

In general, all sentient beings of the three realms, and in particular, the enemies who rise up against you and the obstructors who harm you—are really heartbreaking. Contemplate:

> First of all, there is not a single one of them that has not been my father and mother. At that time, they kindly took care of me and protected me from harm. How sad! Secondly, they are without any refuge protectors. Previously they have wandered endlessly in cyclic existence. Currently they must wander endlessly in cyclic existence. How sad! Thirdly, it is as if they are blind and crazy; they are unable to understand virtue and vice or recognize cause and effect. They desire only happiness, but they achieve only suffering. How sad!

Don't just mouth the words. Eventually, compassion will arise automatically through your wholehearted meditation. Your obscurations will end, merit accumulation will be completed, and enhancement on the path will inevitably come. Until that happens, meditate again and again.

Taking on the adversity of intense adverse circumstances in between

[Contemplate:]

> Until now, I have cycled through the three realms, wandering among the six kinds of beings, and have not attained emancipation and knowledge of everything. What is the problem? It is that I harbored hatred for enemies and love for relatives, valued wealth, cherished my body, clung to my life, and was attached to the reality of appearances. I did nothing but adopt or discard all happiness and suffering, high and low, and did not equalize their values. That is the culprit. Now, in this essence of my mind, there is absolutely no birth and death, no clean and dirty, no likes and dislikes of enemies and friends, no tasty and nasty, no disgust and appeal, no shame and pride. But in this deluded appearance of relative reality, I have grasped on to its validity and am unable to let it go. I cannot blend it and cannot practice cutting it off. That is the culprit. I am tangled up in self-fixation, fenced in by shame, walled in by hypocrisy, and obscured by discursive thinking. Now, you [adverse circumstances], do what you like, go where you want, come what may.

Throw off dualistic thinking. Utterly destroy the characteristics of fixation on solid reality. Let go of the appearances of fixated true existence. Whatever is difficult to sever, blend with it without the commotion of fear and trepidation. Keep training until you realize that appearances are untrue and of no concern.

First, intensify awareness. Arouse the bravado of the view. Arouse the courage of the conduct. Then blend without the least concern. At that time, engage in crazy conduct—crying, laughing, dancing, calling out, and so forth—whatever pops up in your mind. Shame, pretense, outward appearance, stoicism, and so forth—leave behind the trappings of this life and stay far from the madding crowd. However, when you do that, don't expect praise such as, "That is a realized one, that is a yogin, what an amazing person who needs only to practice the Dharma in this way." Don't hope for fame and good luck to increase. Through training that way again and again, at some point delusions will naturally subside. Attachment will naturally reverse. Conceptual reifications will naturally liberate. And realization will suddenly arise. From [Machik's] scattered sayings:

> Whatever is difficult to sever,
> trample upon it without fear.
> That will enhance experiential realization
> and complete the training and qualities.

The benefits

38cd. *Whoever grasps this supreme Object Severance, the victors' intent,*
finds the path of freedom and vast, immeasurable qualities.

Sixteen great benefits accrue from taking up this practice, the esoteric instruction Severance of Evil Object, which is the elixir of all sugatas' speech, the awakened intent of all the victors, and the heart of the profound precepts of the Perfection of Wisdom. (1) The practice of this profound meaning will actualize the realization of the timeless awareness that is inherently present. (2) The sight of the mind's suchness within prevents harm from outer devils and negative forces. (3) Abandonment of adopting or discarding characteristics releases every knot of subject-object dualism.

(4) Confidence in the conduct of equalizing severs all bonds of attraction and aversion. (5) The collapse of the false structure of conventional reality prevents one from coming under the power of adverse conditions and obstacles. (6) Triumph over the wrong thinking of seeing a self annihilates the seeds of afflictive emotions. (7) Swift severance of what is to be discarded actualizes signs and results. (8) The realization that apparent reality is not true uproots the poisonous tree of fixating on real things. (9) Not accepting or rejecting happiness and sorrow topples the mountain of the eight concerns. (10) The realization that everything is an apparition of mind instantly reveals the difference between samsara and nirvana. (11) The pursuit of adverse circumstances liberates from the ocean of samsara. (12) The knowledge that whatever appears is not real vanquishes the entire net of existence. (13) Not regarding what is to be rejected as unfavorable frees your mind from hopes and fears. (14) The integration of whatever arises expands skills and qualities impartially. (15) Your own benefit will be to attain nonabiding nirvana in one lifetime. (16) For others' benefit, you will be able to place all sentient beings on the genuine path through seeing, hearing, recalling, and touching you. The great qualities, such as these sixteen benefits and many others, will be gained. It states in the sutra:

> Whoever holds in their hands this Perfection of Wisdom
> will swiftly gain supreme awakening before very long.[152]

CONCLUSION

How It Is Better than Others

39ab. *Profound and vast, this precious holy Dharma that benefits everyone everywhere is especially elevated in adherents, is compatible with all tenets, and dispels conditions.*[153]

This holy Dharma, Severance of Evil Object, is endowed with six especially elevated features. (1) It is especially elevated since it is fit for any individual to practice. (2) It is especially elevated since it is fit to combine with any other teaching. (3) It is especially elevated since it is fit to deploy directly on any circumstances. (4) It is especially elevated since it is fit to practice in any place. (5) It is especially elevated since it is fit to practice at any time. (6) It is especially elevated since there is no need to wait for signs of accomplishment at a later time.

(1) First, the individual who is the support can be a monastic, a mantrin, a man, a woman, a nonbinary person, a leper, disabled, blind, old, chronically sick, poor, insane, or afflicted by heart-wind. Everybody can practice. For example, it's like a balanced diet that everyone can eat.

(2) It is fit to combine with any practice because it accords with the outer Three Baskets, the inner four classes of tantra, the Mantrayāna [and Mahayana path of] characteristics, and the new and old Mantra [schools]. It does not fall into any camp and is suitable for all. For example, it is like the crossroads of four great highways that anyone can traverse, from kings to beggars.

(3) It is fit to deploy directly on any circumstances because one can practice severing with whatever occurs: adverse and favorable conditions, attraction and aversion and the eight concerns, sickness and suffering, happiness and sadness. For example, it's like a cannon: having an excellent cannon when engaged in battle can beat an army with its four divisions [of infantry, cavalry, elephants, and chariots].

(4) It is fit to practice in any place, including mountain retreats, cities and countryside, homesteads, monasteries, graveyards, haunted places, cliff caves, empty valleys, ravines, forests, and so forth—pleasant isolated places or terrifying places that make you shudder. You can practice in any

place. For example, it's like a horse chariot with good wheels; wherever you steer it, there it will go.

(5) It is fit to practice at any time, whether you are happy or sad, early or later in your life, during fall or spring, under the waxing or waning moon, in daytime or nighttime, or even the moment you encounter it. For example, the springs where nāgas bestow spiritual powers flow continuously, never rising or diminishing.

(6) There is no need to hope for signs of accomplishment at a later time because you trample upon each circumstance each time it occurs. By equalizing circumstances and integrating them on the path, you are freed from them, and unprecedented special experiential realization will arise each time. For example, it is like when you eat different foods, various sublime tastes will arise each time. It says in the *Appendices*:

> Go to a haunted place and relax awareness.
> Practice by encountering circumstances.
> Others aim for results later on.
> In this, they actually manifest now.[154]

It Is Accepted by All

39cd. *Uphold this priceless precious teaching with devotion,*
like someone who has who found a gem and cherishes it.

A person with devotion who requests this teaching and has received the reading transmission may receive this complete guide in the assembly. Do not teach it to persons with small minds, no good fortune, or wrong views. Be respectful toward the teaching. Restrict the texts. Do not give the instructions to such people who are not interested in Dharma and who reject their guru. Although there are many who have heard the instructions, maintained the guidance, and own many books on Object Severance,

there are few who hold the tradition of this Severance. Keep it very secret.
From [Machik's] *Another Bundle*:

> Teach those who are faithful and fortunate,
> who have interest and devotion.
> Those individuals driven by circumstances
> will gain oral instructions through great persistence.
> Since what happens after the cure is unknown,
> do not give them various texts.[155]

And from [Machik's] scattered sayings:

> Those who desire the contents but shun the container,
> who take the qualities by covert methods,
> and who flatter and beguile by deceit:
> do not teach them—keep it very secret.[156]

And from *The [Eight Common] Appendices*:

> There are certainly many who desire Object Severance,
> but apart from desiring its renown,
> doing actual practice is quite rare.
> Therefore, do not give it to them.[157]

Dedicating the Virtuous Roots of Composition

40. *Through the brief arrangement of this Heart Essence of Profound
    Meaning*
    distilled from the vast ocean of the many profound Severance sources,
    may all migrators reach the culmination of Object Severance, fully
    realize its meaning,

and gain the supreme Mother Perfection of Wisdom in the pure realm of phenomena.

From among the sources of Severance and the vast ocean-like profound instructions, this brief collection has been distilled like a drop of elixir. The virtue of doing so is dedicated to the welfare of all sentient beings beyond measure.

The instructions of the Perfection of Wisdom, the Buddha's word; the intention of the scriptures in the Three Baskets; the essence of the Dharma in the four tantras; and the personal instructions of all the guru adepts [are all contained] in this Severance of Evil Object commentary called *Heart Essence of Profound Meaning*. It was composed by the Śākya monk, holder of the vajra, Mañjughoṣanātha. This completes the Dharma that is difficult to find in this world.

sarva maṅgalaṃ

oṃ ye dharmā hetuprabhavā hetun teṣāṃ tathāgato hyavadat teṣāṃ ca yo nirodha evaṃvādī mahāśramaṇaḥ svāhā

oṃ supra tiṣtha vajra svāhā

3

The Seven-Day Severance
Retreat Experiential Guide[158]

Dharmakāya free of embellishment, the lady Perfection of Wisdom
and the royal mother Tārā who taught those [doctrines];
the sublime path of exceptional esoteric instructions on Object Severance;
and Machik, the ḍākinī of timeless awareness: I bow at your feet.

In response to respectful entreaties for an experiential guide,
I supplicate for permission to write this down.
With your compassionate blessings, may I realize the meaning,
and through the power of aspiration, may all migrators triumph.

First of all, a person who has properly received the empowerment and
introduction to mind's nature can then take up the main practice. There are
three parts to [the instructions]: the explanation in the general guide, the
sustaining practice of the experiential guide, and the teaching of personal
advice. *The Big General Guide* was presented previously. This is the *Experiential Guide*. It is said to offer a way to distinguish Severance from the general
Dharma, enhance realization, bring the gods and demons under control, be
a source for the two spiritual powers, and to dry out completely in water.[159]

If you wish to roam in mountain retreats and develop experiential realization, there is no way to wander in haunted retreats without practicing

Severance. For that, one should adhere to four special features: the special place to go, the special time to go, the special person who goes, and the special instruction to practice once you arrive.

The special place to go

The places to enact Severance, such as graveyards or shrine rooms, must have the power to cause fear and trembling, alarm and terror, doubt and superstition. Without those affects, there is nothing to sever. Once you arrive, do not harm the gods and demons, do not seek to blame them, and do not hope that they will grant powers or blessings. The conceit of gods and demons in that frightening external place exposes the internal concepts of the frightened person. That was thoroughly explained in the previous section on the [*Big General*] *Guide*.

The special time to go

In general, go when you are afraid, frightened, terrified, anxious, or sick. In particular, go alone, like at night without friends or companions. Even briefly relying on conceits such as companions or equipment or mountain forts, and so forth, will lead to getting lost in the mind's erroneous impasses.[160] So, no matter what, be absolutely decisive about such inflation.

The special person who goes

The special person is one who has become a worthy recipient through empowerment and is resolved with certainty that, in general, appearance is mind, due to having received the introduction [to mind's nature]; this person has also cut through outer and inner superimpositions by receiving the instructions. Regarding that, in the beginning, see whether you are capable or incapable of going to practice Severance. In the middle, see whether you can equalize apparitions or not when they arise. At the end, see whether you will travel the Buddhist path or not.

In the beginning, the first reason that you may be incapable of going to do Severance is having little courage. Therefore, once you arouse courage and take on direct action, there is no reason at all that you wouldn't be capable [of going to do the practice]. For example, fire, water, precipices, and the like may appear in a dream, but they are not truly existent. Second, the problem may be not understanding that samsara and nirvana are in the mind. You should know that everything is an apparition of the mind. If you just become free of fixating on the true existence of the mind, then there is nothing at all to fear. It is like a fearful child who has never seen a mask before, but then is no longer afraid once it has become familiar. Third, the problem may be not having received the profound instructions. Once you have those profound instructions, you know that all phenomena contained in the six realms of samsara and nirvana appear in a variety of forms, and yet there is not a single one that is actually true. The donkey doesn't gore, just as the rabbit doesn't bite. Fourth, the problem may be meager fortitude. Once fortitude is aroused, there is nothing you could not do for the sake of the Dharma—even sacrificing your own body and life. Past adepts even endured various hardships for the sake of each word of the Dharma.

In the middle, see if you can equalize apparitions when they arise. Does mental regret arise or not when obstacles and apparitions occur? Are happiness and suffering integrated on the path or not when sickness and suffering arise? And can you equalize or not when adverse circumstances and brutal conditions occur?

In the end, to see whether you will travel the Buddhist path or not, see if you have respect or not for those above and concern for the welfare of those below. Consider whether you improve or not in your own views and realizations. See if you are accompanied by emptiness and compassion or not. If you have all that, then go practice Severance. If not, then you shouldn't go.

Again, all those who go to practice Severance should not do so with a competitive mind or machismo. Don't go for the sake of prideful notoriety or pretense. Don't go with the goal of profit or honor. Don't go concerned with self-assurance or rejuvenation. So then, how should one go? Someone who has fully embraced the [meaning of] the words once they have completed the Severance instructions, has ascertained samsara and nirvana by obtaining the guidance introductions, has cut through outer and inner superimpositions by seeing mind's suchness, and can take circumstances on the path by letting go of self-fixation of the body—that person should go to practice Severance.

The special instructions to practice once you arrive

The special instructions are [as follows]: The Buddha's precepts are the meaning of the Perfection of Wisdom; the practice is Severing Evil Object; the camping place is a fierce mountain retreat; the view is no gods, no demons; the meditation is lying in bare untangled simplicity; the conduct is directly trampling and equalizing; the ritual is to carry flesh, carry blood; the practice is to delight in sickness, old age, and death; the integration on the path is casting out the body aggregate as food; the sacred pledge is no virtue, no vice; and the result is nondual spontaneous presence. This is how to take it into experience.

Day One

The practice on the first evening [of a Severance retreat] is to give away the body, release self-fixation from the object, and cast out the form aggregate as food.

Giving away the body

Meditate on your own body as youthful and in its prime, beautiful, and attractive. Meditate on your mind arising from your heart as glorious Vajrayoginī. She comes before you with a flaying knife in her hand and faces your body, a heap of leftovers devoid of mind itself. She separates out the body parts—head, limbs, upper body, lower body—and cuts them into pieces and portions. She pulls out the organs and heart and piles them in front. The pile of flesh is heaped up as high as the worlds of Brahma. The lake of blood swirls as far as the outer oceans. Vajrayoginī blesses them to be received as whatever anyone desires. Then, she summons the ones who cause you harm and the gods and demons who create obstacles. Meditate that they fill the entire space of the sky. They've been dispatched to the banquet of your body and noisily mill about with delight, eager to eat the flesh and drink the blood. At this point, do not entertain even a speck of attachment to that body. Without even a hair's worth of proprietary claim, think, "Gods and demons from afar, eat it cold; those nearby, eat it cooked." Mentally give it away totally, and immediately let go with your mind. Say *phaṭ* and rest relaxed in an unconditioned state. Rest in the total expulsion. Do the same with whatever fear or anxiety arises. Then think, "I don't see this mind as any more mine than yours. As for the body, there is nothing to do other than giving it away to all the gods and demons of apparent existence. Now I don't have to endlessly care for it and take anything under advice. I don't need to cherish it as mine." With those thoughts, cast it out.

Releasing self-fixation from the object

In giving away the body like that, this merely appearing body—whether moving, sitting, or lying down—is without an owner, like an empty house, a corpse thrown in a graveyard, or rocks tossed on the road. No appearance, no attachment, no fixation, no concern, no self, no need, no truth. Rest in that state.

Casting out the form aggregate as food

Then, think that whatever happens to this body—whether it gets sick, harmed, hurt, killed, or beaten—does not matter: "The 'I' has no power, no agency, no clinging to a self by me. You [spirits] have the power—do whatever you want. You even have the power to carry me to hell." Think that and don't be anxious or feel that it is unbearable.

Afterward, don't think at all about the self, the god-demons, and the severance; relax mind into the threefold emptiness and let it go wherever it likes. In that way, the accumulations will be completed, obscurations purified, karmic debts cleared, self-fixation on the body relinquished, and mind itself realized.

Day Two

At first, when you set out to practice Severance, you need to have obtained stability in the introduction, a great spirit for practice, and the ability to trample upon joy and sorrow.

Stability in the introduction

The introduction in the preliminaries should have properly transmitted the nature of the mind. This evening, no matter what apparitions and obstacles arise, they are the apparitions of the unborn mind. Moreover, all phenomena included in the six realms of samsara and nirvana are the apparitions of the unborn mind. Ultimately, think that there is not even one instant of true existence. You must know that.

The great spirit of practice

When you are in possession of the excellent confidence of experience and realization, whatever adverse conditions and obstacles arise, you will be without fear and anxiety. Like brandishing a sword within a thick forest, all adverse conditions will be dispatched by the severing of the subtle and the obvious. Confronting them face-to-face will be like snow falling on hot rocks. That realization and the subsequent knowledge of realizing the lack of true existence are like a sword striking water. You should understand this.

The ability to trample upon joy and sorrow

Whatever highs and lows or joys and sorrows arise, they are superficial—shaky and shifty. In fact, there is not even a split second of any true existence to them. Understand the idea of the sixteen examples of illusion, and go on your way.

Once you arrive there, the practice is to investigate the gods and demons of the outer frightening place, investigate the conceptual thinking of the inner fearful person, and investigate the essence of fear in between.

Investigating the gods and demons of the outer frightening place

Observe where those gods and demons of the frightening place came from in the first place. Look for where they abide in the meantime. Look for where they have gone in the end. Rest in the thought that they don't exist. Consider what kind of shape those gods and demons have: whether square or round, and so forth. Consider their color: white, red, yellow, and so forth. See if they are male, female, or neuter. Rest in the state of not finding anything. Consider whether you can see gods and demons with your eyes, hear their sounds with your ears, smell their odor with your nose, talk to them with your mouth, or grab them with your hands. Rest within the state of absence and emptiness.

Investigating the conceptual thinking of the inner fearful person

Turn your attention inward to the very mind of the one who is frightened of demons. Look everywhere for that person—from the crown of your head above to the soles of your feet below, outside, inside, and in between. Consider the shape, color, and essence of that scared one. Then rest in that absence and emptiness.

Investigating the essence of fear in between

Consider the essence of this so-called fear. Look for its location. Consider its shape and color. Once you have observed in this way, you will not find a frightening object externally, a fearful person internally, or essential fear in between. If there were really such things, you would find them. But since they don't exist, you can't find them. Rest lightly relaxed in that very discovery.

Day Three

At first, when you set out to practice on the third evening, you should go with great bravado of the view, experience in meditation, and great courage in conduct.

Great bravado of the view

The buddha kāyas and timeless awarenesses are apparitions of the mind. They don't exist on the ultimate level. Although there are explanations of the lifespans, physical forms, and hot and cold sufferings of beings in the hells below, they are not truly existent in the ultimate sense. In the conventional sense, they are alluring deceptions for the childish. Arbitrarily, the joys and sorrows, highs and lows, powers of gods and demons, and demonic obstacles are all mind made. In fact, an atom of true existence has never been experienced. Think about that.

Experience in meditation

Always stay connected to the practice of the previous introduction that introduced the nature of your mind. Resting in equipoise, all phenomena were never truly existent; they are nothing but appearances, like the center of space. In subsequent attainment, there are mere appearances, but know that they are not true, like dreams and illusions.

Great courage in conduct

Whatever arises—whether sickness, suffering, adverse conditions, obstacles, brutality, or apparitions—have no fear or trepidation. Don't entertain doubts and uncertainty. Don't reject or accept, deny or affirm. Be without hopes and fears or hesitation, like a wolf among sheep or a lion moving among antelope. Go without dread or anxiety.

Once you arrive, put into practice these three pieces [of advice]: thoroughly investigate discursive thoughts based on gods and demons; thoroughly investigate self-fixation based on fear; thoroughly investigate samsara and nirvana based on obstacles.

Thoroughly investigate discursive thoughts based on gods and demons

This mind itself is currently not experienced as an existent thing. It has never been experienced previously as an entity. In the future, it is impossible for it to arise as an entity. When you yourself as the owner cannot find this mind itself, make a thorough search to find the demons. Is the notion that there really are demons true and constant? Meditate on a great black one with multiple waving arms and legs carrying various weapons. Think that you will sustain various kinds of harm from it. See whether the mind that is a nonentity will be helped or harmed. Look at whether that nonthing mind becomes real or not. Look at whether the gods and demons are truly existent or not.

Thoroughly investigate self-fixation based on fear

When you are afraid, increase that fear even more. Make yourself even more terrified and more anxious. Based on that, look at whether you can find this moving consciousness that is not an entity. Look at the nature of the one who is afraid. Look at the nature that causes the fear.

Thoroughly investigate samsara and nirvana based on obstacles

Fears about the occurrence of obstacles, hopes that they won't come, the actual obstacles that occur—all of those are the mind's apparitions. Moreover, even samsara and nirvana are the mind's creations. Fears of wandering in samsara, hopes of attaining buddhahood—all are the apparitions of your own mind. There is nothing other than the discursive thoughts of hope and fear between samsara and nirvana, between happiness and sorrow, between fear and fearlessness. Come to that definitive conclusion. In going to stay in a haunted place, you don't go because there are demons, you don't go to see demons, and you don't go because you have hopes and fears about demons. You go to thoroughly investigate the awareness of the inner fearful one based on that outer scary place. You ascertain the consciousness that fixates on the inner demon based on the pretext of demons.

Day Four

At first, when you set out to practice Severance, you should go in possession of three greatnesses: great support of blessings, great knowledge of the instructional teachings, and great capacity for surrendering your body and life.

Great support of blessings

In general, you need devotion to the guru and Three Jewels and to have received their blessings. In particular, when you set off to practice Severance, you must supplicate them in earnest, saying, "Please grant your blessings so that I can integrate gods, demons, and obstacles on the path. Bless me to equalize adverse conditions, obstacles, joy, and sorrow. Bless me that sickness and suffering arise as supports for virtuous activity." Mentally offer the mandala and perfect fourfold offerings, including your body and possessions, without holding back. Think, "From this evening on, I do not own my body, speech, and mind. Since I have offered them to the guru and the Jewels, only they know whether they will promote or demote me."

Great knowledge of the instructional teachings

Great knowledge means to have, in general, knowledge from listening to all the teachings of the Mahayana, and in particular, all the instructions on integrating joy and sorrow on the path. Especially, it is to have heard the whole range of instructions on Severance. As for mastering and integrating the meaning of all the words, [you should know that] whatever apparition and ferocity occurs, it is the mental apparition of inner awareness. Externally there is not even a moment of true existence to it. Remember those explanations from the Severance instructions.

Great capacity for surrendering your body and life

When going to practice Severance, don't go out to welcome your qualms by thinking, "What if sickness and obstacles arise?" and don't have the motivation of realization. Instead, think "This Severance is the teaching from the Perfection of Wisdom, the word of the genuine perfect Buddha. All the adepts, such as the Lady Mother, developed realization and qualities based on this approach." On the relative level, once born, this fourfold aggregate body will not escape death. Even a thousand weapon-wielding warriors cannot protect it. On the ultimate level, even if a million devil hordes surround you, they cannot interfere with or damage you. What will you do with this body, a heap of impurity, a bag of pus and blood, a package of lymph, a trunk of snot? If demons need it, give it to them on the spot. In general, give it as the supreme ransom for the six kinds of migrators. In particular, cast it away in generosity without attachment, thinking, "I give all gods and demons this body without even a speck of attachment to it."

Once you arrive, this is the practice: decisively ascertain emptiness through the view, rest in the state of mindlessness through meditation, and equalize all joy and sorrow through conduct.

Decisively ascertain emptiness through the view

What's called *the view* is to look at the emptiness of nonexistent objects. This manner of looking does not apprehend whatever arises and does not mentally fixate on anything at all. Blend object and subject in the space of emptiness, and rest there. From within that state, even if gods, demons, obstacles, and ferocious and malicious ones rise up, do not view them as harmful demons. Don't fixate or meditate on them. Don't look for helpful Dharma instructions or protective gods and gurus, and so forth—just rest in the absolute nonexistence of the unborn, empty nothing.

Rest in the state of mindlessness through meditation

Whatever apparition occurs, don't hold it as demonic or entertain fearful thoughts. Don't be frightened or apprehensive. Don't react with discursive thinking, no matter what adverse circumstances or offensive obstacles occur. Don't meditate. Don't generate. Don't visualize. Whatever thought arises in the moment, do not follow it with mindfulness. Do not engage in thinking or pondering. Forget it. Be vague. Be distracted. Be scattered. Rest in the state of self-vanishing self-liberation. If you try that but it doesn't help and you are still discursive, then investigate that and rest in the state of its ultimate lack of intrinsic nature.

Equalize all joy and sorrow through conduct

If you are afraid, employ the technique of facing whatever is fearful. If you are terrified, employ methods of facing terror. If you are alarmed, despairing, and anxious, meditate on fear that is a hundred or a thousand times greater than before. Then look nakedly at that rampant fear and the essence of what is fearful. Investigate thoroughly where it came from, where it abides, and what it's like. When you follow it and can't find it, rest in that state. By acting in that way, fear will be liberated on its own.

Day Five

At first, when you set out to practice Severance, you should go in possession of three experiences: outwardly, know that the Severance object is empty; inwardly, realize that the Severance practitioner is nonexistent; intermediately, understand that the system of Severance is not truly existent.

Outwardly, know that the Severance object is empty

Know that all the interfering demons, *tsen* spirits, devils, malignant spirits, obstructors, nāgas, earth lords, male and female malignant spirits, custodian and king spirits, male and female knife spirits, and so forth—all are empty. Disruptive circumstances [that occur] around the hearth and burning, contamination from spite and mourning, and defilement—know that all those are empty. The very essence of obstacles, such as leprosy, burn blisters, tumors, ascites, diphtheria, painful epidemics, sickness, suffering, obstacles to body and life, obstacles to life and breath, hindrances to higher realms and ultimate emancipation, theft of donations, interferences to virtue, and robbers of the life force of meditative stability and absorption—know that all of those are empty.

Inwardly, realize that the Severance practitioner is nonexistent

Realize that the practicing yogi or yoginī's own body, speech, and mind; aggregates, constituents, and sense fields; karma and afflictions; the consciousness and intellect performing the practice; armors and antidotes—have all been empty since forever.

Understand that the system of Severance is not truly existent

Understand that the intention of the Buddha's sutras and tantras; the lineage gurus' teachings; the Severance instructions; your own practice of view, meditation, and action; the teachings about the antidotes for demons and spirits that are the objects of Severance; and the Severance practices of view, meditation, and action—are all empty.

In short, the outer interference of bad spirits and obstructors, inner interference of the individual practitioner, and intermediately the essential cause—the antidote to those is to know that all Severance practice is emptiness. Emptiness cannot impinge on emptiness. Signlessness cannot impinge on signlessness. Nonentity cannot impinge on nonentity. With the total purity of the three spheres, set out in the state of emptiness.

Once you arrive, this is the practice: meditation on compassion for gods and demons, meditation on the emptiness of fear, and direct subjugation of self-fixation.

Meditation on compassion for gods and demons

Meditate on immeasurable love and compassion for all sentient beings in general that pervade space, headed by the ground masters of that haunted place. Especially [meditate on compassion for] the gods and demons who favor the dark side, and more particularly, for the gods and demons that create obstacles for you. Why compassion? The primary reason is that those beings have not eliminated ignorance and afflictive emotions. The secondary condition is that they are not free of anger and cruelty. The result is rebirth in the lower realms and wandering in bad places. In their deeds, they inflict harm on others. In their actions, they are violent to beings. Their desire is to have happiness, but they commit negative deeds and accomplish only suffering. If you think about having compassion for those reasons, feel the compassion not merely from your mouth but from the center of your heart, the soles of your feet, and the marrow of your bones, and repeat a hundred times: "May they be happy. May they be free of suffering. May they attain perfect buddhahood." And think, "For that reason, I will engage in virtue with body, speech, and mind, and take up the practice of this instruction on Severance."

Meditation on the emptiness of fear

In general, all phenomena of the apparent existence of samsara and nirvana are emptiness. In particular, the obstructing devils and elemental spirits have never existed for even a moment. In the first place, there is no cause of arising; in the middle, there is no condition for acting; and in the end, there is no support for abiding.[161] This is the spoken word from all the Buddha's sutras and tantras and has been taught by all the holy gurus. Clearly one should put it into one's own practice. While nonexistent, the occluded and shifting appearances are your own deluded ephemera or mistaken conceptions. Outside, they do not validly exist. They are inconstant, a hollow fraud. If [phenomena] existed, gods and demons would exist. Whatever exists should be manifestly appearing, and yet there is no actual cause for their appearance. [Phenomena] should withstand reason and analysis, and yet when they are analyzed, they disappear in nonbeing. You should know that.

Direct subjugation of self-fixation

In general, don't be attached to or stuck on external objects of attachment, such as wealth, possessions, spouses, and close relatives. Don't have pride, proprietary selfishness, attachment, or conceit about the inner objects of attachment—your view, meditation, and action; hearing, contemplating, and meditating; experience and realization; clairvoyance and miraculous ability; accomplishment signs and the qualities of your lineage—no matter how subtle. Be without self-fixation and passionate attachment regarding all the intermediate objects of attachment—your body, life force, longevity, breath, power, charisma, radiance, and physical appearance—whatever you cherish and cannot detach from as your "self." Expel it like vomiting bad food. Flush it out like snot and spit. Let whoever likes it, take it. Whatever they want, let them have it. A strong, brave person does not have even a speck of need of it, without even a hair's tip of attachment and desire. With that, stay and sleep there.

Day Six

At first when you set out to practice Severance, go like a lion without attachment, go like a tigress with strength, and go like a stone rolling down a mountain unhindered, without fear or trepidation.

Go like a lion without attachment

Even when enemies rise up—anywhere from the highest peak of existence above, down to the lowest hell realm below—they are the apparitions of your mental awareness. They have not even a moment of true existence. Within that state, go without fear or trepidation.

Go like a tigress with great strength

Endowed with the experience of understanding emptiness, endowed with the confidence of realizing the unborn, and endowed with the knowledge of the lack of true existence, your awareness sharpens, consciousness intensifies, the senses brighten, and conduct toughens. Say *phaṭ* and go.

Go like a stone rolling down a mountain unhindered

No matter what fear and trepidation you feel, respond directly to that without wavering. Don't be wishy-washy or hesitant. Like a mad elephant or a hailstorm or a rolling stone, go unhindered.

Once you arrive, this is the practice: put the pressure on gods and demons, get on top of discursive thought, and release self-fixation from the object.

Put the pressure on gods and demons

Putting pressure on gods and demons is the action of smiting pestilence directly with pestilence. Therefore, whatever place you fear that supports gods and demons, such as water, cliffs, or trees, suddenly go directly to that place. By that, those gods and demons will immediately leave. For example, if you seem to grab a trembling watchdog by the face, it will run away. When a layperson with no Dharma practice goes to sleep at night, the mere entrance of gods and demons inside the house will create panic, a clouded consciousness, cold sweats, anger, and [fear of] demonic harm. That is the demon's charisma. But when a Severance practitioner arrives at a place occupied by gods and demons, their power and ability weakens, their strength and charisma disperses, and all their magical ability subsides, so they leave. Similarly, if you put antivenom at the entrance of a venomous snake's nest, the snake's venom subsides, its power disperses, and its awareness weakens, so it leaves.

Get on top of discursive thought

At first, you are unable to go to the haunted ground. In the middle, you can't stay there. In the end, you can't give your body. You need to trample upon those issues. Whatever you cannot do, go directly to that. If you're afraid, go directly to the fear. If you experience dread, lie down and remain directly with that dread. Then, awareness will decisively cut through inflation, the fetters of self-fixation will release, the cave of fear will collapse, and dread and fear will be destroyed. For example, it is like [the animals] with small eyes such as horses, donkeys, or cows that do not want to cross over water or narrow bridges. It is said that if you have led them along an easy path, they will become spoiled and refuse to cross over. But wherever they won't go, in that very place you must pressure and push them to go. Later on, they will go over the unpleasant path without hesitation.[162]

Release self-fixation from the object

Look at the one who is scared, the one who has trepidation, and the one who feels incapable. Where is it? What is its essence? Why is it there? Pursue that self-fixation like a dagger or an arrow. Follow it far [with] awareness. Act like an old woman pointing a finger and totally cut through the root source of that self-fixation. By acting in that way, that self-fixation will vanish because of your sudden lack of concern. It will be destroyed as false and liberated. It will be released as nonexistent and lost. Thus, rest in that state and remain.

Day Seven

At first, when you set out for the haunted retreat, assume these four modes: make your body in the mode of a corpse, make mind itself in the mode of a corpse-carrier, make your bed in the mode of a charnel ground, and make gods and demons in the mode of jackals. Think, "Whoever desires this decrepit body, take it away."

Once you arrive, these are the five practices: the view without truth and without fixation, meditation without mental engagement, conduct without adopting or discarding, sacred pledge without limiting safeguards, and results without a cause of accomplishment.

The view without truth and without fixation

Since the view is neither permanence nor nihilism, birth nor cessation, center nor circumference, nor fixation on true existence, don't hope for benefit from gods and their gifts of spiritual powers. Don't supplicate them or make offerings. Don't fixate on the harm that comes from demons. Don't fear the occurrence of obstacles. Don't fight or beat them.[163] Don't even fixate on "no gods, no demons." Rest in a state without pondering or contemplating.

Meditation without mental engagement

Other than simply resting in the original emptiness of the three spheres and great primordial liberation without contriving or creating and destroying, don't heed your fears about harm from incidental gods and demons or the arising of obstacles. Don't engage in the antidote of deity meditation and recitation to save you from fear. Don't even meditate on emptiness.

Conduct without adopting or discarding

When practicing Severance, there is no practice of the ten virtues and no renunciation of the ten negative actions. Rest without denial or affirmation in the uncontrived basic ground, unsullied by virtue and vice.

Sacred pledges without limiting safeguards

Remain unsullied by any kind of virtue and vice, such as the outer śrāvaka vows, the bodhisattva trainings, and the Secret Mantra's sacred pledges. In the end, do not be sullied even by the Severance practice and the Dharma. Mind itself is original dharmakāya. Rest without contrivance in the state of original purity, the original liberation.

Result without a cause of accomplishment

No need to yearn for the Buddha above—since that is not truly existent, there is no accomplishment of kāyas and timeless awareness. No need to fear the hells below—since it is false and not truly existent, there is no need to avoid the sufferings of heat and cold. In between, since gods and demons and bad spirits and obstructors have no true existence, there is no rejection of adverse conditions and obstacles. Sentient beings to be benefited have no true existence, so there is no performing of awakened activity for the sake of others. Settle in that realization.

Those are the esoteric instructions to collapse the false structure of conventional reality. They are the practices that thoroughly sever conceptual thinking. This is the teaching that differentiates samsara and nirvana. Therefore, put into practice this experiential guide for seven days.

In general, although there are differences in the level of difficulty or ease in practicing Severance, corpses, charnel grounds, decrepit temples, and burial mounds with many deceased people provide temporary fright but not much in the long run. They are easy to become familiar with, and shallow. Rock crevices, cliff caves, gorges, and wide plains are not scary in the short run or the long run. They carry little weight and are easy to suppress. Lone trees, springs, lakes, and boulders are not immediately frightening, but they are deep and weighty and difficult to get used to. *Pekar* spirits, king spirits, custodian spirits, male and female ghosts who whirl the consciousness and cause great fluctuation of awareness are temporarily fierce and produce big apparitions, but they are easy to conjure, less populous, and easy to suppress. Oath-breaker spirits, female *sen* spirits, and *mamo*s arouse desire in the mind, rob vital essence, scatter the awareness, and make you want to leave. Don't be attached; they are easy to conjure and suppress. [However], they will follow after you later. Nāgas, devils, pestilent spirits, earth lords, and earth *sinpo* spirits produce excessive sleep, heavy consciousness, muddled awareness, and much sinking and dullness [in the mind]. They are not immediately frightening but are difficult to conjure, difficult to sever, very populous, and difficult to suppress. In the short run, the apparitions are small and they don't show up as fierce, but deep down they are vicious. *Tsen* spirits, *theurang*, local gods, and impure hybrid spirits[164] manifest as a lot of tumult, random dreams, being [mysteriously] called by name, and bartering. They display many apparitions but pose little danger and are less populous, quite weak, easy to conjure, and easy to suppress.

It is crucial to continue practicing with everything that has not been conjured and suppressed. It is more difficult to sever sickness and suffering than severing corpses and demons. Even more difficult to sever humans.[165] And severing attachment and the eight concerns is even more difficult than that. It is a greater enhancement to sever internally than to sever externally. The qualities are greater and the spiritual powers come more quickly.

The meaning of the stainless Perfection of Wisdom, Mother of the victors,
is known infallibly by both mother and son.
I have rendered that meaning accurately here.
May I attain buddhahood and realize the welfare of all.

This is the unified intention of the Buddha's word in the Perfection of Wisdom that clearly teaches the timeless awareness of nondualism. It is the sole path traversed by all buddhas of the three times, the source of spiritual powers of all adepts and realized ones, and the unmistaken instructions of both mother and son.[166] From the *Perfection of Wisdom Severance of Evil Object*, this cycle of practice called *An Experiential Guide*, carefully composed by the Śākya monk, holder of the vajra, Prājñāsvabhāva,[167] is complete. May virtue prevail.

Appendix

Did Machik Labdrön Really Teach Chö?
A Survey of the Early Sources
by Sarah Harding

Adapted from a paper presented at the International Association of Tibetan Studies conference held in Ulaanbaatar, Mongolia, 2013.

This provocative title is a result of a persistent question in the back of my mind for several years while I was researching and translating the early Severance (*gcod*) texts from Jamgön Kongtrul's *Treasury of Precious Instructions* (*Gdams ngag rin po che'i mdzod*, volume 14), an ambitious project of the Tsadra Foundation. As I patiently went through the marvelous teachings in each text, I kept wondering when I would find the actual instructions on Chö, or "Severance," that I was so familiar with from translating *Machik's Complete Explanation* and from my own three-year retreat practice. The following is a short survey of these texts and my findings therein, which suggest that there is no clear attribution of the body-offering practice, and certainly not in the elaborate form that we find commonly practiced today.

Severance is primarily known, now quite famously, as a visualization practice in which one separates one's consciousness from the physical body, and then turns around to cut up the remaining corpse and prepare it for distribution to gods, demons, and spirits of all kinds. The ritual offering may involve going to specific places where such spirits might be found, such as isolated, frightening, or haunted places. It is immediately obvious that several terrifying psychological experiences are invoked: fear of the unseen spirit world, of wilderness, and of the maiming and dismemberment of one's body. It is thus widely recognized as a practice of "facing your fears" and overcoming them.

Severance was developed, also famously, by the woman Machik Labdrön in the late eleventh century, during the time in Tibet when many other lineages were forming. Although technically it is known as a subsidiary of the Shijé (*zhi byed*) or Pacification teachings of Dampa Sangyé, clearly Machik is the single mother (*ma gcig*) of this baby. In the records of Machik's brief encounters with Dampa Sangyé, and in the only Indian Severance source text (*gzhung*) by Āryadeva the Brahmin, there is little about this specific practice. It therefore seems to be solely a result of Machik's own realizations, and so is famous as an original Buddhist teaching indigenous to Tibet that uniquely spread to India in a reverse trajectory from all other doctrines.

The realization that gave birth to Machik's *gcod* is said to have occurred during her recitation of a Perfection of Wisdom (*Prajñapāramitā*) text, which she regularly performed as part of her job as a household chaplain. Specifically, it occurred while reading "the chapter on *mara*." Many suggestions have been offered as to which section that could be, but in any case, none of them throw light on the subject.[168] The fact that it is mentioned at all, however, is very provocative. Māra, of course, is the antithesis of Buddha, and has been personified perhaps in the same way as enlightenment is personified as a buddha. Māra represents obstruction of the spiritual path or spiritual death (from Skt. *mṛ-*, "to die") in all its forms. Besides the Buddha's antagonist, a variety of *māras* were eventually classified into two sets of four, but there are many more examples in the texts I have translated.[169] It is tempting to imagine Machik's inspiration as a profound encounter with the dark side, eventually resulting in the overcoming of that duality through the integration of the Perfection of Wisdom teachings.[170]

There is no shortage of reference to *māras* throughout the texts on Severance and their sources, and no question that the primary goal of these teachings is to deal with them, whether conceived of as demons, adverse circumstances, ego, or ultimate evil and ignorance. Simply put, the term used to describe that process is "chö." But it comes in two homonymic interchangeable spellings: *gcod*, which means "to cut" or "sever," and *spyod*, which means "behavior" or "action." I have seen either used in alternate editions of the same text. *Spyod* and *spyod yul* instantly conjure up the bodhisattva's conduct in the Perfection of Wisdom literature, as in the recurring phrase: "In this way one should train in performing the activity of the profound Perfection of Wisdom."[171] Chö as severance also has its Buddhist antecedents. The classic definition in Severance source material comes from Āryadeva's verses called *Esoteric Instructions on the Perfection of Wisdom*:

> Since it severs the root of mind itself
> and severs the five toxic emotions,
> extremes of view, meditational formations,
> conduct anxiety, and hopes and fears;
> since it severs all inflation,
> it is called "severance" by semantic explanation.[172]

It is clear that the specific practice of cutting up the body is not alluded to in this definition, as well as all others that I encountered. In fact, it may just be an unfortunate parallel of usage that the process of resolution and integration of problems uses the same term as does the ordinary function of an ax or kitchen knife, or dragon glass, for that matter. We can think of the common term *thag gcod pa* ("decide, put an end to, determine, handle, deal with, treat") to get more of a sense of this term, recalling also the interchangeability with *spyod pa* as "conduct and behavior." What to do when things get tough? Act with determination.

Similarly, the term *yul* ("object") in the longer name for this practice, *bdud kyi gcod yul* ("the devil/evil that is the object to sever"), is used in the most abstract way and is attested in the Abidharma by Kongtrul and others. Consider the first verse in Machik Labdrön's source text, the *Great Bundle* (*Bka' tshom chen mo*):

> The root devilry is one's own mind.
> The devil lays hold through clinging and attachment
> in the cognition of whatever objects appear.
> Grasping mind as an object is corruption.

Or again, from the same text, a reference to a more refined state of practice:

> The conceit of a view free of elaboration,
> the conceit of a meditation in equipoise,
> the conceit of conduct without thoughts—
> all conceits on the path of practice,
> if engaged in as objects for even a moment,
> obstruct the path and are the devils' work.[173]

The vast majority of the instructions in these early texts are on the practice and theory of the Perfection of Wisdom, as clearly indicated by their titles. These instructions are often reminiscent of mahāmudrā, and in fact later took on the epithet Severance Mahāmudrā (*gcod yul phyag rgya chen po*). For instance, from Machik's *Great Bundle*:

> Everything is self-occurring mind,
> so a meditator does not meditate.
> Whatever self-arising sensations occur,
> rest serene, clear, and radiant.[174]

Even the earliest source text by Āryadeva the Brahmin employs such mahāmudrā signature phrases as "clear light" ('od gsal) and "mental non-engagement" (yid la mi byed pa),[175] while the commentary on those passages cites scriptures such as Maitreya's *Highest Continuum* and other sources usually associated with the third turning of the wheel of Dharma. There is constant reiteration of this basic instruction to rest relaxed without doing anything. One of the more famous sayings attributed to Machik, often used as a reference to the Severance practice, does not particularly give an instruction to sever and offer the body, but is more of a straightforward Perfection of Wisdom or mahāmudrā instruction:

> Rest the body in the way of a corpse.
> Rest in the way of being ownerless.
> Rest the mind in the way of the sky.
> As a candle unmoved by the wind,
> rest in the way of clarity with no thought.
> As an ocean unmoved by the wind,
> rest in a way serenely limpid.[176]

So where are the references to the practice of casting out the body as food that has made this practice so sensational? A quick survey of the ten early texts (two source texts plus Machik's eight), making up 134 folios, turns up sixteen references to the catchphrase "separating the mind from the body," all but one of which merely give mention to the term. This in itself, however, does not constitute the body-offering practice per se. Separating out the consciousness and "blending it with space" (byings rig bsre ba or 'dre pa) or the later nomenclature "opening the door to the sky" (nam mkha' sgo byed) became signature Severance practices. Jamgön Kongtrul asserts that this is the main practice and relegates the body offering to post-meditation (rjes thob) or a branch (yan lag).[177] Reference to the actual body dismemberment is very rare, and, as I will suggest, limited to the texts of dubious origin. I will briefly survey the texts in the order they are found in the *Treasury of Precious Instructions*.

The verse text by Āryadeva the Brahmin, *Esoteric Instructions on the Perfection of Wisdom*, which is the only source text said to be of Indian origin, mentions the body offering only once, in the context of a classic graded path suitable for the three kinds of individuals:

> Those with superior meditative experience
> rest in the nondual meaning of it all.
> The average practitioners focus on that and meditate.
> The inferior offer their body aggregate as food.[178]

The Great Bundle is taken as the earliest and most basic text attributed to Machik. As the story goes, she responded to three Indian inquisitors with an explanation of this composition and proved to them that her teachings were indeed words of the Buddha (hence *bka'* in the title).[179] It contains only one reference to a body offering:

> Awareness carries the corpse of one's body;
> cast it out in an unattached way
> in haunted grounds and other frightful places.[180]

The third text, classified as a source text by Jamgön Kongtrul, is called *Heart Essence of Profound Meaning*. That name came to indicate a whole cycle of teachings, but this source text is signed by Jamyang Gönpo (b. 1208). In most records of the lineage, his name appears right after that of Machik's son, Gyalwa Döndrup, making him the earliest commentator on Machik's teachings that I have yet encountered, nearly a century earlier than Rangjung Dorjé, the third Karmapa (1284–1339), who is often given that credit. In this text, again, there is only one passage indicating the body-offering practice:

> Free the mind of self-fixated cherishing by casting out the form
>   aggregate as food.
> Disperse the self-fixater by separating out body and mind.
> Liberate fear on its own ground by inspecting the fearful one.
> Obstacles will arise as glory by tossing away fixation on the body
>   as self.[181]

We then come to an interesting text in the *Treasury* attributed to Machik called *Precious Treasure Trove to Enhance the Original Source, A Hair's Tip of Wisdom: A Source Text of Severance, Esoteric Instructions on the Perfection of Wisdom.*[182] It is evident that this is not a text by Machik, but a commentary on what may have been her teachings, which can be reconstructed by extracting the quoted segments. There is not a single mention of casting out the body as food. The entire commentary, including the words apparently spoken by Machik, concern the Perfection of Wisdom.

Then there are two or three or more "bundles" attributed to Machik. *Another Bundle* (*Yang tshom*) is in verse form and captures a dialogue with her son, Gyalwa Döndrup. The longer title is *Another Bundle of Twenty-Five Instructions as Answers to Questions,*[183] although not surprisingly there are actually twenty-eight questions in this version. Tacked on to that and unmentioned in any source or catalogue is a set of eighteen more questions with very cryptic verse answers, called *Vajra Play* (*Rdo rje rol pa*). Then, from an altogether different collection of ancient Severance texts[184] found at Limi monastery in Nepal, there is a text called, again, *Bundle of Precepts* (*Bka' tshom*). The colophon titles it *Thirty-Five Questions and Answers on the Bundle of Precepts, the Quintessence of the Mother's Super-Secret Heart-Mind.*[185] While this text bears no resemblance to Machik's *Great Bundle of Precepts* (*Bka' tshom chen mo*), it is strikingly similar to *Another Bundle*. Of the thirty-five questions, twenty-six of them appear in *Another Bundle*. There is some suggestion in the colophon that this bundle may have been gathered by, again, Jamyang Gönpo. What all of this indicates to me is that there was more than one set of notes circulating as records of Machik's dialogues, and that Jamgön Kongtrul ended up with this particular set for his *Treasury*, while his contemporary, Khamnyön Dharma Sengé, apparently had access to another one, judging from the citations found in his *Religious History of Pacification and Severance*.

To return to my point, there are but two brief mentions in *Another Bundle* concerning body offerings. The first is in a list of things to explain the term "unbearable" in response to the question, "What is the meaning of 'trampling upon the unbearable'?" (*mi phod brdzi ba*), a phrase describing Severance. It says, "Casting out the body to demons is unbearable" (*'dre la lus skyur mi phod*). The second instance is in response to the question, "What should one do when sick?" and the answer is: "Chop up your body and offer it as feast" (*lus po gtubs la tshogs su 'bul*; note the use of *gtubs* rather than *gcod*).

One last bundle is called *The Essential Bundle* (*Nying tshom*). Although it is attributed to Machik, it appears to be a summary of the other bundles, with a structural outline, scriptural citations, and even quotes from Machik, who is respectfully referred to as Lady Mother (*ma jo mo*). This assessment is further supported by the fact that it seems never to be cited in texts such as *The Treasury of Knowledge*, and is not mentioned in Kongtrul's *Record of Teachings Received*,[186] nor in Kunga Namgyal's short list of ten Indian teachings.[187] In any case, again there are only two references here: (1) If afraid, "Immediately hand over the body to those gods and demons without concern," and (2) "Those of inferior scope give over the body to the dangerous obstructors and rest in nonaction within the state of mental nonrecollection."[188]

Finally, we have another set of three texts that I've called "*Appendices*" (*Le lag*), attributed to Machik. Here they are neatly divided into *The Eight*

Common Appendices, *The Eight Uncommon Appendices*, and *The Eight Special Appendices*. However, in other supporting material when quotations are extracted from the *Appendices*, it is inevitably from the first set only, *The Common Appendices*. Moreover, in the aforementioned set of Severance texts from Limi Monastery, there are just two sets of appendices: *The Thirteen Appendices* and *The Eight Appendices*.[189] The latter corresponds loosely to the *Eight Common Appendices* in the *Treasury*. The *Thirteen* correspond neither to the *Uncommon* nor *Special Appendices*. I therefore feel comfortable confirming only the *Common Appendices* (of the three sets) as part of original teachings by Machik.

The Eight Common Appendices mention the body-offering practice twice: once simply stating, "The body is a corpse, cast it out as food" (*lus ni ro yin gzan du bskyur*), and then again reiterating the threefold gradation of practice:

[Recite] "unspeakable, unthinkable, inexpressible,"
or else rest in the separation of body and awareness,
or else cast out the body as food
and rest within the state of evenness.[190]

The Eight Uncommon Appendices is a very interesting text, albeit of doubtful origin. The eight sections are less arbitrary and present a progressive analysis of important elements in the practice. These are (1) the meaning of the name, (2) the vital points, (3) practices applied to faculties, (4) clearing away obstructions, (5) deviations, (6) containing inattention, (7) how to practice when sick, and (8) enhancement. The biggest surprise in this text is in the seventh appendix, which concerns various healing ceremonies, the nature of which is not found in any of the other texts, and involves such items as leper brains and widow's underwear. However, there is a basic principle here—that of dealing with the most difficult circumstances by facing them directly and employing a kind of "like heals like" practice. Thus, substances normally considered unclean may be used to cure disease resulting from contamination. Or, as in modern homeopathy theory, the text offers a prescription to "pacify the heat of feverish illness in fire and resolve cold illness in water."[191] In some ways, this could be taken as the essence of Severance practice, though it might be more difficult to identify Buddhist elements. Of the five references to giving away the body, whether one's own or the patient's, two of them are in this section. For example: "To treat *sriu*,[192] take [the affected] to a haunted place and completely give over the flesh and blood to the harm-doers. The mind will be blessed in emptiness."[193]

The last text of all those attributed to Machik Labdrön is *The Eight Special Appendices*, and if the attribution is true, then this is where my theory falls apart. But I am somewhat skeptical. Stylistically, it is very different from the ancient source texts, being comprised of eight sections outlining a progressive practice from beginning to end, much like a practice manual (*khrid yig*). The eight main headings are (1) the entry: going for refuge and arousing the aspiration, (2) the blessing: separating body and mind, (3) the meditation: without recollecting, mentally doing nothing, (4) the practice: casting out the body as food, (5) the view: not straying into the devils' sphere of influence, (6) pacifying incidental obstacles of body and mind, (7) the sacred oaths of Severance, and (8) the results of practice. The first four of these have further subcategories that contain not only descriptions, but also actual liturgy to be recited in the practice. And as the contents make clear, there is a whole section devoted to casting out the body as food, though not in the specific detail found in later works, such as Kongtrul's *Beloved Garden*. In any case, this is the only text in the group where one can recognize the implementation of the practice of Severance as we have come to know it today. And after the seemingly shamanic-type healing described in *The Uncommon Appendices*, it brings it all back into the Buddhist context with statements such as:

Casting out the body as food is the perfection of generosity, giving it away for the sake of sentient beings is morality, giving it away without hatred is patience, giving it away again and again is diligence, giving it away without distraction is meditative stability, and resting afterward in the abiding nature of emptiness is the Perfection of Wisdom.[194]

The refuge visualization includes not only Machik herself, but also her son, Gyalwa Döndrup, and grandson or grandnephew, Tönyön Samdrup, which would seem to indicate that it was composed at least a second if not third generation after Machik herself. More research needs to be done, and hopefully more will come to light as I continue with the translations on Severance and Pacification.

The question I proposed: "Is there enough material here to warrant attributing the body-offering practice to Machik?" has led to much speculation. I would have to say that so far, I have not seen much evidence linking Machik with the culinary detail of the spectacular charnel ground practices we call Chö. Yet this is not much different from any investigation of the sources of a full-blown tradition. Did Virupa teach the Path with Its Result (lam 'bras)? Did Niguma teach Six Yogas? The ḍākinī's warm breath cools down and the trail is lost, leaving us chilling in a nice cool spot. Buddhist and non-Buddhist elements mix and mingle and we drink, hoping for a good brew to warm us.

Abbreviations

BDRC   Buddhist Digital Resource Center. Online catalog at www.bdrc.io.

DNZ   Jamgön Kongtrul Lodrö Thayé, compiler. *The Treasury of Precious Instructions. Gdams ngag rin po che'i mdzod.* 18 vols. (Shechen printing). (Delhi: Shechen Publications, 1999). Also dnz.tsadra.org.

Dingri Volumes   *The Volumes of the Root Teachings of the Sacred Dharma Pacification of Suffering, and the Subsidiary, Severance of Evil Object. Dam chos sdug bsngal zhi byed rtsa ba'i chos sde dang / yan lag bdud kyi gcod yul gyi glegs bam.* Edited by Ngawang Sangyé. (New Delhi: Dingri Langkor Tsuglag Khang, 2013).

Limi (version)   *Practices of the Severance Collection and So Forth. Gcod tshogs kyi lag len sogs: A Collection of Gcod Texts Representing the Ancient Practices of the Adepts of the Tradition.* (Bir, Himachal Pradesh, India: D. Tsondu Senge, Bir Tibetan Society, 1985). BDRC W23390.

Longchenpa (version)   Volume 26 in *The Collected Works of Kunkhyen Longchen Rabjam. Kun mkhyen klong chen rab 'byams kyi gsung 'bum.* 26 volumes. (Beijing: Krung go'i bod rig pa dpe skrun khang, 2007).

Peling (version)
Cycle of Severance of Evil, the Heart Essence of Profound Meaning, "A collection of Gcod texts reflecting the teachings of Padma-gliṅ-pa. Reproduced from a manuscript collection from Padma-bkod." *Zab don thugs kyi snying po bdud kyi gcod yul gyi skor, padma-glin-pa'i lugs.* (New Delhi: P. K. Tashi, 1981). BDRC WIKG9819.

Skt.
Sanskrit

Toh
A Complete Catalogue of the Tibetan Buddhist Canons. Edited by Hakuju Ui, et al. (Sendai, Japan: Tohoku University, 1934).

TOK
Jamgön Kongtrul Lodrö Thayé, *Shes bya kun khyab* (*Theg pa'i sgo kun las btus pa gsung rab rin po che'i mdzod bslab pa gsum legs par ston pa'i bstan bcos shes bya kun khyab*). *The Treasury of Knowledge.* 3 vols. (Lhasa: Mi rigs dpe skrung khang, 1982).

Glossary 1

Glossary of Selected Terms

This glossary is meant to elucidate some of the terms and translation choices in these ancient texts that are either archaic or used in a unique way. It is not a comprehensive glossary, not even of Severance terminology.

apparitions (*cho 'phrul*). Generally equated with *rdzu 'phrul*, the miraculous ability of buddhas and bodhisattvas to effect emanational forms and transformations as part of their skillful methods to benefit beings. In the context of Chö, it refers to the perceptions attributed to the magical activities of spirits. In particular, in this tradition, it is the second stage of a practitioner's experience in a haunted place, after first raising the spirits or sensing their presence. *See* "uprising" (*lhongs*).

bravado / boasting (*rbad kham*[*s*]). In all dictionaries consulted this means a kind of boasting, puffed up arrogance, or exaggeration, which seems to make sense in context. However, note that Lodrö Tulku Rinpoche explains that it is the view of emptiness, and refers to a whole range of phenomena.[195] Used alone, *rbad* means "to incite."

congested constituents (*khams 'dus ba* / *khams 'du* / *'dus nad*). A physical response to certain conditions usually considered problematic, although also applied to progressive meditation experience. It involves an unhealthy gathering or concentration or merging of the three elemental humors—wind, bile, and phlegm—in the body, particularly the vital winds. In that, it is similar to *lung nad* ("wind sickness"). Most translations have focused on psychological symptoms, such as drowsiness, depression, disheartenment, anger, shock, and even insanity. In one story, a woman's husband and six sons were murdered, which ". . . acted as a catalyst, her grief caused a gathering of the essential constituents, and she went insane."[196]

The same term, *khams 'dus ba,* is used in a very different positive sense to describe the yogic experience in three stages:

The first, middle, and the final gatherings represent the gradual clearing and purification of the nine or ten essential constituents within the body. The four or five vital winds and the five enlightenment minds gather into different channel locations within the body due to the practice of yoga. When these nine or ten essential constituents (the ḍākinīs and ḍākas or buddhas) gather into those specific locations, the ordinary body is transformed into a rainbow body.[197]

However, that usage is not found in the many descriptions of *khams 'dus* in the present texts on Severance. A section by Jamyang Gönpo called "Curing Congested Constituents" in another text discusses methods of diagnosis to find an exact cause and then prescribes specific remedies, intersecting with the medical arts.[198]

contrary or *reverse meditation* (*zlog sgom / log sgom*). A text devoted to this subject by Lorepa (1187–1250), Jamyang Gönpo's teacher in the Lower Drukpa Kagyü tradition, states, "The essence of contrary meditation is the actual antidote to all things to be abandoned (*spang bya*). The literal interpretation is as follows: 'Contrary' means that things that are [considered] objects to be abandoned by others in this [practice] are objects that are to be cultivated; therefore, it is the reverse or opposite of others' practices. It is called 'meditation' because the meaning of this is cultivated and retained." Lorepa also lists six types in addition to meditation on emptiness: reversing conceptual thinking, afflictive emotions, gods and demons, suffering, sickness, and death.[199] These are basically the same as the *Six Cycles of Equal Taste* attributed to Rechungpa, which was rediscovered by Tsangpa Gyaré. In this text, it is described primarily for feelings of disgust toward filth, which fall under the category of conceptual thinking:

> Subjectively, this consciousness that fixates on clean and unclean, if left unexamined and unanalyzed, manifests as repulsion or fear toward appearances. Yet, when examined and analyzed, it is conceptual thinking that creates this nonthing. In fact, there is not even an atom of an entity or a true existent. What is the one who is repulsed and what is the object of repulsion? What is clean or unclean? What is the pure or impure? And where is the agent who fixates on repulsion and uncleanliness? Who is it? How is it? In contemplating these thoughts, look vividly at the nonthingness of appearances. Completely jump into emptiness. Meditate in the immediacy of nonbeing.[200]

crazy vanquishing conduct (*smyon pa'i brtul zhugs*). Sometimes translated as "yogic conduct," *brtul zhugs* is a term used throughout tantric teachings indicating nonnormative and sometimes outrageous behavior that puts previous meditation realization to the test in the field, so to speak. A dictionary definition is "concluding one's previous actions, beginning new actions. That is, vanquishing one's ordinary common conduct, and entering and dwelling in uncommon conduct."[201] In the context of this volume, it is always prefaced by *smyon pa* ("crazy") and recommended as a radical way of raising and confronting spirits. Examples include digging up earth, breaking rocks, and other methods of causing disturbance. Alternatively, it is used simply as energizing spontaneous behavior, such as "crying, laughing, dancing, calling out, and so forth— whatever pops up in your mind."

drying out completely in water (*skam thag chu nang du chod pa*). A paradoxical proverb in which one employs counterintuitive methods, such as drying something in or with water. It is used to describe the signature Severance practice of confronting and resolving adverse circumstances and fears.

equalize (*[b]snyoms / mgo bsnyoms / ro snyoms*). In general, to "equalize" means to respond equally to both positive and negative situations, to make them even or level, or even to demolish them. Often it is translated as "equal taste" or "single value," as in the well-known practice Six Cycles of Equalizing Tastes (*ro snyoms skor drug*). It is very similar to the idea of integrating or carrying on to the path (*lam du khyer ba*) in the sense of accepting and working with whatever presents itself. In the practice of Severance, with its emphasis on confronting frightening and difficult situations that expose one's fear, it is the prime directive. In fact, achieving this ability to face anything with equanimity is the purpose of the practice. Among the many examples from this volume: "Integrate [experiences] on the path with the three equalizers: Vanquish the things that you fixate on as truly existent through emptiness, vanquish attachment to self-fixation through contrary meditation, and vanquish superstitious thinking about cleanliness and uncleanliness."

evidence of success (*tshar tshad*). The evidence or measure (*tshad*) of completion or termination (*tshar*) is used throughout Severance literature. A similar term with the same meaning is *chod tshad*, literally "measure of cutting." A helpful description of such evidence comes from Rangjung Dorjé's *Practice Manual on the Profound Severance of Evil Object*: "The immediate evidence of success is the subsiding of apparitions and a sense of well-being, clear consciousness, respectful bowing of humans and nonhumans, and so forth. The ultimate evidence of success is that although things occur, they occur as apparitions of the mind."[202]

extreme measures (mtha' la gtad pa / mtha' gtad). Both *mtha' gtad* and *log non* ("pushback") are described in these texts as techniques to apply as ultimate solutions when the regular Severance practices are not effective. It might involve "smiting pestilence directly with pestilence" and other direct countermeasures for raising spirits that are resistant or especially vicious. Indeed, the visualization for extreme measures (*mtha' gtad kyi dmigs pa*) described in some old texts reiterate methods of disrupting the landscape to incite spirits. Literally, *mtha'* means "extreme" or "limit," and *gtad* is "to focus" or "to examine." Thus, an alternative understanding might be to examine the essential nature of the extremes of existence, nonexistence, and so on. But in *The Eight Uncommon Appendices*, a source text attributed to Machik Labdrön, we find a very down-to-earth example:

> If, no matter what you do, obstacles still start up, then you need the vital point that is like cornering deer. In this analogy, hunters who are pursuing deer cannot catch them in the open plains no matter what they do. But if they spot an edge (*mtha'*) like a cliff and then chase them there, the deer will be trapped, with nowhere to go. In haunted retreats, [spirits] might cause some harm to the yogin. When a slight sickness occurs and diverting it or giving ritual objects [as ransom] does not help, [disturb] their dwelling places: dig the earth pestilence, stir up water pestilence, cut down tree pestilence, or create a great

hearth contamination. Then, remain right there at ease, and the malicious spirits will disperse and be incapable of causing harm.[203]

false structure or *innermost falsehood* (*rdzun phugs*). This refers to a whole worldview that is based on ignorance of the true nature of reality. It is used here, for example, in the phrase "false structure of samsara and nirvana." Elsewhere it has been translated as "false cave," interpreting *phugs* as *phug*. It also means the innermost falsehood of our assumptions and the source (*phugs*) or long-term (*phugs*) effects of those assumptions.

haunted places / grounds (*gnyan sa*) and *haunted retreats* (*gnyan khrod*). These are places where pestilent or fierce spirits live. Similar to power spots, this is much more than the usual translation as "wild places" or "wilderness," which might be quite benign and not helpful for Severance practice. "Haunted retreat" also suggests the term *dur khrod*, which can be "charnel ground" or "graveyard," and *ri khrod*, "mountain retreat." The salient point is the place is frightening, hence my use of "haunted."

lethargy (*ltengs pa*). According to Lodrö Tulku Rinpoche, it is an old word now mostly replaced by *'bying ba*—"dullness," "sinking," or "stupor"—one of the two major faults of calm abiding meditation (*zhi gnas*; Skt. *śamatha*).

loss of focus or *diffusing* (*'byams pa*). This can also mean flowing over, excess, and diffusion. It is an old word, now mostly replaced by *rgod pa* (Skt. *auddhatya*)—"agitation" or "excitement"—one of the two major faults of calm abiding meditation. (See above.)

opening the sky door (nam mkha' sgo 'byed). The phrase "opening the sky door" is distinctive to the Severance tradition and refers specifically to the practice of separating consciousness from the body and sending it out the cranial aperture, a kind of transference (*'pho ba*). However, it has become a more generalized designation for a cycle of Severance teachings, including an enumeration of a set of ten instructions, called door openings, attributed originally to Jamyang Gönpo. Khamnyön's *Religious History of Pacification and Severance* reports that Machik received the empowerment originally from Kyo Sakya Yeshé during the transmissions of a teaching called the *Six Pieces* and attained liberation after receiving only four of the six instructions. In any case, the term is most commonly associated with the empowerment ritual that is required before commencing Severance practice and the pointing-out instructions or introduction to mind's nature.

pestilence or *pestilent spirits (gnyan).* The word *gnyan* has a wide range of meanings, starting with "pestilence" or "pestilent," which matches pretty well, according to Merriam-Webster: "1. destructive of life: deadly; 2. injuring or endangering society: pernicious; 4. infectious." The spirits that cause pestilence or epidemics are also called *gnyan*; they are basically fierce or malignant earth lords (*sa bdag*). Places (*sa*) or retreats (*khrod*) that are inhabited by such spirits are here termed "haunted" or "fierce" places.

pushback (log gnon / mgo gnon). Also "suppression practices" or "counter measures." My very literal translation of *log* ("back," "reverse") *gnon* ("push," "suppress") refers to the second kind of "extreme measure" (see above) to be used as a last resort when difficulties and resistance occur in the practice. It must take into account the particular use of the term *log* in the context of Severance, referring to the resistant spirits (see "resistance" below). A more comprehensive description would be pushing back on or suppressing resistance by spirits.

put pressure on (*ur/ar la mnan*); *get on top of* (*ar la gtad pa / ar gtad*). Both of these expressions mean "to focus intently on" something in particular. *The Big Chinese-Tibetan Dictionary* defines closely related phrases as "to focus on pressure" (*nan la gtad pa*) or "to segregate or isolate the vital point" (*don gyi gnad la bkar ba*).

putting constellations under darkness (*skar chen thibs 'og tu gzhug*). A phrase that appears in several source texts, it is described in *The Eight Uncommon Appendices*:

> In this analogy, it is like the predawn constellations or stars that grow dimmer at daybreak. Then, when the sun rises and the sunlight completely overwhelms them with its brilliance, they do not appear at all. In the same way, yogis and yoginīs who rest within the great pervasiveness of their own minds overwhelm all the gods and demons of spirit-appearance with the brilliance of the nature of phenomena so they cannot rise up.[204]

And here in the *Big General Guide*:

> *Putting the stars under darkness* makes them unable to rise up. For example, anything in the sky—such as the moon and constellations—is overwhelmed by the brilliance of the light of the rising sun. All the great stars are put under darkness and are of no consequence. Just so, the yogin who realizes the view is like the sun, and does not attend to or mentally engage in the external obstacles of devils or the internal eight concerns of attraction, aversion, and so forth. All those subtle or coarse

discursive thoughts are like the constellations; they cannot show up because they are overwhelmed by splendor.

resistance / resistant (*log pa / log*). By itself, *log* means "to return, revert, turn back, mistake, or oppose." As it is used in these Severance texts, it refers to the opposition or resistance of spirit apparitions to the normal efforts in the practice to overcome them, or even to raise them. Thus, there are occurrences of minor resistance (*log byung*) and major resistance (*log chen*), which require special techniques. This is clear in the recurring phrase "extreme measures for major resistance" (*log chen mtha la gtad pa*). Also see above under "pushback" for the suppression methods (*log gnon*).

reverting (*zlog pa / ldog pa*). In general, *zlog pa* means to "reverse" (similar to *log pa*), "negate," and especially to "avert" or "turn back," as in turning back an invading army or exorcising spirits. However, in these texts it is only used in the sense of failing in one's efforts to accomplish the practice.

Severance (*gcod / spyod*; "chöd"). In most explanations of the term *chö* (*gcod*), its use in this context is said to derive from its homonym *chö* (*spyod*; Skt. *caryā*), meaning "conduct" or "activity," as it is used throughout the Perfection of Wisdom literature. It appears, for example, in the line: "In this way one should train in performing the activity (Skt. *caryāṃ cartukāmaḥ*) of the profound Perfection of Wisdom." The Tibetan word *gcod* means "to decide" as well as "to cut" or "to sever." The meanings converge, for instance in the common term *thag gcod pa* ("decide, resolve, put an end to, determine"). The two terms (*gcod* and *spyod*) are often tellingly used interchangeably in Severance texts, and both point to the original intent of putting one's understanding of the Perfection of Wisdom to the test in the field. In Severance visualizations, the verb *gcod* is almost never used for cutting up the body, which instead is *stub pa* ("to chop").

sleep / stay / lie down / camp out (nyal ba / nyal la sdod). The term *nyal ba* is used throughout these texts in a way that seems to indicate simply to "stay" or to "abide," sometimes even in the compound *nyal la sdod*. Normally it is defined as to "lie down" or to "sleep." Here it is used in cases where a practitioner would travel and occupy a haunted ground at night, as in English vernacular "to camp out." Lodrö Tulku Rinpoche suggested a connection with *mal gcod* ("bed Severance"), an archaic term for Severance that is not used anymore.[205]

smiting pestilence directly with pestilence (gnyan thog tu gnyan dbab pa). The word *gnyan* can also be understood as "powerful" or "fierce." Pestilence or pestilent spirits are confronted directly and overwhelmed by the practitioner's own power or ferocity, which is even more fierce because it comes from their understanding of emptiness. For instance, in this text, "Outside, the palace of the nāgas is pestilent (or powerful), but more pestilent is the mind itself with the realized view." This is also used in the phrase "smiting pestilence directly in haunted places" *(gnyan [sa] thog tu gnyan dbab pa).*

take on the load/adversity (thog 'gel ba / thog tu bskal). The literal translation of taking on the load, or loading up the yak, as it were, affords a clear picture in context. Generally, it means to "take on intense adverse circumstances" *('gal rkyen drag po la thog 'gel byas pa)* and accept the responsibility of working with them, another way of describing the attitude and action of all Severance practice.

trample upon / direct subjugation of (thog brdzi; thog tu brdzi ba). To directly stamp down or immediately subjugate whatever circumstance or adverse condition is occurring. The verb *rdzi* (*brdzis, brdzi, rdzis*) means to "squeeze, press, stomp, and so on," and *thog tu* means "directly upon" or "on top of." Of course, it is meant in an abstract sense as "subjugate" or "suppress," but the literal "trampling" or "stomping" gives a clearer picture and was favored by my test audience. It is an important antidote in Severance practices, particularly in the conduct after meditation, along with "equalizing" (*ro snyoms*); the two are often used as a compound: *ro snyoms thog brdzi*. Jamgön Kongtrul advises: "Do not be without the reinforcement (literally, "army") of the antidotes of trampling and equalizing" (*thog brdzis dang ro snyoms la gnyen po'i dpung dang ma bral bar bya*).[206]

In our texts, one way to trample is to use crazy vanquishing conduct. The idea of immediacy is conveyed by the line: "Trample upon each circumstance each time it occurs. By equalizing circumstances and integrating them on the path, you are freed from them" (*rkyen re byung res kyis thog brdzis bya/ ro snyoms byed cing lam du khyer bas de las grol pa*). And the ultimate power of trampling upon circumstances is to realize that "whatever occurs—highs and lows, happiness and sadness—is relative reality" (*thog brdzis nus pa ni/ mtho dman skyid sdug ci byung yang 'di kun rdzob*).

uprising (*lhong[s]* / *slong ba*). The verb *lhongs* can mean "to be successful," but the similar sounding *slong ba* (*bslangs, slong, bslang, slongs*) means "raise" or "lift up." The two spellings do not share the same etymology, yet generally both mean something that arises suddenly (*glo bur lhong*), and seem to be used interchangeably here. As a noun, it refers to something that has arisen, such as an uprising or upheaval. The *Big Tibetan-Chinese Dictionary* also gives "hindrance" (*gegs*) or "obstacle" (*bar chad*) as definitions. In the context of Severance, this is an experience that is desired and even conjured, a raising of the spirits, so that the practitioner can engage in the practice. Here it is used to describe the first stage of sensing the presence of spirits, or even the presence of fear, in anticipation of an actual apparition. Sometimes it is called "activation"; even "the heebie-jeebies" has been suggested.

Glossary 2

Glossary of Spirits

The various spirits mentioned in these texts are only described in terms of their abodes in the landscapes of Tibet. Therefore, their names here have either been rendered literally into English or kept in Tibetan. (The one exception is the more widely known Sanskrit term *nāga*). The following is a list and minimal description, just to clarify the translations and provide the Tibetan, and the Sanskrit where relevant. Some translated names are purposefully general, allowing the practitioner to entertain their own version of spirits.

custodian spirits (*dkor bdag*). Local spirits in charge of sacred images and monastic wealth.

death lords / death lord minions (*gshin rje*; Skt. *yama/yamāri*). A class of supernatural beings regarded as the entourage of Yama, the lord of death.

demons (*'dre*). General term for malicious and evil spirits.

devils (*bdud*; Skt. *māra*). See the introduction, page xxiii.

earth lords / earth owners (*sa bdag*; Skt. *bhūpati*). Spirit kings of an area and lords or owners of land.

elemental spirits / spirits (*'byung po*; Skt. *bhūta*). A very general term referring to any being, but usually spirits that simply exist. Not necessarily
associated with the four elements (*'byung ba bzhi*) per sé, but rather
what just arises or occurs. Once described to me by Chagdud Tulku
Rinpoché as "just popping up" (*'byung ba tsam*).

female sen *spirits* (*bsen mo*). A type of demoness often found in company
with the king spirits; the male and female spirits symbolize desire and
anger, respectively.

flesh-eaters (*sha za*; Skt. *piśāca*). Associated with wild places, and thought to
devour flesh.

gods and demons / god-demons (*lha 'dre*). See the introduction, page xxiii. Also
see Harding 2003, 123.

gongpo spirits (*'gong po*). A type of evil spirit symbolizing ego-clinging. Also,
an enchanter, sorcerer, bewitching demon, craving spirit, or a demon
who causes disease.

ground masters (*gzhi bdag*; Skt. *bhūmapati*): Local spirits and guardians of
particular regions, similar in meaning to *sa bdag* and *yul bdag*.

harm-doers (*gnod sbyin*; Skt. *yakṣa*). A class of supernatural beings, in India
often the attendants of the god of wealth. They were generally por-
trayed as benevolent, but the Tibetan translation of harm-doer indicates a more dangerous kind of spirit.

king spirits (*rgyal po*). A type of mischievous spirits that can cause insanity,
although when subdued by a great master, they can also act as guardians of the Dharma.

knife ghosts, male and female (gri bo dri mo). Ghosts of those murdered with knives.

life-force rulers (srog bdag). Spirits with the power of taking or sustaining one's life force.

local lords / country owners (yul bdag). Similar to ground masters.

malignant spirits (gdon; Skt. graha). This term is used broadly to refer to multiple classes of beings who can affect a person's physical and mental health. Often used in conjunction with "sickness," as in *nad gdon*, it can be interpreted either as "sickness spirit" or "sickness *and* malignant spirit."

mamo (ma mo; Skt. mātṛkā). Ferocious female (literally "mother") spirits that can cause sickness and trouble, or provide help and protection if propitiated.

nāgas (klu). Subterranean water spirits subject to the same caste system as Indians: outcaste, brahmin caste, nobility caste, royal caste, and low caste. Described as having the upper body of a human and the lower body of a serpent. They possess wealth and religious interest, but cause disease if the bodies of water that they inhabit are disrupted.

oath-breakers (dam sri). Nine sibling spirits who have violated their commitments.

obstructors (bgegs). Any situation that obstructs or hinders, but most often personified as interfering spirits.

pekar spirits (*[d]pe dkar [po]* / *pe har*). Chief custodians of monastic property. The pekar spirits may have a negative influence, however Pekar as a proper name is a more god-like spirit, whose main shrine is in Nechung.

pestilent spirits (*gnyan*). See the glossary of terms.

serak spirits (*bse rag*). A kind of hungry ghost, called "rhinoceros" because they live alone, have trouble interacting, and have a single horn (*Big Tibetan-Chinese Dictionary*).

sinpo spirits (*srin po*; Skt. *rākṣasa*). A class of nonhuman beings often considered demonic. They are often depicted as flesh-eating monsters who haunt frightening places and are ugly and evil-natured with a yearning for human flesh, and who additionally have miraculous powers, such as being able to change their appearance (*84000*).

theurang (*the'u rang*). Evil-natured spirits who move in the sky and cause illness in children. They ride goats and carry a bellows and hammer as patrons of blacksmiths.

tsen spirits (*btsan*). Wrathful, warlike spirits or hungry ghosts, often associated with mountains, that can cause disease and destruction. Associated with fire and the color red.

Notes

1 *Sgrub brgyud shing rta chen po brgyad*. A system of categorizing the esoteric instructions (*man ngag*) that flowed from India to Tibet, used extensively by Jamgön Kongtrul Lodrö Thayé (1813–1900) as an organizing principle for his massive anthologies. It was first suggested by Sherab Öser (1518–1584), who listed eight "charioteers" who founded the lineages of Nyingma, Kadampa, Shangpa Kagyü, Lamdré, Marpa Kagyü, Shijé, Jordruk, and Dorjé Sumgyi Nyendrup. See Jamgön Kongtrul 2016, xii–xiii.

2 This may be present-day Tsome, administered from the capital of Tamzhol. (Dorje, 2004, 215–16). See my attempt to unravel the prevailing confusion regarding Labdrön's birthplace in Jamgön Kongtrul 2016, 540n8.

3 *Bdud bzhi*, Skt. *catvārimārā*: (1) *phung po'i bdud*; Skt. *skandhamāra*, (2) *nyon mongs pa'i bdud*; Skt. *kleśamārā*, (3) *'chi bdag gi bdud*; Skt. *mṛyupatimāra*, and (4) *lha'i bu yi bdud*; Skt. *devaputramāra*. The fourth one, literally "child of the gods," indicates the state of being extremely spoiled or complacent.

4 Three of these four were also mentioned in a poem by Āryadeva the Brahmin (translated in Jamgön Kongtrul 2016, 3–11). He was a maternal uncle of Dampa Sangyé, not Nāgārjuna's student Āryadeva, and his poem is often cited as the Indian source text for Machik's tradition. However, it is not clear if Machik ever even saw this text. Such a claim seems like a stretch, but is nevertheless important to give Indian authenticity to Tibetan indigenous work, not to mention male authenticity to the risky business of being a female saint.

5 Harding 2013b, 117.

6 Those consulted for this summary were Gö Lotsāwa, 2:793–96 (translated in Roerich 1976, 676–80); Koshul Drakpa Jungné, *Treasury of Names*, 634–37; Pema Karpo, *The Sun that Opens the Lotus of the Doctrine*, 448; and Dan Martin 2008, "Jamyang Gonpo," Treasury of Lives.

7 Gtsang is usually divided into *g.yas ru* and *ru lag*. Ferrari 1958, 141n405.

8 'O yug; a district in Central Tibet.

9 Lo ras Dbang phyug brtson 'grus, 1187–1250, a.k.a. Dbus ras pa or Dbu ri pa. For an interesting and readable version of events in Lorepa's life, see Miller 2005. Also see "The Songs and Story of Jetsün Lorepa" in Nālandā Translation Committee 1980, 246–55.

10 Tsangpa Gyaré (Gtsang pa rgya ras Ye shes rdo rje, 1161–1211) was also apparently a recipient of *zhi byed* teachings, and he was the treasure revealer of *The Six Cycles of Equalizing Tastes* that Rechungpa had brought back from India and later hid. This discovery made him the first Kagyü tertön. Both of these facts are important in his connection to Severance.

11 *Thubs pa lnga*. See Jamgön Kongtrul's version of Lorepa's system in DNZ, 10:235–39. The five capabilities are (1) to fathom mahāmudrā (*phyag rgya chen po gting thub*); (2) to wear the cotton robe of the fierce inner heat (*gtum mo ras thub*); (3) to practice secret conduct in the mountains (*gsang spyod ri thub*); (4) to stir up sickness and spirits (*nad gdon 'khrugs thub*); and (5) to apply antidotes to circumstances (*gnyen po rkyen thub*). Obviously the fourth capability is closely connected with the teachings of Severance. Also see DNZ, 18:338–39, for the practice in Kunga Drolchok's Ninety-Ninth Guidebook, translated by Gyurme Dorje in Jamgön Kongtrul 2020, 18:475–77.

12 BDRC lists Nyang stod Jam dbyangs mgon po as a contributing author of a three-text volume on *The Five Capabilities* preliminaries. His name is not in the text as an author, but appears at the end of the lineage as Lama Jamyang.

13 That is to say, he attained what is known as the "rainbow body," a very advanced spiritual attainment where no physical remains are left. Pema Karpo, Kunkhyen, 448. The second title mentioned here has not been definitively identified.

14 See vol. 2, 3225–26.

15 Khamnyön, 75a. Regarding the possible alias Sangyé Tenpa mentioned here, there is a text called *Short Practice of Severance* attributed to one Chöjé Sangyé Tönpa who might be the same as Sangyé Tenpa (491).

16 For a brief summary of Gyalwa Döndrup and his descendants, see Harding 2013b, 101–02. Also see Roerich 1988, 985–86. (Jamyang Gönpo is not mentioned in this telling.)

17 See for instance Jamgön Kongtrul's colophon in *Distillation of the Profound*, where he states: "The traditions of Gyalthangpa Samten Öser and Chöjé Jamyang Gönpo's direct lineages are found in the teachings of the great Jonang Jetsun [Tāranātha] and Minling Terchen Rinpoché" (DNZ, 14:330).

18 *Opener of the Wisdom Eye*, 455. The author, Könchok Gyaltsen of Labrang (1764-1853), was the third Balmang tulku, a Gelukpa line.

19 Most famously, the beautiful song addressed to his mother Machik at her funeral ceremony: *Supplication Stirring the Intention*. In Tāranātha, *The Required Liturgies on the Occasion of Venerable Tāranātha's Severance Empowerment*, translated in Jamgön Kongtrul 2016, 240–44.

20 An exception is a three-folio confession liturgy addressed to Machik and the Severance lineage signed as the "Tibetan Paṇḍita Dönyö Dorjé." Thank you to Lodrö Tulku Rinpoche for giving me this text and identifying it as authored by Jamyang Gönpo.

21 Those are *Sgrub thabs dngos grub sgo 'byed kyi shog dril lhan thabs* and *Zab don thugs kyi snying po'i drag las / gcod kyi nyams len bsdus pa gegs sel zhal gdams* (folio 69b).

22 Perhaps differentiated only by a variant spelling of "heart essence"—*thugs kyi sny-ing khu* rather than *thugs kyi snying po*—although this is not consistent, probably due to editorial variation.

23 Dingri Volumes, 9: 50; Limi, 278. Thank you to Ringu Tulku Rinpoché for clarifying this passage (personal communication, November 2, 2023).

24 DNZ, 18:75. Translation by Gyurme Dorje in Jamgön Kongtrul 2020, 162.

25 Tashi Chöpel notes that Kongtrul received the blessing empowerments of Profound Severance of Evil Object in the Gyalthang tradition of Samten Öser based on Tāranātha's text (*Record of Teachings Received*, 772).

26 DNZ, 14:22. Translation in Jamgön Kongtrul 2016, 38.

27 Ban rgan (or Rtogs ldan) Bstan 'dzin rnam dag, a master in the Surmang tradition of Severance, *White Crystal Mirror*, DNZ, 14:228. See the translation and notes in Jamgön Kongtrul 2016, 257–96. In that previous translation, I mistakenly speculated that the "great Drukpa" referred to Pema Karpo (who was, of course, also great).

28 In Limi, 95–96.

29 Thank you to Gelong Sean Price and his source for this information.

30 Pemakö is the name of a magical hidden land (*sbas yul*) in southeastern Tibet, though it is not clear if that location is meant here.

31 *Shes rab kyi pha rol tu phyin pa zab mo gcod kyi gzhung dang man ngag mtha' dag gi yang bcud zab don thugs kyi snying po.* An earlier iteration of my translation of these verses was published in Jamgön Kongtrul, *The Treasury of Precious Instructions, Volume 14: Chöd: The Sacred Teachings on Severance*, Shambhala Publications, 2016. Used with permission of the Tsadra Foundation and Shambhala Publications.

32 *Bdud gcod zab mo don gyi nying khu las / zab don gyi spyi khrid chen mo.*

33 *Sde snod* (Skt. *piṭaka*), generally the Three Collections (Skt. *tripiṭaka*) that represent the early teachings of Buddhism, namely, the Vinaya, Sūtra, and Abhidharma. The word originates from the term "baskets," which were originally used to hold the collections written on palm leaves.

34 *Rgyud sde bzhi.* These are action tantra (Skt. *kriyātantra*); performance tantra (Skt. *caryātantra*), yoga tantra, and highest yoga tantra (Skt. *anuttarayogatantra*).

35 Verses in italics represent the source quotations from Jamyang Gönpo's root text called *Heart Essence of Profound Meaning: The Quintessence of All Source Texts and Esoteric Instructions on Severance, the Perfection of Wisdom*. However, this first verse does not appear there, other than the last line of homage, which begins that text. Note that there are many spelling variations. Here I have followed the version in this current text.

36 *Dbu ma.* This is the opening homage in Āryadeva's *Lamp for Integrating the Practices*, found in in the tantra section of the Tengyur, 57a.2–3.

37 *Prajñāpāramitāsaṃcayagāthā*, 15a–b. Translation in Conze 1983, 57.

38 Śāntideva, *Bodhicaryāvatāra*, 32a4. Translation in Shantideva 1997, 142.

39 *Śatasāhasrikāprajñāpāramitā*, appearing multiple times between 254b and 259a. Gandharvas (*dri za*), or "scent eaters," are a class of benevolent nonhuman beings who inhabit the skies or cities in the clouds and subsist on smells.

40 *Śatasāhasrikāprajñāpāramitā*, 141b, 142b, etc.

41 *Prajñāpāramitāsaṃcayagāthā*, 10b.

42 Here *dam khrid* (which makes no sense) should be *dmar khrid* ("red guides"), according to Lodrö Tulku Rinpoche. Red guides are direct instructions using examples—by analogy, like a physician who cuts open a cadaver and points directly to various internal organs. The phrase "carrying flesh carrying blood" (*sha khyer khrag khyer*), referencing the body offering, further elaborates the dissection imagery.

43 In the root text, this last line belongs to the next verse. Here it is repeated in the first line of that verse, though I have translated it somewhat differently.

44 The version in the Longchenpa edition seems to say the opposite: "If you follow the Secret Mantra Vehicle, just conferring the torma empowerment opens the Dharma door, because the torma empowerment includes the ten empowerments . . ." (137).

45 Again, a different interpretation in the Longchenpa edition suggests that even if you do all those things, from empowerment through completion phase, yet one's conduct contradicts the sacred pledge, the results will not arise (138). However, Lodrö Tulku Rinpoche says the version here is correct (personal communication, May 12, 2023).

46 *Bka' tshoms chen mo*, DNZ, 14:13. Translation in Jamgön Kongtrul 2016, 21. Some variations on the third line are as follows. DNZ: *bsam pa yul min de nyid yin* ("No object of thought; that's exactly it!"). Longchenpa version: *bsam pa'i yul ni de nyid min* ("The object of thought; no such thing.")

47 Dags po rong dga'i Skye med dga' yan. One of Machik Labdrön's eight disciples said to be equal to herself (*rang dang mnyam pa*); in this case, equal to her in omniscience. Jamgön Kongtrul, TOK, 1:545.

48 *Dgyes rdor*. *Hevajratantrarāja*, part 1, 2a. See Callahan 2012, 1:26.

49 *Verse Summary of the Perfection of Wisdom*, first line: 15b, second line: 3b. Conze 1983, first line, 59.

50 Though not the exact wording here, the original verse is from Machik Labdrön, "The Great Bundle of Precepts," as found in DNZ, 14:7; translated in Jamgön Kongtrul 2016, 14.

51 *Tshar tshad*, "evidence of success," literally "measure of terminating" (see glossary of terms). Alternatively, in Limi: "obstacles don't arise" (*bar chad mi 'byung*). That is, there is nothing to practice with.

52 *Bdud rtsi lnga*: excrement, urine, blood, flesh, and sexual fluids.

53 *Sūryagarbhasūtra*, Lhasa Kangyur, H 258, 342b3. Spoken by the nāga daughter. Translation based on the version in 84000: "The Noble Very Extensive Sūtra, the Quintessence of the Sun."

54 *Dhvajāgramahāsūtra*, 265a–266a. This is really a gloss of several statements in this short sutra.

55 *Nad pa'i sngas srung byed pa.* "Pillow guarding: The practice of watching the corpse day and night to make sure there are no demonic attacks (or possibly also to make sure it won't be reanimated in one way or another)" (Rangjung Yeshe Wiki - Dharma Dictionary, n.d.).

56 Machik Labdrön, *Yang bka' tshoms* (elsewhere just *Yang tshoms*). The first two lines are not in *Another Bundle* verbatim, but are elsewhere attributed to an unidentified text called Machik's *Vajra Verses*. See for instance *The Body Donation and Feeding Ritual*, DNZ, 14:275. The last four lines are in DNZ, 14:109, translated in Jamgön Kongtrul 2016, 133. There are various versions of the texts known as "bundles." See introduction to *Another Bundle* in Jamgön Kongtrul 2016, 123–24.

57 The first two lines are in DNZ, 14:107, and are famously quoted in many places. The second two are found in the explanation that follows on the same page. Both appear in the translation in Jamgön Kongtrul 2016, 131.

58 Alternative in Longchenpa version: "By grabbing hold of malignant spirits, fearful objects are realized as empty."

59 This bracketed phrase, missing here, is present in all three other editions, and the text makes more sense when it is included: *gdon de'i nus pa ci yod pa de.*

60 *Bas ldags*: A disease of the skin that looks like it has been licked by a cow. *Big Dictionary of Tibetan Medicine* 2006, 515.

61 Here and in other places, I would like to thank Tenzin Leksang, doctor of Tibetan medicine, and Kunga Lama, RN, for their help with medical terminology.

62 A short text called *Presentation of the Sixteen Ridicules of the Devils* is contained in Dingri Volumes, vol. *ta*, 303–7. The only notable difference is the colophon: "Find most other instructions elsewhere. Copied from the holy lama's text at the secluded place of Margom" (*man ngag gzhan rnams phal cher logs na gsal/ bla ma dam pa'i phyag dpe las/ dben gnas dmar sgom du zhal bshus so*). Possibly Dmar sgom Bsod nams blo gros, 1456–1521 or 1516–81), abbot of Margom in Dolpo.

63 DNZ, 14:109. Only the first two lines are an exact match with the edition of *Another Bundle* in DNZ, 14:132–33. There are many editions, and this quotation points to an older version.

64 This verse might be traced to a verse in Āryadeva's *Grand Poem*, which is said to be the Indian source text or antecedent of Tibetan Severance. The DNZ version reads: "Set pestilence upon pestilence, directly in the flesh. / Stick the hot needle precisely there. / Go for refuge in the Three Jewels. / Put the morning star under darkness. / Reject closeness and distance toward gods and demons. / Use extreme measures for major pestilence" (14:8). An earlier antecedent could be in the *Verse Summary on the Perfection of Wisdom.*

65 This sentence is notably different and maybe better in the Limi version: "When you first arrive at haunted retreat, practice the instructions on severing. If there are [spirit] uprisings, follow the explanations on the signs of uprising."

66 This line is missing here, but has been added based on the three other sources. (*Brag gam pha bong bra ma yin a de ka la btags*, Limi, 137).

67 *Gag lhog*: "Diphtheria or inflammation associated with the throat (*gag*) and the vulnerable diseases of the smooth muscles (*lhog*)" (Drungtso and Drungtso 1999, 39).

68 The author uses Sanskrit here, whereas elsewhere the Tibetan *gnod sbyin* has been translated as "harm-doer."

69 Alternately, other editions state: "will cause regret in the minds of the gods and demons who would initiate obstacles."

70 This event is recorded in Tsangnyön Heruka, *A Hundred Thousand Songs of Milarepa*, 134b, and translated in C. C. Chang 1962; see chapter 28, "The Goddess Tseringma's Attack," 2:296–311. For the eighteen great malignant spirits (*gdon chen bco brgyad*) see Nebesky-Wojkowitz 1956, 310–11.

71 This event is described in Gö Lotsawa, 2:1144. It was based on Machik's instructions to her son Drupché, later known as Gyalwa Döndrup. The translation in Roerich 1988, 985, contains several misinterpretations, and names only a single magician as Tengkawa (Stengs ka ba).

72 This appears in many sutras, for example in the *Verse Summary*, where the second line reads "no body, no mind, and even no name" (15a), rather than as it is rendered here, by "no perception/conception (*'du shes*)." I have followed the *Verse Summary*, since it is often referenced in the Severance material.

73 *Verse Summary*, 15b. Translation: Conze 1983, 59.

74 Not located. Since Gyalwa Döndrup was said to be Jamyang Gönpo's teacher, this was likely a personal instruction.

75 There are a number of variations or mistakes regarding the term for darkness here: *thigs*; DNZ root text: *thibs*; Āryadeva: *thims*; Longchenpa, Limi, and Peling: *thebs* (that led to my previous mistranslation as "put under thumb"!). Based on a similar iteration from the *Verse Summary* (see following note), I believe the correct, if archaic, spelling should be *thibs po*: "darkness." For another variation in an early teaching known as *The Six Pieces* that Machik received from Dampa Sangyé, we find four vital points of the view: burning the stars in the hearth (*skar chen thab tu sreg pa*); extreme measures for major resistance (*log chen mtha la gtad pa*); going to gamble on great pestilence (*gnyan chen skugs su gcar ba*); and overwhelming with Mahayana's brilliance (*theg chen zil byis gnon pa*) (75). See the commentary from that text in Jamgön Kongtrul 2016, 548n14.

76 Perhaps based on the *Verse Summary*, ch. 23: "When the sun rises, free from clouds and one blaze of rays, / having dispelled the entire blinding and confusing darkness, / it outshines all animals such as glowworms, / and also all the hosts of the stars, and the lustre of the moon" (Conze 1983, 53).

77 Here, *skab su rig pa rbad khams ma btangs na phra mo'i rnal 'byor kyis mi non gsung*. In a text of Dampa's answers to his heart-son Kunga, *Clarifying Mirror of the Mind*, it is quoted as "Occasionally raise the boasting of intrinsic awareness. A subtle yoga won't sever the place" (*skabs su rig pa'i rbad kham slong/ pra mo'i rnal 'byor gyis sa mi chod*), 67–68. Perhaps expanded in *The Eight Uncommon Appendices*: *de yang dang po rig pa la ngar btags la lta ba'i rbad khams bskyed la* (Dingri, vol. *ja*, 275). Lodrö Tulku Rinpoche said this is a fixed expression meaning "application of analysis" (personal communication May 8, 2023). I cannot find support for this interpretation.

78 As mentioned elsewhere, the word being translated as pestilence (*gnyan*) has a wide range of meaning. Basically, it is a name for dangerous spirits that are thought to cause harm if disturbed. They can occupy, or be inseparable from, trees, cliffs, and almost anything. When elements of the natural or even human environment are treated with disrespect, it will result in an uprising of pesitilence unless preventative measures are taken, such as practicing Severance.

79 *Le lag*, here referring to Machik's *Eight Common Appendices*. Only the first two lines appear in DNZ, 14:134 (Jamgön Kongtrul 2016, 162), and in Limi. There the second line reads "devils and king spirits will act as patrons." I have preferred "patrons" (*yon bdag*) rather than, as here, "qualities" (*yon tan*) since it accords with the other versions of *The Big General Guide*. In those versions, the last two lines read instead: "No matter what adverse circumstances occur, taking them as supports is the supreme instruction" (*rkyen snang sna tshogs ci byung yang/ grogs su 'khyer bas gdams ngag mchog*). The whole verse as found here is in the *Abridged Authoritative Teaching on Machik's Severance* by Karma Chakmé, found in his Collected Works (vol. *zi*, 53) and in many other collections. It is also in the Tibetan input for the Dingri Volumes, but is not in the print edition.

80 In Machik, *The Eight Great Appendices*, DNZ, 14:134 (with minor differences); Jamgön Kongtrul 2016, 163.

81 King Maitrībala (Byams pa'i stobs) was a previous incarnation of the Buddha as a king in Varanasi who fed five life-draining yakṣas with his own flesh and blood. From *The Hundred Deeds*, 177–78, part 4.1.

82 King Candraprabha (Zla 'od, Moonlight), the Buddha in a previous life, gave away his own head. Prince Gedön (Rgyal bu Dge don, Prince Virtue), also the Buddha in another life, retrieved the *cintāmaṇi* (wish-fulfilling jewel) from the Golden Isle after much travail and betrayal and caused it to rain down wealth on all the people. Both stories are from the *Sutra of the Wise and Foolish*, translated in Frye 1981, chapter 23, "King Chandraprabha Gives his Head," 109–18, and chapter 34, "Prince Virtuous," 164–73.

83 Not found in the *Hundred Thousand*, but there are several near misses in the *Perfection of Wisdom in Eight Thousand Lines*, 214a–b.

84 Machik, *Yang tshom[s]*, DNZ, 14:111. Previously, I have translated the word *spyod pa* (pronounced "chöpa") in the root text as "activity" (Jamgön Kongtrul 2016, 135), but here, and in many places, it is a synonym and homonym for "severing," *gcod pa*.

85 This is found in several sources (but not in Maitreya, *Ornament of the Mahayana Sutras*) with the first line as "total afflictions completely pure" (*kun nas nyon mong rnam par dag*). See, for instance Maitreya, *Distinguishing the Middle from the Extremes*, 41a3. There is a similar description in *Ornament of the Mahayana Sutras*, 12.13.

86 Found in Maitreya, *Distinguishing the Middle from the Extremes*, 41a5, as well as many treatises.

87 *Hevajratantrarāja*, part 2, 22a5.

88 Not located.

89 *Hevajratantrarāja*, part 2, 22a3. Callahan 2012, verse 69.

90 *Prajñāpāramitāhṛdaya*, 145a.

91 Although all versions say sixteen (*sgyu ma'i dpe bcu drug*), the highest traditional number of examples or similes of illusion is twelve: an illusion, the moon in water, an after-image of a moving light, a mirage, a dream, an echo, a city of gandharvas, a magic play, a rainbow, a bolt of lightning, a water bubble, and a reflection in a mirror.

92 The three continents (*gling gsum*) are the first three of the four continents in ancient Indian cosmology, excluding Unpleasant Sound (*sgra mi snyan*). Functional sex characteristics (*mtshan don byed nus pa*) indicates that eunuchs and hermaphrodites were not suitable for ordination, according to the Vinaya.

93 Vasubandhu, *Abhidharmakośakārikā*, 12a. In this and all commentaries in the Derge canon, the order of lines differs from that found here: "Returning the training and passing away, / if two sex organs develop, / and cutting off the roots and the passing of night, / the personal vows of liberation are cancelled" (*bslab pa phul dang shi 'phos dang / mtshan gnyis dag ni byung ba dang / rtsa ba chad dam mtshan 'das las / so sor thar pa'i 'dul ba gtong*).

94 An added note in this edition lists one version of the names of the thirteen bodhisattva stages as follows: (1) Perfect Joy, (2) Stainless, (3) Illuminating, (4) Radiant, (5) Hard to Keep, (6) Clearly Manifest, (7) Far Progressed, (8) Immovable, (9) Excellent Intellect, (10) Dharma Cloud, (11) Total Radiance, (12) Lotus of Non-Attachment, and (13) Vajra Holder.

95 *Vajracchedikā*, 131a–b. The last two lines, plus two that follow, are instructive: "See buddhas as the nature of phenomena (*dharmatā*); the guides are dharmakāya, so the nature of phenomena is not something knowable, consciousness cannot know it."

96 Found in *Perfection of Wisdom in Eighteen Thousand Lines*, *Aṣṭadaśasāhasrikāprajñāpāramitā*, 17a5 and 198a5 and in several other sutras.

97 *Śatasāhasrikāprajñāpāramitā*. Similar statement on 213a5: "Bhagavat, what is this word 'buddha, buddha?'"

98 *Verse Summary*, 8a.

99 In DNZ, 14:110, the first line reads, "If you don't know occurring circumstances as supports," then one verse later it says, "Bring the instructions inside you. If you don't

gain confidence in your understanding, just hearing the words won't cut it. Think about that, noble child." Translated in Jamgön Kongtrul 2016, 134.

100 There are seventeen passages with this phrase in the *Perfection of Wisdom in Ten Thousand Lines* alone.

101 Other terms in place of "nondistraction" (*g.yeng med*) appear in Longchenpa: "nonduality" (*gnyis med*); Peling: "unwavering" (*g.yo med*); and Limi: "no matter" (*gal med*).

102 The first four lines are in *The Eight Common Appendices*, DNZ, 14:139. Translation in Jamgön Kongtrul 2016, 168. The last five are quoted in several other places.

103 DNZ, 14:11. There and in both the Longchenpa and Peling editions of the *Big General Commentary*, the term is *snyems med*, "without inflation," as translated here because it is more straightforward. However, in this Dingri edition, and in the Limi text, it is not negated: *snyems byed dbyings*, "the space of inflation." This might also be feasible as a paradoxical statement such as the other examples in this section on confronting problems.

104 This seems to be assembled from different places, or else is based on a different edition. The first two lines are in DNZ, 14:10. The second two lines are on 12 and 20, respectively. The last two lines are on 15 and 25, respectively.

105 DNZ, 14:133. Translated in Jamgön Kongtrul 2016, 162. There is an important difference in that in the DNZ edition of this text, the first line is "Don't be attached to appearance; don't meditate on emptiness." I think the version here is probably correct.

106 Śāntideva, 9a. Chapter 4, verses 30–31.

107 Added from Longchenpa version: *gcod 'di 'dre 'dul gcig pu*.

108 Machik's *Le lag, The Eight Common Appendices*, found with variations in DNZ, 14:137. Translated in Jamgön Kongtrul 2016, 166.

109 *The Eight Common Appendices*: Only the last two lines appear on page 135.

110 Attributed to Machik's *Le lag*, but these lines were not located in either the common or uncommon *Appendices*.

111 Not located.

112 *The Eight Common Appendices*, DNZ, 14:135. Lines 1–3 are in different order and there is no line 4.

113 *Kha thor* or *kha 'thor*: the miscellaneous sayings are records (or rumors) of Machik's teachings that are not collected in one specific place, possibly found in the disciples' notes. See Harding 2013b, 101, and Jamgön Kongtrul 2007, 434.

114 *Nag tshur*: ferrous sulphate.

115 DNZ, 14:133. Translation: Jamgön Kongtrul 2016, 161, though quite different.

116 The text here says: *stong nyid chos kyi dbyings su sgrol ba'i phyir*, but all other editions have the negative *ma bsgral* or *ma grol*, which seems a more direct statement than "emptiness [must be] liberated. . . ."

117 *Verse Summary*, 13b.

118 *Root Verses on the Wisdom of the Middle Way*, 15a (24.14).

119 The first line has not been located (despite seeming so appropriate). The second line occurs in *Hevajra Tantra*, part 2, 16a.

120 DNZ, 14:16. Translation in Jamgön Kongtrul 2016, 26–27. The second line there reads "like cauterizing wounds by fire" (*rma byung me yis bsregs btang bzhin*).

121 Not located in the tantra, but also quoted in Karma Chakmé, *Abridged Authoritative Teaching on Machik's Severance*.

122 *Bhūmi-piṭaka*; *Sa'i sde snod* (or Limi, *Mdo sde*). I have not found an original text by that name, though it may refer to the *Yogācārabhūmi*. However, it is quoted widely. Elsewhere, the first two lines are reversed and it is attributed either to a text called *Twenty Verses on the Bodhisattva Vows* by Candragomin (166b), or in some places, to Śāntideva (Zhi ba lha), perhaps a mistake for Śāntarakṣita (Zhi ba 'tsho), who wrote a commentary on the *Twenty Verses*.

123 Not located.

124 DNZ, 14:11. Translation: Jamgön Kongtrul 2016, 19. The last two lines there read instead, "if you attain confidence without inflation, / the gods and demons of apparent existence cannot arise."

125 *Rtsi ma ghi*. According to Rinchen Wangchuk 2012, 10, this is a name for musk: "Musk is called as 'tsimagi' in Tibetan Buddhism which is recognized as an invaluable material that can subdue or ameliorate any illness."

126 Not located.

127 Not in *Piṭaka* (*Sde snod*) as stated here, but in Śāntideva, 22a (7.53) as correctly stated in the Limi version.

128 Machik Labdrön, DNZ, 14:9–10. Translation: Jamgön Kongtrul 2016, 17.

129 DNZ, 14:135, where it is a bit different: "At first you must have great courage. / This severing of evil object instructs you / to remain in a happy mind state with no inflations. / All yogins go to haunted places . . ." (Jamgön Kongtrul 2016, 164).

130 DNZ, 14:10–11, where it is "Afflictive emotions such as the five poisons, / fears about invisible demons, / hopes regarding unreal gods, and / all similar hopes and fears about mental objects / arise from inflation and are the devil of inflation" (Jamgön Kongtrul 2016, 18).

131 Information on these specific Tibetan astrological terms can be found in the glossary to *Tibetan Elemental Divination Paintings* 2001, 412–24. Also see Namkhai Norbu 1995, 147–62.

132 Machik, DNZ, 14:138–39. Translation in Jamgön Kongtrul 2016, 168.

133 Translation is uncertain, and no one was able to clarify it. But the idea is that the Severance practitioner did all the wrong things that would normally be considered very inauspicious and dangerous but had a good outcome nevertheless, thus demonstrating the efficacy of the Severance methodology.

134 Machik, DNZ, 14:16. Translation in Jamgön Kongtrul 2016, 26. Seems to be a variation on the quote given above.

135 DNZ, 14:16. Translation in Jamgön Kongtrul 2016, 27. Lodrö Tulku Rinpoche describes "carry the load" as making good use of circumstances.

136 *Mnyam khrid*: like the miscellaneous teachings, this quotation does not refer to a specific text and has not been located.

137 Appears often in *The Hundred Deeds* and in the *Glorious Deeds of Pūrṇa*.

138 Not located.

139 Found in many canonical sources, such as *The Aparimitāyurjñāna Sūtra*, 222a.

140 Śāntideva, 6b1.

141 DNZ, 14:14. Translation in Jamgön Kongtrul 2016, 23. Note that without added beta carotene, butter is often naturally white.

142 *Verse Summary*, 15 (f. 8a). Translation in Conze 1983, 30.

143 Śāntideva, 16b (6.59). Translation in Shantideva 1997, 86.

144 Nāgārjuna, v. 29, 42a. Translation by Padmakara Translation Group 2006, 39. I've kept the common verse as it is found in the Dergé Tengyur, but in all editions of this text the second line varies slightly: "or kind words and abuse, or fame and disgrace." This might be from a different Tibetan translation, or simply misremembered.

145 DNZ, 14:10. There and in other editions, such as Dingri, vol. *ja*, it reads, "The confidence of Severance is to be without hope. No hope—free of extremes of fear. Other than the decisive cutting of fixation, how could there be definite buddhahood?" Translation in Jamgön Kongtrul 2016, 18.

146 Not located.

147 *Me shel*; Skt. *arkakānta* or *sūryakānta*. A stone that gives off heat when exposed to the sun, like a burning lens.

148 Found in Machik, *A Hair's Tip of Wisdom*, DNZ, 14:90. Translation in Jamgön Kongtrul 2016, 111. This is a text that contains and comments on some original verses attributed to Machik Labdrön.

149 *Khrid pa* ("to guide") should be *mkhris pa* ("bile"), according to Lodrö Tulku Rinpoche.

150 DNZ, 14:13 (with minor differences). Translation in Jamgön Kongtrul 2016, 22.

151 *Ḍākinī Vajra Tent Tantra*, 65b2.

152 *Verse Summary*, 7a.

153 *Rkyen spong.* Alternate reading in some versions: *skyon spang* ("dispelling flaws").

154 *Le lag.* Not found in the DNZ versions, but Kongtrul quotes the same passage in TOK, 3:426, with the one notable difference that the first line reads *gnyan sar song la rig pa slongs* ("arouse awareness," rather than *rig pa glod*, "relax awareness").

155 DNZ, 14:113. Translation: Jamgön Kongtrul 2016, 138.

156 Very similar to a statement attributed to Machik Labdrön in *A Hair's Tip of Wisdom*.

157 Machik, DNZ, 14:136. Translation in Jamgön Kongtrul 2016, 165.

158 *Bdud gcod nyams khrid zab mo* (*Profound Devil-Severance Experiential Guide*), Dingri Volumes, *ta*, 475–501. Title in Limi text: *Gcod kyi lag len nyams khrid du bskyang ba gnyan khrod zhag bdun ma* (*The Seven-Day Haunted Retreat Sustaining Experiential Guide on Severance Practice*), 199–216. The common title in the other editions and references is simply *Nyams khrid zhag bdun ma* (*The Seven-Day Experiential Guide*): Peling, 341–89, Longchenpa, 26:82–100.

159 *Skam thag chu nang du chod pa*: a Tibetan phrase indicating counter-intuitive methods. See the glossary of terms.

160 Preferring *'phrang 'chol* ("impasse"), from Limi text, rather than here the nonsensical *'phra sa 'tshol* ("seeking a place to kick").

161 The version from the other three texts makes more sense than the one here: "In the first place, there is no cause of arising; in the middle, there is no condition for abiding; and in the end, there is no support for leaving."

162 Thank you to Ringu Tulku Rinpoche for sorting out this example. According to him, "small eyes" (*mig chung*) is a euphemism for not very smart (personal communication, November 2, 2023).

163 The Longchen text has *'dzing rdung*, not to struggle with the demonic apparitions, which makes more sense than the version here and that in two other witnesses, where it is *rdza rdung*, "beat clay."

164 *Ma sangs*: the offspring of god-demons and humans.

165 This line is absent from the Limi and Peling texts.

166 *Yum sras gnyis*: This might refer to either Machik Labdrön and her son Gyalwa Döndrup, or to the six principal ("mother") and eleven subsidiary ("son") texts of the Perfection of Wisdom, or to both.

167 Prājñāsvabhāva is a Sanskrit rendering of Jamyang Gönpo's ordination name, Sherap Jungné (Shes rab 'byung gnas), although Prājñāsambhava might be more correct. His name is not recorded in the Longchen and Peling texts, and is added as a note in the margin of the Limi text. But a handwritten version given to me by Lodrö Tulku Rinpoche has a clarifying colophon that identifies all three of his names: Prājñāsvabhāva, Jamyang Gönpo, and Paṇḍita Dönyö Dorjé (*'di shes bya'i dge slong rdo rje 'dzin pa pra jña sva bha ba'am / 'jam dbyang mgon po'am / yongs su grags pa paṇḍita don yod rdo rjes sbyar ba'o*).

168 For examples of the possible lines that inspired Machik, see Harding 2013b, 35 and 97, and Khamnyön, *History of Pacification and Severance*, 2a.

169 Some examples from these texts are the devil of belief in intrinsic existence, of merely mental emptiness, of making Dharma a big project, of clinging to the reality of accomplishing enlightenment, of actual things, of depression and despair, of obstinate reification, and so on.

170 The translation of *māra* as *bdud* in Tibetan has further complicated the issue, given the hordes of *bdud* that roam Tibet. I have everywhere used "devil" or even "evil" for *bdud*, as distinguished from "demon" for *'dre*, although in Tibet the two are often interchangeable.

171 Quoted by Jamgön Kongtrul 2007, 276–77.

172 DNZ, 14:5. Also called *Grand Poem* (*Tshigs bcad chen mo*) and *Fifty Verse Poem* (*Tshigs su bcad pa lnga bcu pa*).

173 DNZ, 14:9.

174 DNZ, 14:9. The last line, *lhan ne lhang nge lham me*, are alliterative words with variable experience-based meanings.

175 DNZ, 14:4.

176 *Another Bundle*, DNZ, 14:107.

177 TOK, 3:426, and *Beloved Garden*: "The main practice [of feeding the spirits] should be understood as an offshoot. But these days, most so-called Severance practitioners don't get the main root and only seem to desire the branches" (DNZ, 14:11).

178 DNZ, 14:6.

179 For this episode, see Harding 2013b, 94.

180 DNZ, 14:13.

181 *Heart Essence of Profound Meaning*, DNZ, 14:18. See also pages 35–36.

182 *Shes rab kyi pha rol tu phyin pa'i man ngag gcod kyi gzhung shes rab skra rtse'i sa gzhung spel ba rin po che'i gter mdzod*, DNZ, 14:81–99.

183 *Shes rab kyi pha rol tu phyin pa'i man ngag yang tshom zhus len ma*, DNZ, 14:101–15.

184 *Practices of the Severance Collection and So Forth*, BDRC W23390.

185 Ibid., 31: *Bka' tshoms kyi zhus lan sum bcu rtsa lnga pa / a ma'i yang gsang thugs kyi nying khu.*

186 Tashi Chöpel 2008.

187 *Explanations of Severance*, 18 (9b) It does include, however, the *Great Bundle* and *Further Bundle*.

188 DNZ, 14:121 and 129.

189 *Le lag bcu gsum pa* and *Le lag brgyad pa* in Limi, 45–66.

190 DNZ, 14:139.

191 DNZ, 14:148.

192 Explained by Ringu Tulku, this refers to a kind of bad luck that occurs when a child dies and the propensity to die carries over to the next born. To remove this jinx (*sriu*), one has to do a ritual or ceremony using either the actual child or its clothing, and so forth (personal communication, April 2013).

193 DNZ, 14:149–50.

194 DNZ, 14:162–63.

195 Personal communication, May 8, 2023.

196 Stearns 2006, 202

197 Lama Dampa Sönam Gyaltsen 2011, 439.

198 *Khams 'dus can gso ba*. In *The Ten Door-Openers: Personal Advice on Severance* (*Gcod kyi zhal gdams sgo 'byed bcu pa*), in Dingri Volumes, 9:560.

199 Lorepa 2008, 2:96. Thank you to Artemus B. Engle for referring me to this text.

200 See page 103.

201 *Big Tibetan-Chinese Dictionary*, 1:1124.

202 Rangjung Dorjé, 251.

203 DNZ, 14:142.

204 Machik, DNZ, 14:142.

205 Personal communication, May 12, 2023.

206 *Self-Arising Dharmakāya*, DNZ, 10:228.

Bibliography

Works Cited in the Texts

Scriptures (Kangyur)

Ḍākinī Vajra Tent Tantra. Ḍākinīvajrapañjaramahātantra. Mkha' 'gro ma rdo rje gur zhes bya ba'i rgyud kyi rgyal po chen po'i brtag pa. Toh 419, rgyud 'bum, *nga*, 30a–65b.

Diamond Cutter Sutra. Vajracchedikāprajñāpāramitā. 'Phags pa shes rab kyi pha rol tu phyin pa rdo rje gcod pa. Toh 16, shes byin, *ka*, 121a–132b.

The Glorious Deeds of Pūrna. Pūrṇāvadāna. Gang po la sogs pa'i rtogs pa brjod pa brgya pa. Toh 340, mdo sde, *aṃ*, 1b–286b.

Heart of the Perfection of Wisdom (Heart Sutra). Bhagavatīprajñāpāramitāhṛdaya. Bcom ldan 'das ma shes rab kyi pha rol tu phyin pa'i snying po. Toh 529, shes rab sna tshogs, *ka*, 144b–146a.

Heart of the Sun Sutra. Sūryagarbhasūtra. 'Phags pa shin tu rgyas pa chen po'i sde nyi ma'i snying po. Toh 257, mdo sde, *za*, 91b–245b (vol. 66). Lhasa Kangyur (H 258) mdo sde, *wa*, 131b–350b (vol. 66).

Hevajra Tantra. Hevajratantrarāja. (Part 1) *Kye'i rdo rje zhes bya ba rgyud kyi rgyal po.* (Part 2) *Kye'i rdo rje mkha' 'gro ma dra ba'i sdom pa'i rgyud kyi rgyal po.* Toh 417 and 418, rgyud 'bum, *nga*, 1b–13b; 13b–30a.

The Hundred Deeds. Karmaśataka. Las brgya tham pa. Toh 340, mdo sde, *ha*, 1b–309a.

The Noble Mahāyāna Sūtra of Aparimitāyurjñāna. Aparimitāyurjñāna Sūtra. 'Phags pa tshe dang ye shes dpag tu med pa shes bya ba theg pa chen po'i mdo. Toh 674, rgyud 'bum, *ba*, 211b–216a.

Perfection of Wisdom in Eight Thousand Lines. Aṣṭasāhasrikāprajñāpāramitā. Shes rab kyi pha rol tu phyin pa brgyad stong pa. Toh 12, shes phyin, *ka*, 1b–286a.

Perfection of Wisdom in Eighteen Thousand Lines. Aṣṭadaśasāhasrikāprajñāpāramitā. Shes rab kyi pha rol tu phyin pa khri brgyad stong pa. Toh 10, shes phyin, *ka*, 1b1–300a.

Perfection of Wisdom in One Hundred Thousand Lines. Śatasāhasrikāprajñāpāramitā. Shes rab kyi pha rol tu phyin pa stong phrag brgya pa. Toh 8, shes byin, *ka*, 1b–394a.

Sacred Victory Banner Sutra. Dhvajāgramahāsūtra. Mdo chen po rgyal mtshan dam pa. Toh 293, mdo sde, *sha*, 265a–267a.

Sutra of the Wise and Foolish. Damamūkanidānasūtra. (Chinese: *Hsien-yü ching*). *Mdzangs blun zhes bya ba'i mdo.* Toh 341, mdo sde, *a*, 129a–298a.

Verse Summary on the Perfection of Wisdom. Prajñāpāramitāsaṃcayagāthā. 'Phags pa shes rab kyi pha rol tu phyin pa sdud pa tshigs su bcad pa. Toh 13, shes phyin, *ka*, 1b1–19b7.

Treatises (Tengyur)

Āryadeva. *Lamp for Integrating the Practices. Caryāmelāpakapradīpa. Spyod pa bsdus pa'i sgron ma.* Toh 1803, rgyud, *nyi*, 57a2–106b7.

Āryadeva the Brahmin. *The Grand Poem (Tshigs bcad chen mo)* or *Fifty Verse Poem (Tshigs su bcad pa lnga bcu pa)* or *Esoteric Instructions on the Perfection of Wisdom ('Phags pa shes rab kyi pha rol tu phyin pa'i man ngag).* In Narthang Tengyur, mdo, *nyo*, 396b–399a; Golden Tengyur, *nyo*, 517a–520a; and DNZ, vol. 14, 7–17.

Asaṅga. *Bodhisattvabhūmi. Rnal 'byor spyod pa'i sa las byang chub sem dpa'i sa.* Toh 4037, sems tsam, *wi*, 1b–213a.

Candragomin. *Twenty Verses on the Bodhisattva Vows. Bodhisattvasaṃvara-viṃśaka. Byang chub sems dpa'i sdom pa nyi shu pa.* Toh 4081, sems tsam, *hi,* 166b–167a.

Maitreya. *Distinguishing the Middle from the Extremes. Madhyāntavibhāga. Dbus dang mtha' rnam par 'byed pa'i tshig le'ur byas pa.* Toh 4021, sems tsam, *phi,* 40b–45a.

———. *Highest Continuum. Mahāyānottaratantraśāstra. Theg pa chen po rgyud bla ma'i bstan bcos.* Toh 4024, sems tsam, *phi,* 54b–73a.

———. *Ornament of the Mahāyāna Sutras. Mahāyānasūtrālaṅkāra. Theg pa chen po'i mdo sde'i rgyan.* Toh 4020, sems tsam, *phi,* 1b–39a.

Nāgārjuna. *Letter to a Friend. Suhṛllekha. Bshes pa'i spring yig.* Toh 4182, spring yig, *nge,* 40b–46b.

———. *Root Verses on the Wisdom of the Middle Way. Prajñānāmamūlamadhya-makakārikā. Dbu ma rtsa ba'i tshig le'ur byas pa shes rab ces bya ba.* Toh 3824, dbu ma, *tsa,* 1b–19a.

Śāntideva. *Bodhicaryāvatāra. Byang chub sems dpa'i spyod pa la 'jug pa.* Toh 3871, dbu ma, *la,* 1b1–90b5.

Vasubandhu. *Abhidharmakośakārikā. Chos mngon pa'i mdzod kyi tshig le'ur byas pa.* Toh 4089, mngon pa, *ku,* 1b–25a.

Tibetan Authors

Machik Labdrön (Ma gcig Lab sgron). *Another Bundle: Answers to Questions on the Esoteric Instructions of the Perfection of Wisdom. Shes rab kyi pha rol tu phyin pa'i man ngag yang tshom zhus lan ma.* In Dingri Volumes, vol. *ja,* 97–114. New Delhi: Dingri Langkor Tsuglag Khang, 2013. Also in DNZ, Shechen Printing, vol. 14, 101–13.

———. *The Eight Common Appendices. Thun mong gi le lag brgyad pa.* In Dingri Volumes, vol. *ja,* 239–53. Also in DNZ, vol. 14, 130–40.

———. *The Great Bundle of Precepts: The Source Text of Esoteric Instructions on Severance, the Profound Perfection of Wisdom. Shes rab kyi pha rol tu phyin pa zab mo gcod kyi man ngag gi gzhung bka' tshoms chen mo*. In Dingri Volumes, vol. *ja*, 97–114. New Delhi: Dingri Langkor Tsuglag Khang, 2013. Also in DNZ, Shechen Printing, vol. 14, 7–17.

Reference Bibliography

Tibetan Texts

Big Dictionary of Tibetan Medicine. *Bod lugs gso rig tshig mdzod chen mo*. Bod rang skyong ljongs snam rtsi khang. Beijing: Mi rigs dpe skrun khang, 2006.

Big Tibetan-Chinese Dictionary. *Bod rgya tshig mdzod chen mo*. Edited by Zhang Yisun et al. 2 vols. Beijing: Mi rigs dpe skrun khang, 1985/1987.

Dampa Sangyé (Pha Dam pa sangs rgyas). *Six Pieces*. *Brul tsho drug* (*Shes rab kyi pha rol tu phyin pa gcod kyi gdams pa brul tsho drug pa'i gzhung gser zhun ma*). In Dingri Volumes, vol. *ja*, 53–96.

Dingri Volumes (*The Volumes of the Root Teachings of the Sacred Dharma Pacification of Suffering, and the Subsidiary, Severance of Evil Object*). *Dam chos sdug bsngal zhi byed rtsa ba'i chos sde dang / yan lag bdud kyi gcod yul gyi glegs bam*. Edited by Ngawang Sangyé. New Delhi: Dingri Langkor Tsuglag Khang, 2013.

Dönyö Dorjé (Don yod rdo rje). *A Confession by the Tibetan Paṇḍita Dönyö Dorjé*. *Bod kyi paṇḍi ta don yod rdo rjes mdzad pa'i bshags pa*. In *Mkhas dbang raghu wīra dang lokesha tsandra rnam gnyis kyis nyar tshags byas pa' i dpe tshogs*, vol. 43, 679–84. BDRC MW1KG26281.

Gö Lotsāwa Zhönnu Pal ('Gos lo tsā ba Gzhon nu dpal). *The Blue Annals*. *Deb ther sngon po*. 2 vols. Chengdu: Si khron mi rigs dpe skrung khang, 1984.

Gyalwa Döndrup (Rgyal ba don grub). *Supplication Stirring the Intention*. *Gsol 'debs dgongs bskyod ma*. In Tāranātha, *The Required Liturgies on the Occasion of Venerable Tāranātha's Severance Empowerment*. In DNZ, vol. 14, 169–71.

Jamgön Kongtrul Lodrö Thayé ('Jam mgon kong sprul Blo gros mtha' yas). *Beloved Garden: Brief Notes on the Offering and Gift of the Body. Lus kyis mchod sbyin gyi zin bris mdor bsdus kun dga'i skyed tshal.* In DNZ, vol. 14, 387–405.

———. *Distillation of the Profound: The Way to Practice the Essence of the Vast Object Severance in a Single Sitting. Gcod yul rgya mtsho'i snying po stan thog gcig tu nyams su len pa'i tshul zab mo'i yang zhun.* In DNZ, vol. 10, 353–60; Dingri Volumes, vol. *ja*, 679–90.

———. *Self-Arising Dharmakāya: An Instructional Guide on the Fivefold Capability, the Special Teaching of the Glorious Lower Drukpa Kagyu Lineage from the Dharma Lord Lorepa. Chos rje lo ras pa las brgyud pa'i dpal ldan smad 'brug bka' brgyud kyi khyad chos thub pa lnga'i gdams khrid chos sku rang shar.* In DNZ, vol. 10, 223–41.

———, comp. *The Treasury of Knowledge. Shes bya kun khyab (Theg pa'i sgo kun las btus pa gsung rab rin po che'i mdzod bslab pa gsum legs par ston pa'i bstan bcos shes bya kun khyab).* 3 vols. Lhasa: Mi rigs dpe skrun khang, 1982.

Jamyang Gönpo ('Jam dbyangs mgon po). *The Big General Guide to the Profound Meaning. Zab don gyi spyi khrid chen mo.* Dingri Volumes, vol. *ta.* 319–474; Limi, 105–97; Longchenpa, 131–248; Peling, 47–339.

———. "Curing Congested Constituents." *Khams 'dus can gso ba.* In *The Ten Door-Openers: Personal Advice on Severance. Gcod kyi zhal gdams sgo 'byed bcu pa.* In Dingri Volumes, vol. *ta*, 560–61.

———. *Heart Essence of Profound Meaning: The Quintessence of All Source Texts and Esoteric Instructions on Severance, the Perfection of Wisdom. Shes rab kyi pha rol tu phyin pa gcod kyi gzhung dang man ngag mtha' dag gi yang bcud zab don thugs kyi snying po* or *Bdud kyi gcod yul gyi gzhung.* In DNZ, vol. 14, 17–22; Dingri Volumes, vol. *ta*, 1–10; Limi, 96–101; Longchenpa, 124–30.

———. *Lives of the Lineage Gurus of the Heart Essence of Profound Meaning. Zab don thugs kyi snying po bla ma rgyud pa'i rnam thar.* In Limi, 83–96.

———. *Self-Arising Dharmakāya: Instructions on the Five Capabilities, The Special Teaching of the Glorious Lower Drukpa Kagyu in the Lineage of Chöjé Lorepa.*

Chos rje lo ras pa las brgyud pa'i dpal ldan smad 'brug bka' brgyud kyi khyad chos thub pa lnga'i gdams khrid chos sku rang shar. In DNZ, vol. 10, 223–41.

———. *The Seven Day Severance Retreat Experiential Guide. Bdud gcod nyams khrid zab mo* or *Gcod kyi lag len nyams khrid du bskyang ba gnyan khrod zhag bdun ma.* In Dingri Volumes, vol. *ta*, 475–502; Limi 199–216; Peling 341–89.

———. *A Structural Analysis of the Profound Heart Essence. Zab don thugs kyi snying po'i bsdus don.* In Limi, 101–103.

———. *The Ten Door-Openers: Personal Instructions on Severance. Gcod kyi zhal gdams sgo 'byed bcu pa.* In Dingri Volumes, vol. *ta*, 503–86; Limi, 216–35.

Jamyang Gönpo, et al. *Practices of the Severance Collection and So Forth* ("Limi"). *Gcod tshogs kyi lag len sogs: A Collection of Gcod Texts Representing the Ancient Practices of the Adepts of the Tradition.* Bir, Himachal Pradesh, India: D. Tsondu Senge, Bir Tibetan Society, 1985. BDRC W23390.

Karma Chakmé (Karma Chags med, a.k.a. Arāga or Rāga Asya). *Abridged Authoritative Teaching on Machik's Severance. Ma gcig gcod kyi gdengs bshad nyung ngur bsdus pa.* In *Collected Works of Karma Chakmé. Mkhas grub karma chags med gsung 'bum.* 60 vols. Yushu, Tibetan Autonomous Prefecture: Gnas mdo dpe rnying nyams gso khang, 2010.

———, comp. *The Body Donation and Feeding Ritual Arranged as Convenient Liturgy. Lus byin dang bsngo ba* [or *bstab pa*] *bya tshul bltas chog 'don 'grigs.* In DNZ, vol. 14, 261–77.

Khamnyön Dharma Sengé (Khams smyon Dharma seng ge). *Religious History of Pacification and Severance: A Precious Garland Ornament of Liberation. Zhi byed dang gcod yul gyi chos 'byung rin po che'i phreng ba thar pa'i rgyan.* In *A Cycle of Teachings on Severance* (*Gcod kyi chos skor*), 411–597. Delhi: Tibet House, 1974. Also in Dingri Volumes, vol. *ta*, 681–862.

Könchok Gyaltsen (Dkon mchog rgyal mtshan). *Opener of the Wisdom Eye: An Esoteric Instruction on Severance. Gcod kyi man ngag blo gros mig 'byed* (*Zab don snyan brgyud kyi gcod gzhung zab mo gcod kyi man ngag blo gros mig 'byed*). In *Gsung 'bum / dkon mchog rgyal mtshan,* vol. 3, 451–638. New Delhi: Gyaltsan Gelek Namgyal, 1974. BDRC W2519.

Koshul Drakpa Jungné (Ko zhul Grags pa 'byung gnas) and Gyalwa Losang Khedrup (Rgyal ba Blo bzang mkhas grub). *Treasury of Names. Gangs can mkhas grub rim byon ming mdzod.* Lanzhou, Gansu province, China: Kan su'u mi rigs dpe skrun khang, 1992.

Kunga (Kun dga'). *Clarifying Mirror of the Mind: Questions and Answers [from Dampa Sangyé]. Zhu lan thugs kyi me long rnam par gsal pa.* In Dingri Volumes, vol. *kha,* 51–86.

Kunga Namgyal (Kun dga' rnam rgyal). *Explanations of Severance: Lamp of Clarity, and Others. Gcod kyi bshad pa gsal ba'i sgron me sogs.* Thimpu, Bhutan: Kunsang Topgay, 1978. BDRC W27477.

Longchen Rabjam Drimé Öser (Klong chen rab 'byams 'Dri med 'od zer). *The Collected Works of Kunkhyen Longchen Rabjam. Kun mkhyen klong chen rab 'byams kyi gsung 'bum.* 26 vols. Beijing: Krung go'i bod rig pa dpe skrun khang, 2007.

Lorepa Wangchuk Tsöndrü (Lo ras pa Dbang phyug brtson 'grus). *Distinctive Features of Reverse Meditation according to Lord Drogön. Zlog sgom bye brag gi gnad rje 'gro mgon gyis mdzad pa.* In *Smad 'brug bstan pa'i mnga' bdag rgyal ba lo ras pa grags pa dbang phyug mchog gi gsung 'bum rin po che,* vol. 2, 93–134. Kathmandu, Nepal: Ven. Khenpo Shedup Tenzin and Lama Thinley Namgyal, Shri Gautam Buddha Vihar, Manjushri Bazar, 2002. BDRC W23440.

Machik Labdrön (Ma gcig Lab sgron). *The Eight Special Appendices. Khyad par gyi le lag brgyad pa.* In DNZ, vol. 14, 155–64.

———. *The Eight Uncommon Appendices. Thun mong ma yin pa'i le lag brgyad pa.* In Dingri Volumes, vol. *ja,* 239–54; DNZ, vol. 14, 140–55.

———. *The Essential Bundle from the Severance of Evil Object, Esoteric Instructions on the Perfection of Wisdom. Shes rab kyi pha rol tu phyin pa'i man ngag bdud kyi gcod yul las nying tshom.* In DNZ, vol. 14, 116–30.

Machik Labdrön and Kunga Paljor (Kun dga' dpal 'byor). *A Hair's Tip of Wisdom: A Precious Treasure Trove to Enhance the Original Source Text of Severance, the Esoteric Instructions on the Perfection of Wisdom. Shes rab kyi pha rol tu phyin pa'i man ngag gcod kyi gzhung shes rab skra rtse'i sa gzhung spel ba rin po che'i gter mdzod* (*Shes rab skra rtse*). In DNZ, vol. 14, 81–99.

Pema Karpo, Kunkhyen (Kun khyen Pad ma dkar po). *The Sun that Opens the Lotus of the Doctrine: A Religious History. Chos 'byung bstan pa'i pad ma rgyas pa'i nyin byed.* Plouray, France: Drukpa Plouray, 2006. BDRC W1KG4304.

Pema Lingpa et al. *Cycle of Severance of Evil, the Heart Essence of Profound Meaning.* (Peling version). *Zab don thugs kyi snying po bdud kyi gcod yul gyi skor.* "A collection of Gcod texts reflecting the teachings of Padma-gliṅ-pa. Reproduced from a manuscript collection from Padma-bkod." New Delhi: P. K. Tashi, 1981.

Rangjung Dorjé, Karmapa (Karma pa Rang byung rdo rje). *Practice Manual on the Profound Severance of Evil Object. Zab mo bdud kyi gcod yul gyi khrid yig.* In DNZ, vol. 14, 173–84.

Rechungpa Dorjé Drakpa (Ras chung pa Rdo rje grags pa). Revealed by Tsangpa Gyaré (Gtsang pa rgya ras Ye shes rdo rje). *Six Cycles of Equalizing Tastes. Ro snyoms skor drug.* In *Dkor mdzod le'u drug pa zhes kyang bya/ yang mdzod thugs kyi me long zhes kyang bya/ ro snyoms skor drug gi don bsdus pa gcig tu dril ba.* Darjeeling, India: Kargyu sungrab nyamso khang, 1978–85. BDRC MW20749.

Samten Öser, Gyalthangpa (Rgyal thang pa Bsam gtan 'od zer). *Cycle of Profound Severance of Evil: A Collection of Gcod Texts Chiefly Connected with the Tradition Transmitted by bSam gtan 'od zer. Bdud gcod zab mo'i skor.* Darjeeling, India: Lama Dawa and Chopal Lama, 1974. BDRC W27506.

———. *Pearl Rosary of Legendary Tales. Brgyud gtam mu tig phreng ba.* In Dingri Volumes, vol. *ta*, 1–51; Limi, 257–79.

Sangyé Tönpa (Sangs rgyas ston pa). *Short Practice of Severance. Gcod kyi nyams len bsdus pa.* In *Cycle of Severance of Evil, the Heart Essence of Profound Meaning*, 467–91. Also in Longchenpa, vol. 26, 273–84.

Tāranātha, Jonang. *Object Severance Empowerment Known as Opening the Sky Door. Gcod yul gyi dbang nam mkha' sgo 'byed du grags pa.* In DNZ, vol. 14, 361–70; Dingri Volumes, vol. *ja*, 691–704.

Tashi Chöpel (Bkra shis chos 'phel). *Record of Teachings Received (Record of How Jamgön Kongtrul Yönten Gyatso Received the Precious Teachings of Sutra, Tantra, and Classical Studies with Their Source Lineages).* 'Jam mgon kong sprul yon tan rgya mtshos dam pa'i chos rin po che mdo sngags rig gnas dang bcas pa ji ltar thos shing de dag gang las brgyud pa'i yi ge dgos 'dod kun 'byung nor bu'i bang mdzod. Beijing: Mi rigs dpe skrun khang, 2008.

Tenzin Namdak, Tokden (Rtogs ldan Bstan 'dzin rnam dag). *White Crystal Mirror: Notes on the Guru's Teaching Tradition of the Visualization Sequence for Severance Feast Activities "Endowed with All Qualities."* Gcod kyi tshogs las yon tan kun ldan gyi dmigs rim bla ma'i gsung rgyun gyi zin bris shel dkar me long. In DNZ, vol. 14, 201–50.

Tsangnyön Heruka (Gtsang smyon he ru ka). *A Hundred Thousand Songs of Milarepa.* Rje btsun mi la ras pa'i rnam thar rgyas par phye ba mgur 'bum. In Rnal 'byor gyi dbang phyug dam pa rje btsun mi la ras pa'i rnam thar pa dang thams cad mkhyen p'ai lam ston. Woodblock print. Ku lu mu na li rang gnas ci ṭa ri'i dgon, n.d.

Unknown. *Presentation of the Sixteen Ridicules of the Devils.* Bdud kyi spyo ba bcu drug bstan pa. In Dingri Volumes, vol. *ta,* 303–307.

English Publications

84000: Translating the Words of the Buddha. https://read.84000.co.

Callahan, Elizabeth M., trans. 2012. *The Two-Part Hevajra Tantra (Brtags gnyis).* Selected chapters, with commentary from *Revealing the Indestructible Vajra Secrets* by Jamgön Kongtrul Lodrö Thayé. Unpublished manuscript.

Chang, Garma C. C., trans. 1962. *The Hundred Thousand Songs of Milarepa.* 2 vols. New Hyde Park, NY: University Books.

Chögyam Trungpa. 1991. "The Pön Way of Life." In *The Heart of the Buddha,* 219–30. Boston: Shambhala Publications.

Conze, Edward. 1973/1983. *The Perfection of Wisdom in Eight Thousand Lines and Its Verse Summary.* San Francisco: Four Seasons Foundation.

de Rossi-Filibeck, E. 1995. "The Transmission Lineage of the Gcod Teaching According to the 2nd Dalai-Lama." In *Contributions on Tibetan and Buddhist Religion and Philosophy*. Proceedings of the Csoma De Körös Symposium Held at Velm-Vienna, Austria, 13–19 September 1981. Edited by Ernst Steinkellner and Helmut Tauscher. Vol. 2. Delhi: Motilal Banarsidass.

Dorje, Gyurme, trans. and comm. 2001. *Tibetan Elemental Divination Paintings: Illuminated Manuscript from the White Beryl of Sangs-rgyas rGya-mtsho with the 'Moonbeams' treatise of Lo-chen Dharmasri*. London, UK: John Eskenazi Ltd.

Dorje, Gyurme. 2004. *Footprint Tibet*. 3rd ed. Bath, U.K.: Footprint.

Drungtso, Tsering Thakchoe, and Tsering D. Drungtso. 1999. *Tibetan-English Dictionary of Tibetan Medicine and Astrology*. Dharamsala, India: Drungtso Publications.

Ferrari, Alfonsa. 1958. *Mk'yen brtse's Guide to the Holy Places of Central Tibet*. Serie Orientale Roma 16. Rome: Istituto Italiano per il Medio ed Estremo Oriente.

Frye, Stanley, trans. (from Mongolian). 1981/2000/2006. *Sutra of the Wise and Foolish, or Ocean of Narratives*. Dharamsala, India: Library of Tibetan Works and Archives.

Gyatso, Janet. 1985. "The Development of the gCod Tradition." In *Soundings in Tibetan Civilization*, edited by Barbara Nimri Aziz and Matthew Kapstein, 320–41. New Delhi: Manohar.

Harding, Sarah. 2013a. "Did Machik Labdrön Really Teach Chöd? A Survey of the Early Sources." Unpublished manuscript. See appendix.

———. 2013b. *Machik's Complete Explanation: Clarifying the Meaning of Chöd*, expanded ed. Boston and London: Snow Lion Publications.

Jamgön Kongtrul Lodrö Tayé (Thayé). 2007. *The Treasury of Knowledge, Book 8, Part 4: Esoteric Instructions*. Translated by the Kalu Rinpoché Translation Group (Sarah Harding). Ithaca, NY: Snow Lion Publications.

———, comp. 2016. *The Treasury of Precious Instructions: Essential Teachings of the Eight Practice Lineages of Tibet, Volume 14: Chöd, the Sacred*

Teachings on Severance. Translated by Sarah Harding. Boulder, CO: Shambhala Publications.

———, comp. 2019. *The Treasury of Precious Instructions: Essential Teachings of the Eight Practice Lineages of Tibet, Volume 13: Zhije, the Pacification of Suffering.* Translated by Sarah Harding. Boulder, CO: Shambhala Publications.

———, comp. 2020. *The Treasury of Precious Instructions: Essential Teachings of the Eight Practice Lineages of Tibet, Volume 18: Jonang, the One Hundred and Eight Teaching Manuals.* Translated by Gyurme Dorje. Boulder, CO: Shambhala Publications.

Karmay, Samten G. 1998. *The Arrow and the Spindle: Studies in History, Myths, Rituals and Beliefs in Tibet.* Kathmandu: Maṇḍala Book Point.

Lama Dampa Sönam Gyaltsen. 2011. *Treasury of Esoteric Instructions: An Explication of the Oral Instructions of the Path with the Result.* Translated by Cyrus Stearns. Ithaca, NY: Snow Lion Publications.

Lodrö Tulku Rinpoche. 2020. *The Profound Heart Essence: Prajnaparamita and the Practice of Chod.* Translated by Mary O'Beirne from the German *Die Tiefgründige Herzessenz: Prajnaparamita und die Praxis des Chöd,* based on Martin Kalff's interpretation of the oral Tibetan. Churwalden, Switzerland: Bhikshu Mati Foundation.

Martin, Dan. 2008. "Jamyang Gonpo." Treasury of Lives. Accessed October 27, 2023. http://treasuryoflives.org/biographies/view/Jamyang-Gonpo/6672.

———. 2021. "Tibskrit Philology: A Bibliography of Tibetan Philology." Self-published.

Miller, W. Blythe. 2005. "The Vagrant Poet and the Reluctant Scholar." *Journal of the International Association of Buddhist Studies.* 28.2: 369–410.

Nāgārjuna. 2006. *Nagarjuna's Letter to a Friend: With Commentary by Kyabje Kangyur Rinpoche.* Translated by the Padmakara Translation Group. Ithaca, NY: Snow Lion Publications.

Nālandā Translation Committee. 1980. *The Rain of Wisdom.* Boulder and London: Shambhala.

Namkhai Norbu. 1995. *Drung, Deu and Bön: Narrations, symbolic languages, and the Bön tradition in ancient Tibet.* Translated into Italian and edited by Adriano Clemente, and into English by Andrew Lukianowicz. Dharamsala: Library of Tibetan Works and Archives.

Nebesky-Wojkowitz, René de. 1956. *Oracles and Demons of Tibet: The Cult and Iconography of the Tibetan Protective Deities.* The Hague: Mouton.

Rangjung Yeshe Wiki - Dharma Dictionary. "Dictionaries/Dan Martin/17026." Accessed August 20, 2024. https://rywiki.tsadra.org/index.php?title=Dictionaries/Dan_Martin/17026.

Rinchen Wangchuk. 2012. "Musk Conservation in Bhutan Himalaya: Status, Distribution, Habitat Use and Potential Threats in Thrumshingla National Park." BS diss., Dolphin (PG) Institute of Biomedical & Natural Sciences, Dehradun, India.

Roerich, George N, trans. 1976/1988. *The Blue Annals.* Calcutta, 1949. 2nd ed., Delhi: Motilal Banarsidass.

Savvas, Carol Diane. 1990. "A Study of the Profound Path of Gcod: The Mahāyāna Buddhist Meditation Tradition of Tibet's Great Woman Saint Machig Labdron." PhD diss., University of Wisconsin–Madison.

Shantideva. 1997. *The Way of the Bodhisattva.* Translated by the Padmakara Translation Group. Boston: Shambhala Publications.

Smith, E. Gene. 2001. *Among Tibetan Texts: History and Literature of the Himalayan Plateau.* Boston: Wisdom Publications.

Stearns, Cyrus, trans. 2006. *Taking the Result as the Path: Core Teachings of the Sakya Lamdré Tradition.* Library of Tibetan Classics. Boston: Wisdom Publications.

Index

About the Contributors

Jamyang Gönpo was born in 1208 in the region of Upper Nyang in southern Tibet. Early on he showed special abilities in learning, meditation, and visionary experience. After his mother died when he was ten, he traveled to Tsang and received ordination and many teachings with Tibetan masters. His main master was Lorepa, also known as Lopön Urepa, who was the source of the Lower Drukpa Kagyü tradition. However, most of his extant compositions relate to his other important lineage connection, that of Machik Labdrön's Severance (*gcod*). He learned these practices primarily from her eldest son, Gyalwa Döndrup—himself a lineage holder in the tradition—and perhaps from others of her immediate descendants. Because of his close connection with Machik's family as well as his visions of her, his writings are considered source texts for the tradition, included with Machik's own teachings, and are likely the earliest written commentaries. Jamyang Gönpo's death date is unknown, for he left for China and is said to have attained rainbow body at Wutaishan mountain without leaving remains.

 Sarah Harding has been studying and practicing Buddhism since 1974, and has been teaching and translating since completing a three-year retreat in 1980 under the guidance of Kyabjé Kalu Rinpoché. She was a professor at Naropa University for twenty-five years, in Boulder, Colorado, where she currently resides, and has been a fellow of the Tsadra Foundation since 2000. She specializes in literature with a focus on tantric practice. Her publications include *Creation and Completion: Essential Points of Tantric Meditation*; *The Treasury of Knowledge: Esoteric Instructions*; *Niguma, Lady of Illusion*; *Ornament of Dakpo Kagyü Thought*; *Four Tibetan Lineages: Core Teachings of Pacification, Severance, Shangpa Kagyü, and Bodong*; and four volumes on Chöd, Zhijé, and Shangpa Kagyü from the *Treasury of Precious Instructions*.

What to Read Next from Wisdom Publications

Four Tibetan Lineages
Core Teachings of Pacification, Severance, Shangpa Kagyü, and Bodong
Translated by Sarah Harding

Drawing primarily from the Pacification, Severance, Shangpa Kagyü, and Bodongpa traditions, *Four Tibetan Lineages* presents some of Tibet's most transformative yet lesser-known teachings on meditative practice.

Ornament of Dakpo Kagyü Thought
Short Commentary on the Mahāmudrā Aspiration Prayer
Rangjung Dorjé
Mendong Tsampa Rinpoché
Translated by Sarah Harding

"Sarah Harding clarifies the essence of mahāmudrā with characteristic humor and penetrating insight, including points of contention. These pithy texts, elegantly translated, are contemplations on lucid awareness and immeasurable compassion, sparking illumination while refreshing one's language skills!" —Karma Lekshe Tsomo, professor of Buddhist Studies, University of San Diego

About Wisdom Publications

Wisdom Publications is the leading publisher of classic and contemporary Buddhist books and practical works on mindfulness. To learn more about us or to explore our other books, please visit our website at wisdom.org or contact us at the address below.

Wisdom Publications
132 Perry Street
New York, NY 10014 USA

We are a 501(c)(3) organization, and donations in support of our mission are tax deductible.

Wisdom Publications is affiliated with the Foundation for the Preservation of the Mahayana Tradition (FPMT).